The Times

The Parnellite Split

Or, the Disruption of the Irish Parliamentary Party

The Times

The Parnellite Split
Or, the Disruption of the Irish Parliamentary Party

ISBN/EAN: 9783744729949

Printed in Europe, USA, Canada, Australia, Japan

Cover: Foto ©Suzi / pixelio.de

More available books at **www.hansebooks.com**

THE PARNELLITE SPLIT:

OR,

THE DISRUPTION OF THE IRISH

PARLIAMENTARY PARTY.

FROM

𝕿𝖍𝖊 𝕿𝖎𝖒𝖊𝖘,

WITH AN INTRODUCTION.

LONDON :

GEORGE EDWARD WRIGHT, THE TIMES OFFICE, PRINTING-HOUSE-SQUARE;

AND

GEORGE ROUTLEDGE AND SONS (LIMITED), BROADWAY, LONDON, E.C.,

AND GLASGOW, MANCHESTER, AND NEW YORK.

1891.

INTRODUCTION.

On the 17th of November last, the jury in the divorce action of
"O'Shea v. O'Shea and Parnell" pronounced their verdict. They
found that the charges against the respondent and the co-
respondent had been proved, and that there had been no con-
nivance on the part of the petitioner. Ten months had elapsed
between the issue of the writ and the trial, and it is impossible
to suppose that during this long interval the effects of a decision
adverse to Mr. Parnell were not a subject of speculation to many
persons actively interested in public affairs. The decision itself
was very generally anticipated by those best qualified to judge,
and practical politicians of all parties must have foreseen that it
might seriously modify the complex relations then subsisting
between Mr. Parnell, the Irish Parliamentary party, and the
British Gladstonians. Yet it may be said that the political consequences of the trial came as a surprise to even the most intel-
ligent observers of current events. No accurate forecast of those
consequences had been made, because the *data* for such a forecast
were, in fact, inadequate. The existence of the two forces which
have proved to be the determining factors in the situation
created by the verdict was indeed known, but there were no
means of calculating the strength of the one, or the probable direction of the other. These forces were the disaffection of the Irish
Nationalists towards their leader, and that curious moral entity,
"the Nonconformist conscience." Persons moderately ac-
quainted with Irish politics had long been aware that the
Nationalist ranks contained elements bitterly hostile to the
supremacy of Mr. Parnell. They knew that he had a band of
personal enemies within the Irish Parliamentary party. They
knew, too, that the Irish priesthood disliked the leadership of a
Protestant, and that prominent members of the old Land League
nourished fierce resentments against the chief of the "constitutional" party. But the force and volume of the disaffection

1—2

cherished by these several sections of the Irish Nationalists towards the common leader of them all, were wholly unsuspected. They were concealed by the iron discipline of the Parliamentary party, by the professional timidity and reticence of the priests, and by the sense of their own impotence entertained by the discomfited Land Leaguers so long as they remained without allies. The power as well as the existence of "the Nonconformist conscience" were well known, but its idiosyncracies are so inscrutable, its operations in the sphere of Irish politics have been for many years so abnormal and so erratic, that any confident prediction of its action under novel conditions was impossible. On the one hand, it had always professed to base its political judgments on a rigid and unfaltering obedience to the precepts of the Decalogue. On the other, it had condoned the flagrant and systematic breach of many of those precepts by the Irish Nationalists for years. To foretell its view of Mr. Parnell's delinquencies was a problem, as events proved, which "passed the wit of man."

Little, however, as the political consequences of the divorce action had been foreseen, they constituted nothing less than a political catastrophe. Nothing like it, either for the dramatic interest of its development, or for the effect it promises to exercise on the fortunes of political parties in the United Kingdom, has occurred within the memory of the present generation. It is believed, therefore, that a permanent record of these events will be acceptable, not only to students of history and politics, but to all who take an interest in public affairs, whether at home or abroad. Accordingly, it has been determined to republish in the present volume the letters, manifestoes, and other documents issued by the several parties to the conflict, together with the reports of the meetings of the Irish Parliamentary party during the crisis. Some portions of the "Interview" with Mr. Davitt of November 26, and also one or two passages of the debates in No. 15 Committee Room, have been omitted, as they appeared to be devoid of permanent interest, and some trifling alterations of a verbal nature have been made in order to preserve the continuity of the narrative. With these exceptions the whole of the present volume has been reprinted from the reports which appeared from day to day in the columns of *The Times*. All the documents quoted have been reproduced at length.

The book contains a minute account of the daily progress of the crisis from November 18, the day following the verdict in " O'Shea v. O'Shea and Parnell," down to Mr. Parnell's departure for Ireland on December 9. The first chapter covers the period from the verdict in the divorce case down to the unanimous re-election of Mr. Parnell as chairman of the Irish Parliamentary party (November 18-25). It begins with the report of the National League meeting in Dublin on November 18, gives the opinions of Mr. William O'Brien and the other delegates to America delivered the same day, and the report of the very important meeting at the Leinster Hall, Dublin, on November 20, and concludes with the unanimous re-election of Mr. Parnell as chairman of the Irish Parliamentary party on the first day of the Session, Tuesday, November 25. Throughout the whole of this period the members of that party vied with each other in expressions of unalterable devotion to their old leader. No voice was raised against him. All agreed that the verdict in the divorce action in no wise affected his public position. The American delegates announced that they stood firmly by his leadership not only out of gratitude for his unparalleled services in the past, but " in profound conviction that Mr. Parnell's statesmanship and matchless qualities as leader are essential to the safety of our cause." At the Leinster Hall meeting Mr. Justin M'Carthy himself moved the first resolution declaring " that in all political matters Mr. Parnell possessed the confidence of the Irish nation," and that the meeting " rejoiced at the determination of the Irish Parliamentary party to stand by their leader." He said that they were not going to change their leader " because of the cry raised against him." He suggested that " chivalrous and generous motives " might have led Mr. Parnell to refrain from defending himself in the Divorce Court. He asked, Were they going to set up " some wholly inferior man " in Mr. Parnell's place, because certain Tory and Liberal Secessionist papers had attacked him ? " No man of common sense," he urged, would dream of doing so. Mr. M'Carthy did not fear the effect of the verdict on British opinion. The Home Rulers, he contended, would not lose the support of any honest allies. Some people, it was true, might fall away from them. He could only say, " Let them fall away. The national cause would go on without them." Mr. M'Carthy's motion was seconded by Mr. Healy, and Mr. Healy's loyalty to Mr. Parnell outrivalled Mr. M'Carthy's. To Irishmen he declared, Mr. Parnell was " less a man than an institution." They had been taxed with servility to Mr. Parnell. Mr. Healy repudiated the charge. The Irish party, he observed, without their chief would be " a very pretty party in the House of Commons." It would include representatives of " the Socialists, the land nationalizers, the barristers, and, probably, the attorneys." The choice of instruments they made to guide them to Home Rule was " a matter for them and not for the English people," and Mr. Healy roundly warned intermeddlers " not to speak to the man at the wheel." Mr. Gladstone's late Attorney-General for Ireland, Mr. Samuel Walker, Q.C., warmly supported the views expressed by Mr. M'Carthy and Mr. Healy, while his colleague in office, the late Gladstonian Solicitor-General, The MacDermot, Q.C., seconded a further resolution.

The unanimity of the Parliamentary party remained unbroken five days later. Mr. Parnell's re-election as chairman was the first business at their meeting. It was proposed by Mr. Sexton, and "agreed to amid loud applause." Seceders from Mr. Parnell's faction have alleged that his re-election was a merely formal honour, and that he was not expected to accept the office tendered him. No hint of such a feeling appears in the report. It is distinctly stated that Mr. Parnell " promised that he would continue to discharge the duties of leader," in response to " the unanimous desire " of the party. Mr. Parnell plainly took the election seriously, and no dissent seems to have been expressed from his view.

The second chapter contains a record of the chief events which happened between the adjournment of the meeting of the Irish Parliamentary party on the afternoon of November 25, and the issue of Mr. Parnell's Manifesto on Friday, November 28. The verdict in the divorce case, it will be remembered, was given on Monday, November 17. Mr. Gladstone has stated, in a speech made at Retford on December 11, that he felt the proceedings in that case " would destroy entirely the moral weight and the moral force " of Mr. Parnell. He did not at once communicate his opinion to Mr. Parnell. He waited for a week, and in the same speech he explains the reason of his inaction. " I determined," he says, " to watch the state of feeling in this country, and I very soon found that the Liberal party in this country had made up its mind to draw a broad distinction between the national cause of Ireland and the person and the personal office of Mr. Parnell." Sir Charles Russell insists, with candour yet more damaging, on the fact that considerations of political expediency alone, and not of outraged morality, wrung from Mr. Gladstone his condemnation of Mr. Parnell. Speaking at Braintree on December 5, he said that " it was not until Mr. Gladstone saw the rising, overwhelming tide of public opinion that he felt bound, in the interest of the party he led and of the cause he advocated, to convey to the leader of the Irish people that his continued leadership must have a chilling effect upon the enthusiasm of many staunch friends." Mr. Gladstone's investigations into the state of feeling in the country were doubtless materially aided by the reports he received from the meeting of the National Liberal Federation held at Sheffield on the Thursday and Friday after the verdict, at a moment, as Mr. John Morley told the delegates, when the country was " peculiarly stirred by anxious incidents and painful disclosures." On Sunday the " Nonconformist conscience " spoke from a hundred chapels, and on Monday Mr. Gladstone announced to Mr. Morley the conclusion to which his studies of the " rising tide " had brought him. It was that Mr. Parnell's continuance " at the present moment " in the leadership of the Irish party would be disastrous to Ireland, while it would render his own leadership " almost a nullity." The Irish members learnt the contents of this document soon after they had unanimously and enthusiastically re-elected Mr. Parnell as their chairman, and had received his pledge that he would continue to discharge the duties of his office. They held a second meeting the same evening, but, as Mr. Parnell had gone home, they adjourned without coming to any decision. Mr. Parnell presided over their deliberations next day (November 26). Mr. Barry and Dr. Commins at once pressed him to resign. Mr. Justin M'Carthy quite forgot his objection to setting up " some wholly inferior man," and seconded their exhortations. Mr. Sexton and other members agreed with Mr. M'Carthy, while Colonel Nolan and Mr. John O'Connor urged Mr. Parnell to stick to his post, and " not to permit himself to be dictated to by Mr. Gladstone." Mr. Parnell, " who throughout the proceedings had maintained the attitude of a listener, closed the proceedings by simply leaving the chair."

The meeting adjourned from Wednesday, November 26, to Monday, December 1. On the Wednesday night Mr. Davitt pronounced a severe condemnation of his old confederate, taxing him with trickery and falsehood, declaring that he would have nothing more to do with him, and suggesting that the leadership should be put into commission.

The third chapter contains the Manifesto issued by Mr. Parnell to "the People of Ireland" on the night of Friday, November 28, the replies of Mr. Gladstone and Mr. Morley published on the following day, and the telegram and manifesto of five of the six American delegates, pronouncing Mr. Parnell's retention of the leadership to be impossible. In his Manifesto Mr. Parnell alleged that the integrity and independence of a section of his party had been "sapped and destroyed by the wire-pullers of the English Liberal Party"; that Mr. Gladstone's letter claimed "a right of veto" on the Irish party's choice of their own leader, and contained a menace that resistance to this claim would involve an indefinite postponement of Home Rule. To enable the Irish people to measure the loss wherewith they were threatened unless they threw him, their leader, "to the English wolves," Mr. Parnell purported to describe the kind of Home Rule Mr. Gladstone was ready to grant. Mr. Parnell declared that he had obtained his information from Mr. Gladstone himself, when on a visit to Hawarden in November, 1889. He said that Mr. Gladstone told him that in his own opinion and in that of his colleagues, the Irish representation in the Imperial Parliament must be reduced from 103 members to 32, that the land question must be reserved from the control of the Irish Legislature, that the Irish constabulary must remain under Imperial control for an indefinite period, and that the appointment of "judges, resident magistrates, &c.," should be kept in the hands of the Imperial authority for some ten or twelve years. Mr. Parnell next stated his own views upon these alleged proposals of Mr. Gladstone's, and, after mentioning certain negotiations he had had with Mr. Morley on questions of Parliamentary strategy, went on to assert that Mr. Morley had lately asked him whether he would be willing to accept the Chief Secretaryship for Ireland himself, or would allow any other member of his party to do so; and that

Mr. Morley had also urged him to allow " a legal member of his party " to become a law officer of the Crown. After a brief reference to the " Plan of Campaign " tenants, for whom Mr. Parnell stated Mr. Morley had informed him it would be impossible for the Liberals to do anything " by direct action," Mr. Parnell concluded his Manifesto by declaring his belief that Home Rule could be obtained only by an Irish party which was independent of any English party ; that Home Rule would be neither endangered nor postponed by any action of the Irish people in supporting him ; and that even a postponement of Home Rule would be preferable to a compromise of Ireland's national rights, by the acceptance of a measure which would not realize the aspirations of the Irish race.

The answers to this remarkable document do not call for any special observation. Mr. Gladstone gave Mr. Parnell's statements a general denial, and asserted that every suggestion made by himself was from written memoranda. He did not, however, disclose what in fact his suggestions to Mr. Parnell had been, or quote from the memoranda to which he referred.

On the night of Saturday, November 29, the day of Mr. Gladstone's reply to Mr. Parnell's Manifesto, Mr. Parnell made another curious and characteristic move, the details of which were disclosed in the debate of the Irish party on Monday, December 1. On Saturday a meeting of Irish members was hastily convened. Mr. Parnell then requested Mr. M'Carthy to see Mr. Gladstone, Sir William Harcourt, and Mr. Morley, and to try to obtain from them letters declaring that on their return to power they would propose a Home Rule Bill vesting the control of the constabulary and the settlement of the land question in an Irish Parliament, and that they would treat these provisions as vital to the Bill. Mr. Parnell assured Mr. M'Carthy that if these two concessions were made he would retire " from public life." Mr. M'Carthy undertook the commission with reluctance, and endeavoured to execute it in the course of the following day. Mr. Gladstone, however, declined to regard Mr. M'Carthy as representing, in any sense, the Irish party, and stated that he could offer no suggestion, sign no document, and give no message for him to convey to that party. Mr. Gladstone further intimated that even were the proposed arrangement otherwise possible, he could not feel certain that any document he might sign would not be divulged. Sir William Harcourt gave a similar reply in curter terms. He said that after Mr. Parnell's Manifesto, he would not give anybody any assurance in writing or by word of mouth, that was to be brought in any way under the notice of Mr. Parnell. Mr. M'Carthy failed to see Mr. Morley at all. Mr. Parnell's object in making these proposals will appear later. They were very dexterously devised, and became the pivot of the adroit and unscrupulous strategy he now proceeded to display.

The fourth chapter contains the reports of the meetings and proceedings of the Irish Parliamentary party from Monday, December 1, down to the abortive close of the attempted negotiations with Mr. Gladstone on Friday, December 5. Throughout the course of these proceedings Mr. Parnell's policy was simple and consistent. He strove to gain time. His followers engaged in systematic obstruction, and Mr. Parnell shamefully abused his position as chairman to abet them. The first two days, Monday, December 1, and Tuesday, December 2, were occupied in debating a dilatory proposal of Mr. Parnell's supporter, Colonel Nolan, to the effect that the question of the chairmanship should be postponed until members had had an opportunity of consulting their constituents, and until the party could meet in Dublin. Mr. Sexton opposed the motion, on the ground that delay would break up the alliance between the people of Ireland and " the only friends from whom they had any reasonable hope—he meant the Liberal democracy of Great Britain." His judgment, he declared, was clear, and not even his constituents could alter it. No power on earth could alter it, " for it was the *fiat* of his conscience," and " he claimed to act on his conscience." Mr. J. Redmond, on the other hand, supported Colonel Nolan. Mr. Parnell's offer to resign upon the conditions laid down on Saturday proved, Mr. Redmond urged, the sincerity of his patriotism. He contended that, although the English alliance was important, " they were asked to sell their leader " to preserve it, and that they were bound to see what they were getting as his price. Mr. Parnell promptly took up his spokesman's words. " Don't sell me for nothing," he exclaimed dramatically. " If you get my value, you may change me to-morrow." Mr. Redmond went on to argue that, in selling their leader, "they were selling absolutely and irrevocably the independence of the Irish party." He pointed out that while Mr. Gladstone had denied Mr. Parnell's statements, "he abstained absolutely from giving to the public or to the Irish nation anything in the shape of a definite or clear statement as to what he proposed." Mr. Redmond, for his part, unhesitatingly preferred Mr. Parnell's word to Mr. Gladstone's. He twitted the majority with having changed their attitude only "when Mr. Gladstone issued his ukase that Mr. Parnell should be trampled under foot," and he warned the champions of the tenants on the "Campaign" estates, that "Mr. Parnell's dethronement would rend the Irish people in America in twain," and so stop "the source of the supply on which these tenants had been depending for so long." Mr. Healy, like Mr. Sexton, based his opposition to the motion on grounds of pure political expediency. He boasted that he "went to the Leinster Hall meeting and pronounced for Mr. Parnell in the face of English clamour." "Aye," he continued, "we stood up for Mr. Parnell against the Bulls of the Pope of Rome. It was not likely we would allow ourselves to be influenced by the declarations of a single Wesleyan pulpit." It was only when Mr. Healy perceived that Mr. Parnell had alienated that body of opinion "which they were bound in this matter to defer to," that Mr. Healy did, in fact, defer to it. "Having neither armies nor fleets," observed this earnest advocate of the "union of hearts," "we are bound to rely upon constitutional and Parliamentary methods." The Home Rule, however, at which Mr. Healy aims, is essentially the same as the Home Rule demanded by Mr. Parnell. "We believe," he said, "that the Home Rule Bill outlined in Mr. Parnell's Manifesto is not one the Irish people could accept. I cordially join in that sentiment. (Loud cheers.) I pledge myself to accept no such measure." Mr. Parnell himself followed Mr. Healy. After bitterly reproaching his former secretary with ingratitude, and exclaiming "That Mr. Healy should be here to-day to destroy me, is due to myself," he went on to inquire who had asked Mr. Healy to second the resolution at the Leinster Hall meeting, calling upon him not to retire, and who had asked Mr. Justin M'Carthy "to travel to Dublin, and to say that he could give secret information to throw a different complexion on hidden events?" "I did not give Mr. Justin

M'Carthy any information," added Mr. Parnell. " Where was Mr. Sexton ?" he went on, " at this meeting ?" " Where were you all ? Why did you encourage me to come forward and maintain my leadership in the face of the world, if you were not going to stand by me ?" Mr. Parnell then reverted to and amplified the argument already used by Mr. Redmond. He was ready to be deposed, provided they got value for his deposition, and as a proof that they would not get adequate value, he told the story of the negotiations conducted on Saturday and Sunday by Mr. M'Carthy. " We are all agreed," he said, " that you will not have this Bill," and the remark was greeted with loud cheers. " There has not been a man to say a word in favour of this Bill. But are you sure that you will be able to get anything better ? " Mr. Parnell assured them they would not. He said he knew what Mr. Gladstone, Sir William Harcourt, and Mr. Morley would do for them. " I know that there is not a single one of the lot to be trusted," he added, " unless you trust yourselves." Therefore the author of the Manifesto adjured the party he had trained so well, to be true to their own selves, and it would follow, as the night the day, they could not be false to any man.

On Tuesday, several hours were wasted in reading telegrams and discussing the communications sent to the delegates in America. The debate was not so interesting as on the previous day, but some lively episodes occurred, and some valuable statements were made. Mr. Barry, a determined anti-Parnellite, " respectfully submitted " that it was not in order for Mr. Parnell's private secretary, Mr. Campbell, to speak of him and his friends as " the infamous caucus in the corner," whereupon the chairman characteristically declared that " he would confirm Mr. Campbell's word, if necessary." Mr. Healy was rebuked for his " most insolent and impertinent " conduct, as he had been compelled to withdraw an imputation of falsehood made against Mr. Parnell the day before. He took his correction very kindly, and presently expressed his sense of the dignity of the chairman's action. A great point was made by some of Mr. Parnell's supporters of the alleged fact that a telegram from the American delegates, hostile to their chief, had been greeted with cheers by some anti-Parnellite members of the party in the National Liberal Club—" in an English Club," as it was bitterly described. Mr. O'Kelly again asked whether any man, knowing Mr. Gladstone's " intellectual subtlety," would assert that there was "anything like real or valuable contradiction" of anything that Mr. Parnell had said, in Mr. Gladstone's letter, and he announced that he had received a telegram from "their old friend, Devoy." Mr. Arthur O'Connor, like Mr. Sexton, thought it necessary to inform the meeting that in repudiating Mr. Parnell, he looked to the approbation of his conscience. He was a party, it is true, to the resolution moved by Mr. Sexton, which proposed Mr. Parnell's re-election to the chair. But he explained his attitude. Like Dr. Tanner and Mr. J. F. X. O'Brien, Mr. Arthur O'Connor "considered himself then in the position of one of the Old Guard of Napoleon giving a parting salute." Mr. W. A. Macdonald reminded the meeting that when Mr. Sexton came down to the House on the first day of the Session, "he told the members of the party that Mr. Parnell's leadership ought to be continued." At length a division was taken, when the Noes were 44 and the Ayes were 29, showing a majority of 15 against Mr. Parnell. Twelve members of the party, including the six American delegates, were absent, and one seat, that for North Kilkenny, was vacant.

A letter from Sir William Harcourt and a joint letter from Mr. Labouchere and Professor Stuart, both of which denied certain statements made by Mr. Parnell in the course of Monday's debate, were issued on Tuesday. The same evening a meeting of the Central Branch of the Irish National League sent a telegram to Mr. Parnell expressing its "undivided allegiance" to him and the Irish cause. On the following day—sixteen days after the verdict in the divorce action—the "Standing Committee of the Archbishops and Bishops of Ireland" issued an address declaring that "they could no longer keep silent." "As pastors," the prelates announced, they did not base "their judgment and solemn declaration on political grounds, but simply and solely on the facts and circumstances revealed"—more than a fortnight before—"in the London Divorce Court." They repudiated Mr. Parnell's leadership, and pronounced him to be "wholly unworthy of Christian confidence." But the Irish Bishops are rarely content in these days to speak "as pastors" only. Political motives, they did acknowledge, stimulated their zeal. "As Irishmen," they confessed, "devoted to their country . . . and earnestly intent on securing for it the benefits of domestic legislation, they could not but be influenced by the conviction that the continuance of Mr. Parnell as leader . . . must have the effect of disorganizing their ranks," and even of causing " inevitable defeat at the approaching general election." With so dangerous a sinner their lordships could no longer prudently co-operate. Accordingly they exhorted the faithful to throw him over.

On Wednesday, December 3, Mr. Parnell fell back upon the ground he had taken up on the previous Saturday. Mr. Clancy, one of his supporters, proposed that the Whips of the party should be instructed to obtain from the Liberal leaders a statement of their views on the control of the constabulary and the settlement of the land question, before any further consideration of the subject under debate. Mr. Clancy argued that there was no reason why, if Mr. Gladstone were prepared to give the assurances desired by Mr. Parnell, the fact should not be made public. The control of the constabulary, he said, was a question " at the very bottom of their demands," and they also wanted the settlement of the land question in their hands. It was further stated that if the Liberal leaders gave assurances of a satisfactory nature upon these points, Mr. Parnell would retire. The meeting was adjourned at Mr. Parnell's request, to afford him an opportunity to determine whether he should reserve to himself the right of accepting or rejecting the assurances to be obtained from the Liberal leaders, or concede it to the majority of the Irish party.

On the Thursday Mr. Parnell announced his decision. He was prepared to let the party be the judge of the sufficiency or insufficiency of the assurances, upon condition that the party took the responsibility off his shoulders on to their own. That responsibility, Mr. Parnell said, depended not merely on his position as chairman of the Parliamentary party, but upon his position as " leader of the Irish nation." If, therefore, he transferred it to the majority of the party, as he professed to be ready to do, he claimed that they should "by solemn resolution" record their judgment in the face of their constituencies. He insisted on the need of caution in dealing with Mr. Gladstone. His own word, he said, had been "grievously challenged" about the Hawarden communications, " but no attempt had been made to contradict him, no attempt had been made to say in what single respect inaccuracy existed, no attempt had been made to show, if there was inaccuracy, what the correction for the inaccuracy ought to be." "In other words," he proceeded, "although I have been contradicted by a wholesale system of slander, we have not been informed, we have not been told that the constabulary will be given." "You are dealing," Mr. Parnell warned his hearers, "with an unrivalled sophist." "You are dealing," he repeated, "with a man with whom, and to whom it is as impossible to give a direct answer to a plain and simple question, as it is for me impossible to give an indirect answer to a plain and simple question." "I know this old gentleman well," he added. "I do say this, having been in communication with him since 1882, upon many important subjects and topics connected with Ireland—I can tell you, gentlemen, I have never yet succeeded in getting a straight answer to a single straight question from him, and they have been many and numerous that had to be laid before him." In his desire to bring home to the meeting the perils they might have to face in treating with this "unrivalled sophist," Mr. Parnell reminded them of an important bit of secret history relating to the Home Rule Bill of 1886—that project which has been invariably represented to the outside public as the happy offspring of the "union of hearts," and as being freely accepted by the Irish party in complete and final satisfaction of all Irish demands. The Home Rule Bill, said Mr. Parnell, was forced upon himself and upon his colleagues, and it was accepted by them *pro tanto* only. Just before it was introduced, Mr. Parnell received a message that if the Irish party "did not accept that Bill as it stood, the Cabinet would resign in a body." Thereupon Mr. Parnell called together Mr. Dillon, Mr. O'Brien, Mr. Healy, Mr. Sexton, Mr. M'Carthy, Mr. O'Kelly, the late Mr. Dwyer Gray, and Mr. Davitt. He said, "Here is the Bill. It is a Parliamentary hit. It is nothing more. I have been told to-day by Mr. Gladstone that it is for us to take or reject that Bill, and if we undertake the responsibility of leaving-it, he will make a statement in the House of Commons to-night declaring that he can do no more, and that the responsibility and the want of solution for the Irish Question must rest upon us." Mr. Parnell then placed the situation before his friends. "Here is the Bill," he said, "with all its defects, absence of sufficient control of the police; will you take it or will you leave it?"

His colleagues, he informed the meeting in No. 15 Committee Room, said to him "that they would accept it *pro tanto,* reserving for Committee the right of enforcing and, if necessary, reconsidering their position with regard to those important questions." Mr. Healy, who replied to Mr. Parnell, supplemented his account of this remarkable transaction. He said that Mr. Parnell displayed true statesmanship in his conduct of this secret conference in 1886. The members present were cavilling over the details, or, rather, over the absence of certain provisions in the Government Bill. "Mr. Parnell," continued Mr. Healy, "rose from the table and said—and it clenched and ended the discussion—' Gentlemen, two great statesmen have left the Cabinet. You have now an opportunity of wrecking another Cabinet,' whereupon they all said, ' Good evening.' That was the way in which the discussion was concluded." Mr. Parnell ended his speech on Mr. Clancy's amendment by repeating his offer to retire from the chairmanship upon the terms he had stated, and he suggested that two resolutions of his own should be substituted for Mr. Clancy's, as defining more exactly his own position and that of his opponents. The good faith of this suggestion was suspected by the anti-Parnellites, and a very heated and angry discussion followed. Two important matters which had cropped up in the debates of the previous days were brought out with fresh clearness. Mr. Sexton once more stated that the only reason why he and his friends desired to get rid of Mr. Parnell, was to satisfy the scruples of the British Gladstonians. It became their duty, he said, to call upon their leader to abdicate " as soon as it became apparent to them, that the result of Mr. Parnell's retention of his leadership would be infallibly to draw away from the Liberal camp a sufficient proportion of the electors of the country to render victory impossible." It was then that Mr. Sexton's conscience uttered its irrevocable *fiat,* and that the man who had proposed Mr. Parnell as chairman, and had told other members that his leadership should be continued, became at twenty-four hours' notice his steadfast opponent. Personal considerations, Mr. Sexton was at pains to insist, had no place in their thoughts. "He, for his part, had no other ambition but to serve his country in the ranks." The anti-Parnellites, indeed, still professed their eagerness to leave to Mr. Parnell the substance of his power. In the debate of Tuesday, December 2,

Mr. M. J. Kenny, an anti-Parnellite, had stated that on the previous Wednesday, the first day upon which the party met after the publication of Mr. Gladstone's letter to Mr. Morley, a compromise had been tendered to Mr. Parnell by his opponents. They had suggested "that Mr. Parnell should retire from the chair for a time, they undertaking not to fill it up in the meantime." Mr. Kenny's statement was now expanded and confirmed by Mr. Sexton. "If they were to change their leader," he declared, "it would be possible for them to surround him with a Cabinet ; and in this connexion he had told Mr. Parnell that in his retirement he could nominate the committee." Mr. Healy, "with much emotion," had already pledged himself on Wednesday that, if Mr. Parnell accepted the judgment of the majority on the sufficiency of the assurances of the Liberal leaders, "his voice would be the first, at the very earliest moment possible consonant with the liberties of his country, to call him back to his proper place as leader of the Irish race." There is no evidence to show that Mr. Parnell was much affected by either the promises or the emotion of the men of whose fidelity he had just experienced such convincing proofs. He adhered to the terms he had offered the majority, and when "the storm in a tea-cup," as he called it, provoked by their suspicions of his proposed substitutes for Mr. Clancy's resolution had been lulled, he explicitly pledged himself to resign if, by vote, the majority of the party decided that the answer of the Liberal leaders was satisfactory. Thereupon Mr. Clancy's resolution was carried in a slightly modified form, with two dissentients only, and the meeting adjourned to give time for the proposed negotiations with Mr. Gladstone, Sir William Harcourt, and Mr. Morley. The Liberal leaders decided that Mr. Gladstone alone, as leader of the Liberal party, could speak in its name, and accordingly Sir William Harcourt and Mr. Morley declined to see the delegates of the Irish Parliamentary party. After a good deal of rather puerile diplomacy, in the course of which Mr. Gladstone granted the delegates an interview, he finally refused to make any statement of the intentions of himself and his colleagues on any provisions of a Home Rule Bill, "in connexion with the question of the leadership of the Irish party." In other words, Mr. Gladstone made Mr. Parnell's deposition a condition precedent to any announcement of his intentions, nor

2

did he give any definite or tangible pledge to make such an announcement, even confidentially, if that condition were fulfilled.

It is difficult to suppose that Mr. Parnell did not from the first foresee that these proceedings would be fruitless. In any event, he risked nothing by the offers he had made. If by any inconceivable piece of fatuity the Liberal leaders had given the delegates clear and positive assurances upon the subjects referred to them, Mr. Parnell's hold over his countrymen and over his party would have become stronger than ever. He had elicited from Mr. Sexton a promise that under no circumstances should he be called upon to retire from Parliament. His retirement from the leadership, accomplished upon such terms, would have been universally regarded by Irish Nationalists as a crowning personal sacrifice to his country's cause—a sacrifice insuring the substitution of true national independence for the sham "self-government" of 1886. In the popularity won by the achievement of so solid an advantage Mr. Parnell would have possessed a real security that the promises of Mr. Sexton and Mr. Healy would be kept—that his retirement would be merely nominal, and that it would be brief. If, on the other hand, assurances had been given which were not clear and positive, and they were nevertheless pronounced to be satisfactory by the solemn vote of Mr. Parnell's opponents, he would have been able to quote their action to their constituents as a convincing proof that they were either "traitors" or fools. When, as actually happened, the Liberal leaders declined to give any assurances at all, Mr. Parnell could plausibly charge both them and the seceders from his own party with treachery, and he had gained a delay of several days.

The fifth and last chapter contains the report of the final meeting of the Irish party on Saturday, December 6, of their disruption that evening by the secession of the majority, of the subsequent meetings of the rival sections on December 8 and 9, and of Mr. Parnell's departure for Ireland on the evening of the last-named day. The book concludes with the observations of *The Times* upon the scene at Euston Station and Mr. Parnell's valedictory remarks.

The earlier part of Saturday's meeting was spent in a prolonged wrangle over a resolution directing the delegates to report upon the negotiations with the Liberal leaders. After the report had been read, Mr. Abraham, an anti-Parnellite, endeavoured to read

a resolution, in defiance of Mr. Parnell's ruling that Mr. John
O'Connor, a member of his own faction, was in possession of the chair.
Mr. Abraham handed his resolution to Mr. M'Carthy. Mr. M'Carthy
rose, "and was apparently about to read it, when Mr. Parnell,
who throughout the scene remained standing, grasped the copy of
the resolution from Mr. M'Carthy, saying, ' I will not receive
it.' " A scene of great uproar followed, but Mr. Parnell adhered
firmly to his ruling, and finally obtained a hearing for Mr. John
O'Connor, who moved a long resolution expressing the regret of
the party that Mr. Gladstone refused to negotiate with them, or to
state his views on the two vital points submitted for his consideration, " except upon the condition that this party shall first
remove Mr. Parnell from the chairmanship." A succession of "scenes" followed. A taunt from Mr. J. Redmond
describing Mr. Gladstone as " the master of the party " elicited
an obvious retort from Mr. Healy, referring to Mr. Parnell's private
life. Mr. Parnell replied by calling his assailant "a cowardly little
scoundrel " for insulting a woman. Mr. Abraham desired to
move, as an amendment to Mr. O'Connor's resolution, a resolution declaring Mr. Parnell's tenure of office at an end. Mr.
Parnell ruled that this was a new substantive motion, which could
not be put as an amendment. Mr. Healy sneered. Mr. Parnell
threatened. Mr. Arthur O'Connor declared they were " in danger
of becoming the laughing stock of the world "—a remark which the
party, with unconscious humour, greeted with " unanimous
cheers "—and adjured them to terminate proceedings which were
" rapidly becoming a disgraceful farce." Other members thought
differently, and Mr. Leamy had just pleaded, amid cheers, Mr.
Parnell's services in having " brought their country to its present
glorious position," when Mr. Justin M'Carthy rose, and called
upon all who thought with him to retire from the room. Forty-
five members thereupon withdrew, and the disruption of, perhaps,
the most perfectly disciplined party Parliament has ever seen,
was consummated. Mr. Parnell remained behind with twenty-six
adherents. After a speech from Colonel Nolan, he rose, and with
much bitterness taunted the men who had " deserted " with
dreading " the lightning of public opinion in Ireland." They
had been false to all their pledges, and Ireland, he declared, had
the power and the will to fill the places of the deserters. Mr. John
O'Connor's motion was then carried unanimously, and the his-

toric series of meetings in No. 15 Committee Room came to a close.

The meetings of the anti-Parnellite faction held between the disruption of the party and Mr. Parnell's departure for Ireland do not call for any extended comment. Mr. Parnell received a characteristically effusive telegram from Mr. William O'Brien, to which he sent a characteristically curt reply. The delegates to America, with the exception of Mr. T. Harrington, gave in a cautiously-worded adhesion to the seceding majority, and on Tuesday, December 9, six days after the Irish Roman Catholic Bishops had issued their tardy repudiation of Mr. Parnell, and when it had now become quite clear that the majority of the Parliamentary party were committed against him, Sir John Pope Hennessy, the selected Nationalist candidate for North Kilkenny, informed Mr. Parnell that " he could not as an Irish Catholic " support him. Sir John Pope Hennessy was at once adopted by the seceders as their candidate, and the same night Mr. Parnell went over to inaugurate his Irish " Campaign."

THE PARNELLITE SPLIT.

CHAPTER I.

THE IRISH PARTY AND THEIR CHIEF.

MEETING OF THE NATIONAL LEAGUE.

At the fortnightly meeting of the National League, held in Dublin on November 18, MR. J. E. REDMOND, M.P., who was in the chair said he felt very highly honoured at the privilege of presiding at that meeting, the more so because it afforded him an opportunity of speaking from a position of some authority a few words on a subject which must be uppermost in the minds and hearts of the Irish people that day. They would read with amusement, tempered only with disgust, the stupid and malicious reports in reference to the political position of their leader, Mr. Parnell (loud cheering), which within the last few days had appeared in the columns of the anti-Irish Press in England. He took leave to say that the talk that Mr. Parnell's political position had been prejudiced in the remotest degree by what had taken place within the last few days was the most grotesque absurdity. (Cheers.) Mr. Parnell's colleagues in the House of Commons were bound to him by the double ties of private friendship and political allegiance. (Cheers.) For himself he might say that for the last ten years Mr. Parnell had been his friend, and nothing had been done that could tend in the remotest degree to weaken that friendship. On the contrary, it did seem to him that when trouble came to him, when a shadow came to burden his life, it was the time for every man who called himself his friend to draw closer and nearer to him. (Cheers.) Private friendship was one thing; political allegiance was an entirely different thing. The Irish party were bound to their leader by ties of absolute confidence and unswerving allegiance, and in that the Irish party reflected the sentiment of the entire Irish people. (Cheers.) The

A

position which Mr. Parnell occupied that day in politics had been won by ten years of unceasing courage and unparalleled success. (Cheers.) He found Ireland weak, hopeless, and despised. He had brought her to-day to a position of power. From the commencement of his political career down to that moment he had been assailed by the remorseless and undying hate of Ireland's enemies. No weapon was too mean to be used in attacks upon him in public and in private, and the measure of Mr. Parnell's fidelity to the Irish cause had been the measure of the hatred of his enemies. He had borne those attacks with patience, and the Irish people were not so foolish and so ungrateful as to forget those things at a moment of this kind. (Cheers.) It is quite possible that if Mr. Parnell were to consider his own selfish interest he might, perhaps, evade the duties and responsibilities of his great position ; but if the Irish people thought Mr. Parnell entertained the remotest idea of taking such a course, he believed the whole Irish race would go to him, and beg of him to maintain his position at their head. But, with that indomitable resolution which was, perhaps, his most prominent characteristic, Mr. Parnell had stated his intention to stand by Ireland to the last, and they would tell him that never, in his whole political career, were the Irish people more determined to stand by him than they were to-day. (Cheers.) It was quite true that the meeting and Mr. Parnell himself would consider that these observations of his were unnecessary. But he thought it was desirable that their friends in England and Scotland should not be misled for a moment by the attacks which were being made by the enemies of Ireland. Mr. Parnell had that day, as he had at the commencement, the enthusiastic devotion and unswerving political allegiance of the Irish people. (Cheers.) He asserted, and he spoke in the name of the whole of Mr. Parnell's colleagues in the House of Commons, that the nation stood united as one man at the back of their leader. He believed if the malicious attacks by their enemies on their political leader should be persisted in they would result in strengthening the power of Mr. Parnell, and rendering more united at his back the forces of the national movement. (Cheers.)

ALDERMAN DILLON said Mr. Parnell would read with pleasure and satisfaction of the reception which had been given to his name that day at one of the largest meetings of the National

League held in that room for some months. This further attempt to hurl him from the leadership would only secure him more firmly than ever in his position as leader of the Irish party.

Mr. LEAMY, M.P., said this question was one between the Irish people and Mr. Parnell, and the Irish people would not accept the interference of any one outside, whether friend or not. (Hear, hear.) Mr. Parnell was the chosen leader, and as long as he was willing to lead they were willing to follow. (Cheers.) The attack on Mr. Parnell was not due to any sense of morality, but was a matter of revenge for the success he had achieved over his enemies. It was not a sense of morals that inspired his enemies, but a feeling of hate, because he had done so much good for Ireland, and would continue to do good for Ireland, and would continue to do good for the country. (Cheers.) The time was opportune for declaring their loyalty to Mr. Parnell, and the Irish party would rally around him next week with more devotion than ever, when he would be again leading the combat in the House of Commons. (Cheers.) He wondered what would be thought of the men who might suggest that it was necessary to get some one else to be chairman of the party. (Laughter.) He would like to see an Irish member who would propose any one else go before his constituency. He would like to see any one who would have the audacity to do such a thing.

Dr. KENNY, M.P., said it was their duty to declare their un-altered attachment to Mr. Parnell through weal and woe. If ever a man was necessary for the cause of a country, Mr. Parnell was necessary for theirs. (Hear, hear.) The Irish people saw in him the wisdom and indomitable courage that were necessary for their leader, and he had now brought them to the gate of success. They would not permit him to give up his position, even if he was inclined to do so. It would be simply effrontery on the part of the English or Scotch people to interfere in this question, and the Irish people had made up their minds that Mr. Parnell was to be their leader. (Cheers.)

Mr. W. A. MACDONALD, M.P., said he entertained strong opinions in reference to this matter. He had been long of the opinion that private matters of this kind had nothing to do, and ought to have nothing to do, with a man's public position. He always regretted the retirement of Sir Charles Dilke, because of his great efficiency in his department. One of the reasons why he felt that Mr. Parnell should continue as their leader was that if the events of the last two days had occurred a year ago, when the English people were wavering, the Irish cause would have been injured (cries of "No, no," and expressions of dissent); but he believed no injury would now be done to the Irish cause by what occurred, and the people of England would be guilty of gross ingratitude if they did not recognize Mr. Parnell's services in Ireland. (Hear.)

COUNT PLUNKETT said Mr. Parnell was not on his trial before the Irish people, who had no reason to change their position towards him.

Mr. W. REDMOND, M.P., said Mr. Parnell had endeared himself to the Irish party, and he looked on him as the greatest champion that ever fought for Ireland. He would not only follow Mr. Parnell in the House of Commons, but would follow him to death, if necessary. (Cheers.)

Mr. J. J. CLANCY, M.P., said that when the matters decided within the last few days were first mentioned, he wrote to Mr. Parnell, telling him that, whatever the consequences might be, he might count on his support so long as he was true to Ireland. (Cheers.)

Mr. J. G. S. MACNEILL, M.P., also expressed his unswerving affection for and allegiance to Mr. Parnell, and said he hoped he would be by his side when Mr. Parnell made his first speech in the Parliament of College-green. (Cheers.)

Other speeches followed in the same strain.

VIEWS OF THE AMERICAN DELEGATES.

In the course of the same day, the following opinions on Mr. Parnell's position were expressed by the undermentioned members of the Parnellite delegation to America :—

Mr. GILL, M.P., speaking for himself and for Mr. Dillon and Mr. O'Brien, said :—" The result of the case of 'O'Shea v. O'Shea and Parnell' cannot affect Mr. Parnell's standing in political life. The issue in the case is of little importance. Mr. Parnell has thought fit not to defend himself. That is his business, and the fact ought not to enter into politics, nor become a factor in legislative questions between England and Ireland. So far as I can see, the Irish Parliamentary party will take no notice of the

Nov. 18.

verdict." Mr. Gill stated the circumstances of the election of Mr. Parnell to the leadership of the party. After the death of Mr. Butt, he said, the party was divided between Mr. Parnell and Mr. Shaw, there being 16 in favour of each, thus causing a deadlock. Then Captain O'Shea, who was the thirty-third member of the party, entered the room and cast a deciding vote for Mr. Parnell. By this act, therefore, Mr. Parnell was made leader of the Irish Parliamentary party.

Mr. O'BRIEN himself, in the course of an interview, said that he regarded the attack of the Tory newspapers on Mr. Parnell as beneath notice. For ten years, he continued, the same papers had assailed Mr. Parnell's character, not from motives of public morality, but on account of his unrivalled leadership. With regard to the O'Shea case, Mr. O'Brien said he knew nothing, but he went on to vituperate Captain O'Shea in extreme terms. He added :—"The Irish party and people may be trusted to safeguard the interests of the cause without the least regard to the rumours set afloat by moralists like Pigott's employers."

Mr. T. P. O'CONNOR was also clear that it was for the Irish alone to choose their leader, that they would cling to Mr. Parnell, and that the Gladstonian Liberals would not interfere with their choice. He said that "the Irish envoys knew that the people at home were resolved to keep Mr. Parnell at the head of the party. With regard to the Gladstonian Liberals, he believed that they would act at the present conjuncture according to their convictions on the Irish question. Their policy was to leave to the Irish the government of their own affairs, and that included the choice of leader. It was for the Irish people alone to choose their leader, and, besides, all the English statesmen acknowledged that Mr. Parnell was the greatest Parliamentary leader that the Irish had ever had. His disappearance from that post would create dismay among the Nationalists."

THE LEINSTER HALL MEETING.

Nov. 20.

Two days later, on Thursday, November 20, a great meeting was held in the Leinster Hall, Dublin. The meeting was convened for the purpose of considering the policy of the Government in Ireland, to reiterate the demand for Home Rule, and to forward the movement in aid of evicted tenants. It was, how-

over, speedily turned into a demonstration in support of Mr.
Parnell. Twenty-five members of the Irish Parliamentary party
attended.

Among those on the platform were Messrs. Justin M'Carthy,
M.P., William Murphy, M.P., William Redmond, M.P., Pierce
Mahony, M.P., T. Healy, M.P., J. Redmond, M.P., Thomas
Condon, M.P., Dr. Kenny, M.P., Swift M'Neill, M.P., J. J.
Clancy, M.P., the Right Hon. S. Walker, Serjeant Hemphill,
The Macdermot, Q.C., &c.

On the motion of Mr. WILLIAM MURPHY, M.P., the chair was
taken by the Lord Mayor of Dublin.

Dr. KENNY read the following telegram, which had been received from the Irish delegates in America :—

" We stand firmly by the leadership of the man who has
brought the Irish people through unparalleled difficulties and
dangers and from servitude and despair to the very threshold of
emancipation with a genius, courage, and success unequalled in
any history. (Cheers.) We do so not only out of gratitude for
those unparalleled services in the past, but in profound conviction
that Mr. Parnell's statesmanship and matchless qualities as
leader are essential to the safety of our cause." (Cheers.)

The LORD MAYOR, in opening the proceedings, said it must be
a great support to Mr. Parnell, whose life and fame and hope
were centred and bound up with the cause of Ireland naturally,
to see that there was no diminution in the number and the
warmth of his followers ; but that, on the contrary, they massed
themselves at his back compactly as on the joyful day when his
heel was planted on the neck of the malignant and fallen foe. It
was living in England that caused any lapse that had occurred
in Mr. Parnell. If he had lived in Ireland he would never have
been contaminated by O'Shea. However, he had chosen to keep
silence, and that was his own affair. They had no more right to
question his private action and motives than they had to interfere with him as a Protestant if he chose not to go to church on
Sunday or eat meat on Friday. (Cheers and laughter.) The only
crime Ireland would know of Mr. Parnell was one which she
knew was impossible in him—the crime of treason to Ireland.
(Cheers.)

Mr. JUSTIN M'CARTHY, M.P., moved :—

" That this meeting, interpreting the sentiment of the Irish people that no side issue shall be permitted to obstruct the progress of the great cause of Home Rule for Ireland, declares that in all political matters Mr. Parnell possesses the confidence of the Irish nation, and that this meeting rejoices at the determination of the Irish Parliamentary party to stand by their leader." (Cheers.)

Mr. M'Carthy said they were not going to change their leader because of the cry raised against him. (Hear, hear.) He did not know whether it might not have been chivalrous and generous motives that induced Mr. Parnell not to enter any defence in the action, but they might take from him the suggestion that if Mr. Frank Lockwood had been allowed to cross-examine they would have a very different story before them. (Cheers.) If they found a leader of consummate skill and absolute devotion, a man who could lead them as no one else was ever able to lead the Irish cause, a man who had raised the Irish cause far beyond the level to which it was raised by Grattan or O'Connell, were they going to change this man and set up some wholly inferior man in his place because some Tory and Liberal Secessionist newspapers said that the man had gone wrong? (Cries of "No, no.") No man of common sense would accept such a doctrine as that. If Mr. Parnell had gone morally wrong, was that the least reason to excuse him from doing his duty to the people whom he was leading to victory? They all knew they could not do without him, and their duty was, firstly, secondly, and lastly, to raise their country. (Cheers.) No one could say that the Irish race was wanting in honour or in virtue, and they certainly should not like to go to the London Press, or the Press of the Tory party, or the Liberal Secessionist party, for instructions in these subjects. (Cheers.) They would say to their opponents in England :— " Look to your own men and women and do not touch Irish men and women." (Cheers.) The speaker, in conclusion, expressed a conviction that the cause would be carried on to most perfect success under the leadership of Mr. Parnell. He did not believe they would lose in this contest one honest Englishman, Scotchman, or Irishman who stood by them from the first. (Cheers.) There might be some who would fall away from them, not only in Great Britain, but over here, and to those people he could only say let them fall away ; the national cause would go on without them. (Cheers.)

Mr. T. M. HEALY, M.P., seconded the motion. He said that for Irishmen Mr. Parnell was less a man than an institution. If he were to-morrow to resign his seat for Cork he would be instantly re-elected. (Cheers.) Mr. Balfour might go down and oppose him with the battle cry of "light railways and heavy sentences." (Laughter and cheers.) They were accused by their opponents of being servile to Mr. Parnell, but who, he would ask, was servile to Mr. Parnell? He (Mr. Healy) was no man's man but Ireland's (cheers), and he supported the resolution, not for the sake of Mr. Parnell as an individual, but for the sake of Ireland as a nation. (Cheers.) He observed that there was from one quarter where he would have expected silence a recommendation to Mr. Parnell to retire. Some of them might have heard of the king who never said a foolish thing, and who said to his brother James, "Nobody, my friend, will ever kill me to make you king." (Laughter and cheers.) When he (Mr. Healy) thought of the possibilities that might occur were they to join in this demand for dethronement of Mr. Parnell he saw a very pretty party in the House of Commons. (Cheers and laughter.) They would see included in it representatives of the Socialists, the land nationalizers, the barristers, and probably the attorneys. (Laughter.) He looked at this question in a very different manner from the way the English people looked at it. They were born Irishmen and Nationalists, and they remembered the time, not yet ten years ago, when Ireland stood ragged and distressed begging at the gate of nations, when the representation in Parliament was a bye-word and a disgrace, when the sacred House of Commons was little better than an auction mart for the honour of Irish representatives, and he would never for a moment forget who it was that had changed all that. (Cheers.) The right to govern Ireland depended on the personal character of no man. If they were convinced of the righteousness of Home Rule, the instruments they selected for the purpose of guiding them towards it was a matter for them, and not for the English people, but for Ireland. (Cheers.) For his part, he declined to take the cork out of the soda-water bottle to see it fizz. (Laughter and cheers.) He was satisfied with a National party, and by the National party and the National leader he would abide. While they owed a duty to Mr. Parnell, the latter owed a duty to them. They had stood by Mr. Parnell, and Mr. Parnell must stand by them. (Hear, hear.) He would only say, in conclusion, that he joined in the metaphor used by Mr. M'Carthy with reference to the ship sailing under experienced hands and at a time of crisis and danger and struggle recommend to them the weather-beaten monition :—" You are requested not to speak to the man at the wheel." (Continued cheers.)

The resolution was supported by Mr. SAMUEL WALKER, Q.C., Mr. PIERCE MAHONY, M.P., and the MAYOR of CORK, and carried unanimously. MR. JOHN REDMOND moved the following resolution :—" That, impressed by the generous sentiments of the masses of the people of Great Britain and their determination to end for ever the misgovernment of our country, this meeting, assuring them of the gratitude of Irishmen, repels with indignation every suggestion of compromise terms with the coercion Ministry, and declares its satisfaction at the policy of combat announced by Mr. Parnell for the coming Session."

THE MACDERMOT, Q.C., seconded the resolution, and MR. J. J. CLANCY, M.P., and COLONEL NOLAN having spoken in support of it, the resolution was carried unanimously.

A vote of thanks having been passed to the Lord Mayor for presiding, the proceedings terminated.

MR. PARNELL RE-ELECTED BY HIS PARTY.

Parliament re-assembled on Tuesday, November 25. Pursuant to the notice which he had issued to his followers on November 15—the first day of the divorce action—Mr. Parnell met the members of the Irish party in No. 15 Committee Room shortly before 3 o'clock. A full muster awaited his appearance, and the welcome accorded to him was enthusiastic in the extreme. Loud cheers were given as he entered the room, and much hand-shaking and many assurances of continued allegiance preceded the business of the day.

On the motion of MR. M'CARTHY, MR. RICHARD POWER, the principal Whip of the Nationalist party, was voted to the chair. The first business was the re-election of MR. PARNELL as chairman of the party, which was proposed by Mr SEXTON, seconded by COLONEL NOLAN, and agreed to amid loud applause.

MR. PARNELL thanked the meeting for this further and fresh proof of their confidence in him, and stated that, in response to their

Nov. 25. unanimous desire, he would continue to discharge the duties of leader. After some further formal business the meeting adjourned, having lasted about an hour.

CHAPTER II.

MR. GLADSTONE'S ULTIMATUM AND ITS EFFECT.

In the course of the afternoon of the same day, November 25, the following letter from Mr. Gladstone ·to Mr. John Morley was communicated to Mr. Parnell :— Nov. 25.

" 1, Carlton-gardens, Nov. 24, 1890.

" My dear Morley,—Having arrived at a certain conclusion with regard to the continuance at the present moment of Mr. Parnell's leadership of the Irish party, I have seen Mr. M'Carthy on my arrival in town, ·and have inquired from him whether I was likely to receive from Mr. Parnell himself any communication on the subject. Mr. M'Carthy replied that he was unable to give me any information on the subject.

" I mentioned to him that in 1882, after the terrible murder in the Phœnix Park, Mr. Parnell, although totally removed from any idea of responsibility, had spontaneously written to me, and offered to take the Chiltern Hundreds, an offer much to his honour, but one which I thought it my duty to decline.

" While clinging to the hope of communication from Mr. Parnell, to whomsoever addressed, I thought it necessary, viewing the arrangements for the commencement of the Session to-morrow, to acquaint Mr. M'Carthy with the conclusion at which, after using all the means of observation and reflection in my power, I had myself arrived. It was that, notwithstanding the splendid services rendered by Mr. Parnell to his country, his continuance at the present moment in the leadership would be productive of consequences disastrous in the highest degree to the cause of Ireland. I think I may be warranted in asking you so far to expand the conclusion I have given above as to add that the continuance I speak of would not only place many hearty and effective friends of the Irish cause in a position of great embarrassment, but would render my retention of the leadership of the Liberal party, based as it has been mainly upon the prosecution of the Irish cause, almost a nullity. This expansion of my views I begged Mr. M'Carthy to regard as confidential, and not intended for his colleagues generally if he found that Mr. Parnell contemplated spontaneous action ; but I also begged that he would make known to the Irish party, at their meeting to-morrow afternoon, that such was my conclusion, if he should find that Mr. Parnell had not in contemplation any step of the nature indicated.

"I now write to you, in case Mr. M'Carthy should be unable to communicate with Mr. Parnell, as I understand you may possibly have an opening to-morrow through another channel. Should you have such an opening, I beg you to make known to Mr. Parnell the conclusion itself, which I have stated in the earlier part of this letter. I have thought it best to put it in terms simple and direct, much as I should have desired, had it lain within my power, to alleviate the personal nature of the situation. As respects the manner of conveying what my public duty has made it an obligation to say, I rely entirely on your good feeling, tact, and judgment.

"Believe me sincerely yours,

"W. E. GLADSTONE.

"Right Hon. John Morley, M.P."*

---

*The verdict in O'Shea v. O'Shea and Parnell was found on Monday, November 17 ; Mr. Gladstone's letter to Mr. Morley is dated November 24. The following passage from a speech delivered by Mr. Gladstone at the Retford Railway Station on December 11, may help to explain his silence during the week that intervened :—

Well, then came the proceedings in the Divorce Court, and those proceedings produced in my mind this effect. I am now telling you what is my own personal impression. I felt that the effect of those proceedings would be, so far as I could judge, to destroy entirely the moral weight and the moral force which are absolutely necessary in Parliament for any one who is to be the leading champion of a great national cause. But I felt also that we ought to look to Mr. Parnell himself to recognize that fact, and I knew very well that it was impossible that the question could reach a satisfactory solution except by his spontaneous action. (Cheers.) Therefore I determined to watch the state of feeling in this country, and I very soon found that the Liberal party in this country had made up its mind to draw a broad

The tenour of Mr. Gladstone's letter soon became known amongst the Nationalist members, and great excitement followed. They gathered in groups in the corridors and lobbies, and consternation marked every face. After some informal consultation of this kind, another meeting of the Irish party was called.

At this second meeting, which was held in the Conference Room at 9 o'clock, and was not so largely attended as the first, a copy of Mr. Gladstone's letter to Mr. John Morley was read, and considerable discussion took place in reference to its contents. All present admitted that after such a pronouncement the gravity of the situation had increased tenfold. Mr. Parnell did not remain at St. Stephen's long after the commencement of the Address, and he was consequently absent from the meeting. For this reason it was resolved to postpone any decisive action for the present. The copy of Mr. Gladstone's letter was sent on to Mr. Parnell, and the meeting adjourned until next day, the member for Cork being apprised of the fact.

Nov. 25.

MEETING OF THE IRISH PARTY.

The adjourned meeting of the Irish Parliamentary Party was held in No. 15 Committee Room at 2 o'clock on Wednesday, November 26.

Nov. 26.

Mr. Parnell, as chairman of the party, presided. Among those present were Messrs. Justin M'Carthy, vice-chairman of the party, J. Huntly M'Carthy, Knox, Tuite, Donal Sullivan, Commins, Hayden, Arthur O'Connor, Leamy, J. J. O'Kelly, Barry, Pierce Mahony, Swift MacNeill, Joseph Nolan, Crilly, W. A. Macdonald, Peter M'Donald, Blane, Condon, Sheehy, John O'Connor, P. J. O'Brien, E. Harrington, Webb, Lane, Morrogh, Molloy, T. A. Dickson, Murphy, Dalton, Fox, Deasy, Pinkerton, Flynn, H. Campbell, Quinn, Sheehan, Foley, R. Power, Stack, Harrison, Clancy, Sir Thomas Esmonde, Colonel Nolan, Dr. Kenny, and Dr. Tanner.

distinction between the national cause of Ireland and the person and the personal office of Mr. Parnell. (Cheers.) In fact, it became clear to me—and I am now speaking only as a witness of the fact—it became clear to me that the persistence of Mr. Parnell in the leadership of the Irish party would be completely fatal to the cause of Home Rule in England, Scotland, and Wales. (Cheers.)

Mr. Parnell formally opened the proceedings, but made no speech.

Mr. Barry, member for South Wexford, was the first to broach the subject of the day. He appealed to Mr. Parnell, as a co-adjutor of 11 or 12 years' standing, not to take a step which might prejudice for years the cause in the promotion of which they had been so long engaged. He referred in touching language to the services which Mr. Parnell had rendered to the party, but urged that the present crisis was one which demanded a personal sacrifice for the good of the country, and he put it to the Nationalist leader whether in the light of Mr. Gladstone's letter it would not be the wisest course for him to retire for a period from the leadership of the party.

Dr. Commins, another old coadjutor of Mr. Parnell's, followed. He said he had been associated with the leader for many years, and he thought he was therefore entitled to speak. He would regret as deeply as any one Mr. Parnell's retirement, but he felt that expediency demanded that he should adopt this course for a time.

Mr. Justin M'Carthy, in an eloquent and impassioned speech, dwelt at length on the sacrifices which Mr. Parnell had made in the cause of his country. Having regard to Mr. Gladstone's letter, however, he had come to the conclusion that the situation had undergone a material change since the previous day, and he endorsed the view which had been expressed by the last two speakers as to the advisability of the position being reconsidered.

Mr. Sexton held the same view, and in a speech which lasted nearly three-quarters of an hour made certain suggestions with a view to an amicable settlement He regretted the absence of Messrs. Dillon and O'Brien at such a juncture, but thought that the best course to adopt would be to ask every member of the party for an expression of opinion on the subject of the leadership. The proposal was received with applause.

Mr. Lane referred to the case of the tenants on the Ponsonby estate, and pressed upon Mr. Parnell the undesirability of taking any action which would be likely to prejudice them. He reminded the member for Cork that the farmers on this estate had been waiting for a prolonged period in the anticipation that their prospects would be improved by a general election, and he expressed an earnest hope that their expectations might not be disappointed just as they were on the verge of realization. He appreciated to the full the sacrifices which Mr. Parnell had made in the cause of Ireland, but he thought the temporary retirement of their chief would be the best thing that could happen at the present juncture.

After some further conversation, in the course of which COLONEL NOLAN and others urged Mr. Parnell to stick to his post, and not to permit himself to be dictated to by Mr. Gladstone when his own party had spoken unanimously in favour of his retention of the leadership, the meeting was adjourned in order to allow members who had charge of Bills to proceed to the House and take part in the ballot, which was fixed for 3 30 p.m.

At 5 o'clock the conference was resumed, and further speeches were delivered.

MR. SHEEHY spoke at some length with regard to the Smith-Barry tenants, on whose behalf he had been labouring for a long time, and, taking the same line as Mr. Lane, asked what would happen to these unfortunate people if the next general election went against the Home Rule party. The people in Tipperary were living on in the hope that an appeal to the constituencies would bring not merely comfort and prosperity to the country, but their own restoration to their homes. For the sake of the Smith-Barry tenants, he appealed to Mr. Parnell to consider carefully whether it would not be best for him to retire for a time from the leadership.

After some further discussion, in the course of which MR. JOHN O'CONNOR spoke strongly in favour of Mr. Parnell's continuance at the head of the party, a suggestion was made that the meeting should be postponed until the following Monday, in order that time might be given for obtaining the views of the absent members. Some members objected to this, and further discussion took place ; but eventually the proposal was adopted amid cheers.

MR. PARNELL, who throughout the proceedings had maintained the attitude of a listener, closed the proceedings by simply leaving the chair.

***

MICHAEL DAVITT ON MR. PARNELL.

The New York *Sun* and other New York papers of November 27

published a long interview with Michael Davitt, in which the following passages occur :--

MR. MICHAEL DAVITT, on leaving the conference held yesterday (Wednesday) evening by the chiefs of the Home Rule movement, gave a complete and categorical statement of his views of the effect of the Parnell scandal upon the cause of Home Rule.

MR. DAVITT, who appeared to be suffering from great depression of spirits, expresses himself as follows :—

" The crisis is unquestionably the most serious that has arisen for the last 20 years in connexion with the Irish cause. It is now a question whether the Irish people are to lose all chance of Home Rule for the next dozen years by clinging to the discredited character and leadership of Mr. Parnell, or whether, by throwing him over, they are to secure that for which Ireland has made untold sacrifices in supporting the Land League and National League movements.

" The decision practically rests with the Irish Parliamentary party. Mr. Parnell has been appealed to in vain—first by men who have worked with him faithfully since he entered public life ; secondly, by the best friends of Home Rule in Great Britain ; and, thirdly, at the meeting held yesterday evening, by Mr. Justin M'Carthy, Mr. Sexton, and his most trusty lieutenants. He is deaf to all these appeals, and still resolves to maintain his position at any cost to the Irish cause.

.   .   .   .

If public feeling in Ireland and the opinion of the Irish in America reinforce that section of the Parliamentary party which is now demanding Mr. Parnell's retirement, he will find it impossible to resist any longer. Should he not retire, and should a majority of the party not force him to do so, then, in my judgment, the cause of Home Rule is completely lost—because Mr. Gladstone has made it clear to the public of this free country that he remains as leader of the Home Rule movement only on condition that Mr. Parnell retires from his present position.

.   .   .   .

"I think the postponement till Monday is a wise step, and will be altogether in favour of the right policy. That is, I think it is a healthy sign that Mr. Parnell is not going to have it all his own way. The night before last he had it all his own way by trickery. Last night he did not have it all his own way. A most signifi-

Nov. 27.

cant incident is that Mr. Justin M'Carthy, the vice chairman of the party, who sided with Mr. Parnell on Tuesday night, addressed a speech last night to Mr. Parnell as chairman, in which he asked him to retire.

Asked whether Mr. Justin M'Carthy could succeed to the leadership in the event of Mr. Parnell's retirement, MR. DAVITT said :—

" As to that, probably he will. He is at present the vice-chairman of the party, but he is not at all, in my opinion, competent to lead a combative party. He is a very amiable, cultured man, and thoroughly faithful to the Irish cause."

On the question being repeated as to who would be the most likely man to succeed Mr. Parnell, and whether he himself had any chance of doing so, MR. DAVITT said :—

" As to who would be the leader I do not know. I am entirely out of the question."

Asked what he thought of Mr. Dillon's chance, MR. DAVITT said :—

" If Mr. Dillon was at home I have not the slightest doubt but what he would get a majority of the votes of the party. He is not only popular in Ireland, but he is very highly respected by the Home Rulers here in Great Britain. He is a man of unquestionable earnestness and great ability, and he would, I think, be the most popular of the five or six men who might have any claims to leadership."

To the question whether he or any other man could command the allegiance of the party, MR. DAVITT replied :—

" As for me, I am entirely out of the question ; I am not even in Parliament and do not want to be."

Asked again to say whether he believed that if it should be decided to retain Mr. Parnell's leadership the cause of Home Rule would be dead, MR. DAVITT said :—

" The cause of Home Rule is not only dead, but, if you will permit me to say so, is damned for at least 12 years, Mr. Gladstone at once throws it up. The Liberal party wipes it off the slate, and, unless the Tories come round and give Ireland Home Rule, which is very unlikely—just about as likely as the Queen sending for me to form a Cabinet—we shall not get it.

B

Mr. Davitt, being invited to take into account the enormous influence which the Catholic question had on the subject and to say what he thought of the attitude of the bishops and priests of Ireland in the present juncture, said :—

" So far that attitude has been—well, I was going to use a very strong word, but I will not ; I will put it this way. They should have spoken out, because, poor as Ireland has been and trampled upon as she has been in the past, she has at her moral bankers' probably greater credit than any other nation. In other words, Ireland has always been remarkable for her regard for chastity and virtue, and especially for the sacred rights of the domestic hearthstone. Well, now, notwithstanding Mr. Parnell's outrage upon his friend, and his being proved guilty of acting the part of a dishonourable man and thereby tarnishing the movement of which he has been a leader, there has not been an expression of opinion from a single bishop or priest in Ireland, and their neglect of their duty to speak out in the name of Ireland puts them, I am sorry to say, in rather a bad light before the Irish people throughout the world. It has been left to the Nonconformists in England to speak out in plain language about this crime of Mr. Parnell's. However, it is, perhaps, not too late. Something may yet be said by Archbishop Croke or Archbishop Walsh before next Monday. But many of us have expected that last week we would have had a pronouncement from some of these quarters, which would have told the world that, although Mr. Parnell is a Protestant and this woman is a Protestant, nevertheless, as Mr. Parnell is our leader, we are morally concerned in his acts ; and all the more so that as a Catholic people we are jealous of the moral reputation of our race ; we should have been before the Nonconformists in expressing our condemnation."

Asked whether it was the fact that in the beginning of the O'Shea case Mr. Parnell had pledged his word to Mr. Davitt that the charge against him was untrue, Mr. Davitt replied :—

" That is almost what occurred when this divorce case was first mentioned in the public Press. I came over from Dublin expressly to see Mr. Parnell, and I succeeded within 12 hours in getting at Captain O'Shea's case and his evidence, and was the first to tell Mr. Parnell what Captain O'Shea's case against him was. Mr. Parnell then spoke to me as follows :—' Davitt, I want you to go back to Ireland to tell our friends that I am going to get out of this without the slightest stain on my name or reputation,' and he repeated those words again. I fully believed, and I think he intended me to believe by those words, that he was entirely innocent of the charge made against him. I immediately went and told John Morley so. I crossed over to Ireland and told Archbishop Walsh. Mr. Morley was delighted and so was Archbishop Walsh; intensely relieved Archbishop Walsh was. I told all these and other of my friends that I had never known Mr. Parnell to lie to me, and that until the charge should be proved at his trial I would believe implicitly in his innocence. That was a few days after the thing was mentioned in the Press.

Nov. 27.

.   .   .   .

Now, when I find that Mr. Parnell is deaf to all appeals, that he will not retire, no matter what the cost of his stubbornness may be to the cause of Ireland, I am no longer bound to stand by him in any way, and, no matter what the issue may be on Monday next, I have nothing more whatever to do with him as long as he lives."

.   .   .   .

Asked with regard to the future leadership of the party, MR. DAVITT said :—

" No matter what happens on Monday next, there will be, I regret to say, dissension for a time. It is inevitable. My own opinion is that Thomas Sexton will be the future leader. He is the ablest all-round man in the party, and I think he would be the best, as he would undoubtedly be the most brilliant, Parliamentary leader. M'Carthy may be the choice of the party, because he is a man with no decided opinions, and would not quarrel with anybody, and is a man nobody would be jealous of. I think it just possible they may put the leadership in the hands of a committee. That would be my suggestion—say, a committee of M'Carthy, Sexton, Healy, and Dillon."

CHAPTER III.

MR. PARNELL'S MANIFESTO.

Nov. 28. The meeting of the Irish Party stood adjourned from Wednesday, November 27, to Monday, December 1. At a late hour on the night of the intervening Friday Mr. Parnell issued the following manifesto to the Irish people :—

"To the People of Ireland.

" The integrity and independence of a section of the Irish Parliamentary party having been sapped and destroyed by the wirepullers of the English Liberal party, it has become necessary for me, as the leader of the Irish nation, to take counsel with you, and, having given you the knowledge which is in my possession, to ask your judgment upon a matter which now solely devolves upon you to decide.

" The letter of Mr. Gladstone to Mr. Morley, written for the purpose of influencing the decision of the Irish party in the choice of their leader, and claiming for the Liberal party and their leaders the right of veto upon that choice, is the immediate cause of this address to you, to remind you and your Parliamentary representatives that Ireland considers the independence of her party as her only safeguard within the Constitution, and above and beyond all other considerations whatever. The threat in that letter, repeated so insolently on many English platforms and in numerous British newspapers, that unless Ireland concedes this right of veto to England she will indefinitely postpone her chances of obtaining Home Rule, compels me, while not for one moment admitting the slightest probability of such loss, to put before you information which until now, so far as my colleagues are concerned, has been solely in my possession, and which will enable you to understand the measure of the loss with which you are threatened unless you consent to throw me to the English wolves now howling for my destruction.

" In November of last year, in response to a repeated and long-standing request, I visited Mr. Gladstone at Hawarden, and received the details of the intended proposals of himself and his colleagues of the late Liberal Cabinet with regard to Home Rule, in the event of the next general election favouring the Liberal party.

" It is unnecessary for me to do more at present than to direct your attention to certain points of these details, which will be generally recognized as embracing elements vital for your information and the formation of your judgment. These vital points of difficulty may be suitably arranged and considered under the following heads :—

" (1) The retention of the Irish members in the Imperial Parliament.

" (2) The settlement of the land or agrarian difficulty in Ireland.

" (3) The control of the Irish Constabulary.

" (4) The appointment of the Judiciary (including Judges of the Supreme Court, County Court Judges, and resident magistrates).

" Upon the subject of the retention of the Irish members in the Imperial Parliament, Mr. Gladstone told me that the opinion, and the unanimous opinion, of his colleagues and himself, recently arrived at after most mature consideration of alternative proposals, was that, in order to conciliate English public opinion, it would be necessary to reduce the Irish representation from 103 to 32.

" Upon the settlement of the land it was held that this was one of the questions which must be regarded as questions reserved from the control of the Irish Legislature, but, at the same time, Mr. Gladstone intimated that, while he would renew his attempt to settle the matter by Imperial legislation on the lines of the Land Purchase Bill of 1886, he would not undertake to put any pressure upon his own side or insist upon their adopting his views—in other and shorter words, that the Irish Legislature was not to be given the power of solving the agrarian difficulty, and that the Imperial Parliament would not.

" With regard to the control of the Irish Constabulary, it was stated by Mr. Gladstone that, having regard to the necessity for conciliating English public opinion, he and his colleagues felt

that it would be necessary to leave this force and the appointment of its officers, under the control of the Imperial authority,
for an indefinite period, while the funds for its maintenance,
payment, and equipment would be compulsorily provided out of
Irish resources.

" The period of ten or twelve years was suggested as the limit
of time during which the appointment of judges, resident magistrates, &c., should be retained in the hands of the Imperial
authority.

" I have now given a short account of what I gathered of Mr.
Gladstone's views and those of his colleagues during two hours'
conversation at Hawarden--a conversation which, I am bound to
admit, was mainly monopolized by Mr. Gladstone—and pass to
my own expressions of opinion upon these communications,
which represent my views then and now.

" And, first, with regard to the retention of the Irish members,
the position I have always adopted and then represented is
that, with the concession of full powers to the Irish Legislature
equivalent to those enjoyed by a State of the American Union,
the number and position of the members so retained would become a question of Imperial concern, and not of pressing or
immediate importance for the interests of Ireland. But that with
the important and all-engrossing subjects of agrarian reform,
constabulary control, and judiciary appointments left either
under Imperial control or totally unprovided for, it would be the
height of madness for any Irish leader to imitate Grattan's example and consent to disband the army which had cleared the
way to victory.

" I further undertook to use every legitimate influence to recon-
cile Irish public opinion to a gradual coming into force of the
new privileges, and to the postponements necessary for English
opinion with regard to constabulary control and judicial appointments, but strongly dissented from the proposed reduction of
members during the interval of probation. I pointed to the absence of any suitable prospect of land settlement by either Parliament, as constituting an overwhelming drag upon the prospects of
permanent peace and prosperity in Ireland.

" At the conclusion of the interview I was informed that Mr.
Gladstone and all his colleagues were entirely agreed that, pending the general election, silence should be absolutely preserved

with regard to any points of difference on the question of the retention of the Irish members.

"I have dwelt at some length upon these subjects, but not, I think, disproportionately to their importance. Let me say, in addition, that, if and when full powers are conceded to Ireland over her own domestic affairs, the integrity, number, and independence of the Irish party will be a matter of no importance ; but until this ideal is reached it is your duty and mine to hold fast every safeguard.

"I need not say that the questions—the vital and important questions—of the retention of the Irish members on the one hand, and the indefinite delay of full powers to the Irish Legislature on the other, gave me great concern. The absence of any provision for the settlement of the agrarian question, of any policy on the part of the Liberal leaders, filled me with concern and apprehension. On the introduction of the Land Purchase Bill by the Government at the commencement of last Session, Mr. Morley communicated with me as to the course to be adopted. Having regard to the avowed absence of any policy on the part of the Liberal leaders and party with regard to the matter of the land, I strongly advised Mr. Morley against any direct challenge of the principle of State-aided land purchase, and, finding that the fears and alarms of the English taxpayer to State aid by the hypothecation of grants for local purposes in Ireland as a counter guarantee had been assuaged, that a hopeless struggle should not be maintained, and that we should direct our sole efforts on the second reading of the Bill to the assertion of the principle of local control. In this I am bound to say Mr. Morley entirely agreed with me, but he was at the same time much hampered— and expressed his sense of his position—in that direction by the attitude of the extreme section of his party, led by Mr. Labouchere. And in a subsequent interview he impressed me with the necessity of meeting the second reading of the Bill with a direct negative, and asked me to undertake the motion. I agreed to this, but only on the condition that I was not to attack the principle of the measure, but to confine myself to a criticism of its details. I think his was false strategy, but it was a strategy adopted out of regard to English prejudices and Radical peculiarities. I did the best that was possible under the circumstances, and the several days' debate on the second reading contrasts favourably with Mr. Labouchere's recent and abortive attempt to interpose a direct negative to the first reading of a similar Bill yesterday.

" Time went on. The Government allowed their attention to be distracted from the question of land purchase by the Bill for compensating English publicans, and the agrarian difficulty in Ireland was again relegated to the future of another Session. Just before the commencement of this Session I was again favoured with another interview with Mr. Morley. I impressed upon him the policy of the oblique method of procedure in reference to land purchase, and the necessity and importance of providing for the question of local control, and of a limitation in the application of the funds. He agreed with me, and I offered to move, on the first reading of the Bill, an amendment in favour of this local control, advising that, if this were rejected, it might be left to the Radicals on the second reading to oppose the principle of the measure. This appeared to be a proper course, and I left Mr. Morley under the impression that this would fall to my duty.

" But in addition he made me a remarkable proposal, referring to the probable approaching victory of the Liberal party at the polls. He suggested some considerations as to the future of the Irish party. He asked me whether I would be willing to assume the office of Chief Secretary to the Lord Lieutenant of Ireland, or to allow another member of my party to take the position. He also put before me the desirability of filling one of the law offices of the Crown in Ireland by a legal member of my party. I told him, amazed as I was at the proposal, that I could not agree to forfeit in any way the independence of the party or any of its members ; that the Irish people had trusted me in this movement because they believed that the declaration I had made to them at Cork in 1880 was a true one and represented my convictions, and that I would on no account depart from it. I considered that, after the declarations we have repeatedly made, the proposal of Mr. Morley, that we should allow ourselves to be absorbed into English politics, was one based upon an entire misconception of our position with regard to the Irish constituencies and of the pledges which we had given.

" In conclusion, he directed my attention to the Plan of Campaign estates. He said that it would be impossible for the Liberal party when they attained power to do anything for these evicted tenants by direct action ; that it would be also impossible for the Irish Parliament, under the powers conferred, to do anything for them, and, flinging up his hands with a gesture of despair, he exclaimed, ' Having been to Tipperary, I do not know what to propose in regard to the matter.'   I told him that this question was a limited one, and that I did not see that he need allow himself to be hampered by its future consideration ; that, being limited, funds would be available from America and elsewhere for the support of those tenants as long as might be necessary ; that, of course, I understood that it was a difficulty, but that it was a limited one and should not be allowed to interfere with the general interests of the country.

" I allude to this matter only because within the last few days a strong argument in many minds for my expulsion has been that, unless the Liberals come into power at the next general election, the Plan of Campaign tenants will suffer. As I have shown, the Liberals propose to do nothing for the Plan of Campaign tenants by direct action when they do come into power, but I am entitled to ask that the existence of these tenants, whom I have supported in every way in the past, and whom I shall continue to support in the future, shall not constitute a reason for my expulsion from Irish politics. I have repeatedly pledged myself to stand by those evicted tenants and that they shall not be allowed to suffer, and I believe that the Irish people throughout the world will support me in this policy.

" Sixteen years ago I conceived the idea of an Irish Parliamentary party, independent of all English parties. Ten years ago I was elected the leader of an independent Irish Parliamentary party. During these ten years that party has remained independent, and because of its independence it has forced upon the English people the necessity of granting Home Rule to Ireland. I believe that party will obtain Home Rule only provided it remains independent of any English party. I do not believe that any action of the Irish people in supporting me will endanger the Home Rule cause or postpone the establishment of an Irish Parliament ; but even if the danger with which we are threatened by the Liberal party of to-day were to be realized, I believe that the Irish people throughout the world would agree with me that a postponement would be preferable to a compromise of our national rights by the acceptance of a measure which would not realize the aspirations of our race.

"I have the honour to remain your faithful servant,

"CHARLES STEWART PARNELL."

REPLY OF MR. GLADSTONE.

On Saturday Mr. Gladstone issued the following reply :—

"Sir,—It is no part of my duty to canvass the manifesto of Mr. Parnell, which I have received this morning, and I shall not apply to it a single epithet, for I am not his judge in any matter, and I believe myself to have shown in the matter of the Pigott Commission that I had no indisposition to do him justice. But the first portion of the document consists of a recital of propositions stated to have been made by me to him, and of objections entertained by him to those propositions. The Irish as well as the British public has a right to know whether I admit or deny the accuracy of that recital, and in regard to every one of the four points stated by Mr. Parnell I at once deny it.

"(1) The purport of the conversation was not to make known 'intended proposals.' No single suggestion was offered by me to Mr. Parnell as formal, or as unanimous, or as final. It was a statement perfectly free, and without prejudice, of points in which either I myself or such of my colleagues as I had been able to consult inclined generally to believe that the plan of 1886 for Home Rule in Ireland might be improved, and as to which I was desirous to learn whether they raised any serious objection in the mind of Mr. Parnell.

"(2) To no one of my suggestions did Mr. Parnell offer serious objection; much less did he signify in whole or in part that they augured the proposal of 'a measure which would not satisfy the aspirations of the Irish race.' According to his present account, he received from me in the autumn of 1889 information of vital changes adverse to Ireland in our plans for Home Rule, and kept this information secret until in the end of November, 1890, and in connexion with a totally independent and personal matter, he produces it to the world.

"(3) I deny, then, that I made the statements which his memory ascribes to me, or anything substantially resembling them, either on the retention of the Irish members, or on the settlement of the land or agrarian difficulty, or on the control of the Constabulary, or on the appointment of the Judiciary. As to land in particular, I am not conscious of having added anything to my public declarations, while as to County Court Judges and resident magistrates I made no suggestion whatever.

" (4) The conversation between us was strictly confidential, and, in my judgment, and, as I understood, in that of Mr. Parnell, to publish even a true account of it is to break the seal of confidence which alone renders political co-operation possible.

" (5) Every suggestion made by me was from written memoranda. The whole purport of my conference was made known by me in the strictest confidence, when it had just taken place, to my colleagues in the Cabinet of 1886, and I assured them that in regard to none of them had Mr. Parnell raised any serious difficulty whatever.

" (6) Neither Mr. Parnell nor I myself was bound by this conversation to absolute and final acceptance of the principle then canvassed ; but during the year which has since elapsed I have never received from Mr. Parnell any intimation that he had altered his views regarding any of them.

" I have now done with the Hawarden conversation, and I conclude with the following simple statement :—

" 1. I have always held in public as well as in private that the National party of Ireland ought to remain entirely independent of the Liberal party of Great Britain.

" 2. It is our duty, and my duty in particular, conformably to the spirit of Grattan and O'Connell, to study all adjustments in the great matter of Home Rule which may tend to draw to our side moderate and equitable opponents ; but for me to propose any measure except such as Ireland could approve on the lines already laid down would be fatuity as regards myself and treachery to the Irish nation, in whom, even by the side of Mr. Parnell, I may claim to take an interest.

" I remain, Sir, your very obedient servant,
                              " W. E. GLADSTONE.
" London, Nov. 29, 1890."

REPLY OF MR. MORLEY.

Nov. 29.
On the same day Mr. Morley also replied to Mr. Parnell as follows :—

" Sir,—The manifesto published by Mr. Parnell this morning contains two or three statements affecting me which I desire, without loss of time, to correct.

" (1) I made no sort of attempt to fetter Mr. Parnell's action in the Land Purchase Bill. He agreed with me, in all our conversations, that the Bill ought to be opposed as omitting the principle of local control, and for other reasons specified by him in his speech of April 21. The only question was as to the form of the motion for the rejection of the Bill. I pointed out to him (April 14) that, as many Liberals objected to the whole principle of the Bill, an amendment stating reasons would be less suitable than a motion for rejection *simpliciter*, and Mr. Parnell assented. Two days later he explained to me his alternative plan for fining down rents. This, at Mr. Parnell's request, I immediately communicated to Mr. Gladstone, and the same evening I wrote to Mr. Parnell that Mr. Gladstone felt that we could have nothing to say about his plan one way or another, but that, of course, he was perfectly free to propound it on his own responsibility. So completely did we recognize that our relations with the Irish party were an independent alliance, and not a fusion.

" (2) Mr. Parnell imputes to me that, in our conversation of November 10 (five days before the proceedings in Court), I made a ' remarkable proposal,' with the object of absorbing the Irish party into English politics by means of office. I made no proposal. It was natural that, in a free and confidential discussion of a possible future, I should wish to make sure, for Mr. Gladstone's information, that Mr. Parnell still held to the self-denying declaration of 1880. His answer to my inquiry was what I had fully anticipated.

" (3) Mr. Parnell's account of what passed on the same occasion on the subject of the evicted tenants on Campaign estates is wholly incorrect. I observed that some direct action might become necessary, though, of course, I foresaw that there were difficulties in the way of legislation. I never said that either I or any of my colleagues had formed any conclusion against legislation. I never said or hinted that it would be impossible for an Irish Parliament to do anything in the matter. I did say that, whether by direct or indirect action, the evicted tenants ought not to be allowed to suffer. As to Tipperary, there is all the difference between sensible perception of difficulties and the despair which Mr. Parnell ascribes to me.

" Mr. Gladstone is well able to deal with his own share in the manifesto, but I am bound to say that on November 10 I was under the most distinct impression that Mr. Parnell did not object to the suggestions thrown out a year ago at Hawarden as subjects for provisional examination, if those suggestions were likely to make a scheme generally acceptable to Great Britain.

" I am, Sir, yours faithfully,

" November 29."   " JOHN MORLEY."

Mr. Gladstone further referred to Mr. Parnell's manifesto in the subjoined letter, written the same day to Mr. Mellor, the Gladstonian candidate for the Bassetlaw Division of Nottinghamshire :—

" 9, Carlton-gardens, S.W., Nov. 29.

" Dear Mr. Mellor,—I learn with gratification that you have undertaken to be the candidate of the Liberal party in the Hundred of Bassetlaw, and I feel assured that all your political friends elsewhere as well as there will consider that in the present perhaps unparalleled crisis of affairs you take a wise and patriotic decision. The manifesto of Mr. Parnell, to which you will see my reply in a couple of hours, has made still wider the gulf which since the recent disclosures had separated him from the Liberal party, who have now to consider the great and noble cause of justice for Ireland apart from an individual name. But I am glad to think that, so far as appears, there will not be a severance between us and the Nationalist party of Ireland, for the manifesto of Mr. Parnell throws over his Parliamentary colleagues, acknowledges in them no right or authority, and goes past the constitutional representatives of his country in a fancied appeal to the nation which has chosen them to speak its wants and wishes.

" Believe me very faithfully yours,

" W. E. GLADSTONE."

VIEWS OF THE AMERICAN DELEGATES.

Nov. 29.

November 29th was also the day on which five of the six delegates sent by the Irish party to America first expressed their decisive condemnation of Mr. Parnell. They did so in the following telegram to Mr. Justin McCarthy despatched from Indianapolis, Indiana :—

" We suspended judgment at Mr. Parnell's request, pending the appearance of his manifesto. We have this morning read the manifesto with the deepest pain. It fully convinces us that Mr. Parnell's continued leadership is impossible. We will cable our views fully to-morrow, for the information of the Irish party and the Irish people.

" JOHN DILLON.
" WM. O'BRIEN.
" T. D. SULLIVAN.
" T. P. O'CONNOR.
" T. P. GILL."

MANIFESTO BY THE IRISH DELEGATES IN AMERICA.

Nov. 30.

On Sunday, November 30, they followed up this telegram by the accompanying manifesto :—

" Our sense of the matchless genius displayed by Mr. Parnell as leader of the Irish party, of the imperishable services which he has rendered to the Irish cause, of the courage, integrity, and splendid success with which he has led our people for ten years, and the comradeship, personal respect, and affection which for years have bound us to him, have made us suspend to the latest possible moment our judgment against his further leadership. The obligation to express that judgment is to all of us the most painful duty of our lives. No earthly consideration could have moved us to our determination except the solemn conviction that we have been driven to choose between Mr. Parnell and the destruction of our country's cause. So painfully alive were we to all that might be involved in the loss of such a leader that we eagerly co-operated with our colleagues in every effort to retain his influence in our councils. The manifesto of Mr. Parnell just issued, however, cuts us off from the last hopes to which we clung. Anxious to avoid a word that might embitter this controversy, we shall not dwell on the cruel injustice with which he treats the members of the party who followed him with loyalty and affection such as no leader ever experienced before. His recollection of their fealty to him in many an hour of trial might well save them from the imputation that even a section of them could have allowed their integrity to be sapped by Liberal wirepullers ; nor would we do more than enter a protest against this violation of all constitutional principle in flouting by anticipation the decision of the elected representatives of the people from whose votes the chairman of the Parliamentary party receives his authority, and resorting to a vague general appeal over their heads. Considerations like these we should readily have waived in the interest of the national solidarity, but the method in which, ignoring the origin of the present calamitous situation, Mr. Parnell endeavours to fasten the responsibility for it upon Mr. Gladstone and Mr. Morley compels us to dissociate ourselves in the strongest manner from the imputation, which we believe to be reckless and unjust.

" We view with abhorrence the attacks made upon Mr. Parnell by his public and private enemies under cover of his present difficulty. To attacks of this kind, addressed to a man of proud and strong spirit, we attribute many of the terrible dangers with which Ireland is now threatened, and we fear that they may do further mischief by diverting the minds of many from grave national to purely personal issues in the natural resentment against the ungenerous attack made upon the great leader in the hour of his stress and disaster. But, while making every possible allowance for Mr. Parnell's feeling on this score, we consider it very unjust to the English people, and lamentable from the point of view of international good feeling, to describe as " English wolves howling for his destruction " those who have not been able to bring themselves to the same view to which gratitude and the necessity for union impelled Mr. Parnell's own colleagues and countrymen.

" Mr. Parnell's plea that Mr. Gladstone's letter to Mr. Morley involves a claim to dictate to the Irish party, and thereby strike at its independence as a strictly Irish national body, is one calculated to inspire every Irish national aim. If that plea be not an obvious fallacy, the Irish party having been formed for the purpose of winning Home Rule, any attempt to divert the Irish party from that object in the interest of English parties would be an invasion of the independence of the Irish party, and would, we believe, be repelled by no one more sternly than our colleagues and ourselves, who are now in opposition to Mr. Parnell. But the very basis of our independent alliance with the Liberals is the adoption by them of the programme for which the Irish party was formed and the recognition of it. It must be the first object of a Liberal Cabinet to realize that programme. Whatever differences of opinion may exist as to the motive with which Mr. Gladstone's letter was communicated to the public, it was obviously not his hostility to Home Rule, but his earnest desire to save it from disaster, that prompted him to write the letter. We deplore that the difficulties of Mr. Gladstone's position were not frankly recognised by Mr. Parnell, and that, on the contrary, friendly private communications, obviously made with a view to smoothing the passage of the Home Rule Bill, have been made the basis for insinuations of treachery to the Irish cause. By his conviction, again and again expressed, Home Rule to be effective must be such a measure as will satisfy the Irish. Mr. Gladstone is bound to a full and ample measure of self-government for Ireland. To offer any other scheme would be an act not only of incredible baseness, but of incredible folly, and we emphatically separate ourselves from any such charge against Mr. Gladstone. We think it deplorable that Mr. Morley's suggestion that some of the Irish party should co-operate for carrying out the Irish programme of the Liberal Home Rule party should be so strangely interpreted by Mr. Parnell. Every member of the Irish party will, of course, agree with Mr. Parnell that the acceptance by any Nationalist member of office from an English Ministry would be a breach of the elementary principles upon which the party was founded; but nobody knowing Mr. Morley's character could doubt that the suggestion was made in the honest belief that a Liberal Ministry would be helped in the difficult work of carrying through the details of the Home Rule Bill by co-operation with Irish colleagues, and that it was not an insidious attempt on the integrity and independence of the Irish party. We have now to confront the statement that Mr. Parnell's leadership opens an impassable gulf between the representatives of Ireland and the Liberal party, who faithfully observed their part of their side of the agreements as to the national claims of Ireland; and the situation is aggravated by the deplorable expressions of ill-will towards the British people, who again and again during the past five years manifested their determination to do justice to Ireland, and who have, by their votes, paralyzed the arm of coercion. In deliberately bringing things to this position Mr. Parnell has entered upon a rash and fatal path, upon which every consideration for Ireland's safety, as well as our personal honour, forbid us absolutely to follow him.

" In the future of the party thus isolated and discredited we cannot imagine how any Irishman can see anything but destruction to the hopes of self-government, happiness, and peace, which but a few weeks ago were on the point of being realized for our people, so tried by many years of sacrifice and suffering. What Mr. Parnell asks us to do, stripped of all side issues, is to sacrifice all hopes of an early settlement of the Irish struggle to his resolve to maintain his personal position. We are driven to choose between the leader and the cause, and in that sad choice we cannot hesitate. We lay these views respectfully before all our colleagues of the Irish Parliamentary party, in the earnest belief that a decisive vote on their part will deliver Ireland from the fearful anxiety that now overhangs her people. We are convinced that a calm but resolute course of action on our part in this cruel emergency will redound to the advantage of our cause by furnishing conclusive testimony of the capacity of the party and people for self-government.

" We cannot relinquish the hope that, in face of such decisive action by the elective representatives of the Irish people, Mr. Parnell's sense of patriotism will withhold him from plunging Ireland into those horrors of dissension which so often already in her tragic and unhappy history have robbed her of liberty at the moment when it was within her grasp, and save him from undoing in one passionate hour the results of all his incomparable services to our country.   " JOHN DILLON.
                                    " WILLIAM O'BRIEN.
                                    " T. P. O'CONNOR.
                                    " T. D. SULLIVAN.
                                    " T. P. GILL."

The sixth delegate, Mr. T. Harrington, who has had sole charge of the National League organization as secretary from its foundation in 1882, did not sign this message, and has consistently given Mr. Parnell his support.

CHAPTER IV

MEETINGS AND PROCEEDINGS OF THE IRISH PARTY.

MEETING OF THE IRISH PARTY—THIRD DAY.

DEC. 1. Monday, December 1, was the date fixed for the resumed meeting of the Irish party. At half-past 10 o'clock Mr. Parnell held a private meeting of his supporters at the Westminster Palace Hotel. He was in excellent spirits, and made no secret of the fact that he had not altered his determination not to relinquish the leadership of the party voluntarily.

Mr. Parnell and his secretary were joined by Mr. Edward Harrington, Mr Joseph Nolan, Mr. John Redmond, Mr. W. Redmond, Mr. R. Power, Mr. E. Sheil, and Mr. J. J. O'Kelly. The meeting lasted for over an hour. In reply to the representative of an Irish newspaper, who spoke to him as he was leaving the hotel, Mr. Parnell said, " Tell them I will fight to the end." Mr. Parnell with his supporters then walked across to the House of Commons. As they crossed to the House, Mr. Parnell's supporters passed several of their dissentient colleagues hurrying to the meeting, one of them being Mr. T. M. Healy, who drove up looking much flushed and excited, and did not appear to notice his former colleagues.

Mr. Parnell, accompanied by Mr. Henry Campbell, arrived at a quarter to 12, and at once went to Committee Room No. 15. Mr. Parnell took the chair at half-past 12. There were then 74 members present. Messrs. Carew, Gilhooly, and Lalor were away through illness. The absentees also included the American delegates, the O'Gorman Mahon, Mr. P. O'Brien, who was undergoing a sentence of imprisonment, and Mr. Leahy. The following official account of the proceedings was supplied for publication, through special reporters of the *Freeman's Journal*, who were admitted to the meeting.

The following is a complete list of those who attended :— Messrs. W. Abraham, J. Barry, A. Blane, G. Byrne, H. Campbell, P. Chance, J. J. Clancy, Dr. Commins, T. J. Condon, M. Conway, W. Corbet, J. Cox, D. Crilly, J. Dalton, J. Deasy, T. Dickson, Sir T. Esmonde, J. Finucane, Dr. Fitzgerald, J. C. Flynn, P. J. Foley, Dr. Fox, E. Harrington, H. J. Harrison, L. P. Hayden, M. Healy, T. Healy, J. Jordan, Dr. Kenny, M. J. Kenny, D. Kilbride, E. Knox, W. J. Lane, E. Leamy, M. M'Cartan, J. M'Carthy, J. H. M'Carthy, P. M'Donald, W. A. Macdonald, Sir J. M'Kenna, J. G. Swift MacNeill, R. Maguire, Pierce Mahony, B. Molloy, J. Morrogh, W. Murphy, Col. Nolan, J. Nolan, J. F. X. O'Brien, P. J. O'Brien, A. O'Connor, J. O'Connor, T. O'Hanlon, F. O'Keeffe, J. O'Kelly, J. Pinkerton, P. J. Power, R. Power, T. Quinn, J. Redmond, W. Redmond, W. Reynolds, J. Roche, T. Sexton, J. D. Sheehan, D. Sheehy, E. Sheil, J. Stack, Donal Sullivan, Dr. Tanner, J. Tuite, and A. Webb.

Some time was occupied at the outset by the reading of correspondence bearing on the issue raised.

Messrs. R. Lalor and Leahy wrote announcing their determination to support Mr. Parnell. There was also a large batch of telegrams from various league branches in Ireland and Great Britain, Irish Town Commissioners, and Boards of Guardians, addressed to Mr. Parnell, and read to the meeting by Mr. Campbell. The substance of these communications was an expression of unabated confidence in the member for Cork as leader of the Irish Nationalist party. From Rhode Island and Philadelphia there were also telegrams couched in such terms as " Meeting representing 60,000 supports your leadership," and " Overwhelmingly for you."

As president of the party, Mr. Parnell took the chair, and at the conclusion of the preliminary proceedings,

MR. SEXTON said,—Mr. Parnell, I wish to submit a question to the chair concerning a matter of procedure. Sir, at the opening of the meeting to-day, and before the admission of the Press, you asked the secretary to read to the meeting a number of telegrams which had been received, and amongst them was a telegram from the delegates in America communicating in very brief terms their views, and promising a further communication for the guidance of the party. Since then a further telegram from the

c—2

American delegates has appeared in the Press, addressed to Mr. Justin M'Carthy, and I am informed by him that, not having been at his home since 10 o'clock this morning, he has not received the original, which is probably lying there. Sir, unless this further telegram is now read to the members it may not come to their knowledge upon this supreme question before the vote is taken, and therefore I submit that this further telegram, further explaining and amplifying their views, should be read.

Mr. PARNELL.—Whenever it is put into my hands I will read it.

Mr. SEXTON.—The original ?

Mr. PARNELL.--Yes.

Mr. SEXTON.—But we have not the original. It appears in the newspapers.

Mr. PARNELL.—Has Mr. M'Carthy verified it ?

Mr. M'CARTHY.—No.

Mr. PARNELL.—If you cannot find the original I will read the newspaper copy.

Mr. HEALY.—I move that it be read now *quantum valeat*.

Mr. PARNELL.—I rule that a newspaper paragraph should not be read, as having no bearing on our proceedings, but I do not want to put you to any disadvantage.

Mr. HEALY.—It is not a question of disadvantage.

Mr. PARNELL (to Mr. Campbell).—Will you now continue to read the telegrams ?

Mr. Campbell then continued to read the telegrams, those only being excluded which came from private individuals.

The CHAIRMAN said,—Now, Dr. Tanner, it is your request to address the chair.

DR. TANNER.—Before I move any resolution I should like to know what is the proposition before the meeting.

The CHAIRMAN.—The proposition before the last meeting was, " That a full meeting of this party be held on Friday to give Mr. Parnell an opportunity to reconsider his position," whereupon that debate was adjourned until Monday, and the question now is, " That a full meeting of the party be held on Friday, to give Mr. Parnell an opportunity to reconsider his position."

Mr. HEALY.—That was last Friday.

The CHAIRMAN.—No ! it is clearly next Friday.

Mr. SEXTON.—Have all the telegrams been read ?

The CHAIRMAN.—If there are any more they must be read at the end of the meeting. An exception, of course, will be made in favour of the communication from the Irish delegates when it arrives.

MR. SEXTON.—I merely ask because I have had a telegram from the Bishop of Sligo, and I want it to be supposed that it was not in any way slighted.

The CHAIRMAN.—Of course, no.

DR. TANNER.—I would respectfully urge upon you, Sir, that the resolution which was placed before the meeting on last Friday had reference to the following Friday. But if it has reference to Friday week I presume I cannot speak to a resolution which deals with a past date.

The CHAIRMAN.—This resolution was proposed and seconded on Tuesday. The adjournment of its consideration was to the following Friday. The resolution was duly proposed and seconded, and the party arrived at a unanimous resolution to adjourn the consideration of this resolution until Monday. Therefore the resolution is still before the chair, and I rule that it is still before the chair, and will have to be disposed of before you go on with anything else.

MR. T. M. HEALY.—I would suggest that the better course for those who think that a technical objection should not stand in the way would be that we should vote against the resolution, and allow it to be put at once. (Hear, hear.)

The CHAIRMAN.—You are perfectly willing to vote against your own resolution.

MR. SEXTON.—I suppose it will be perfectly competent for any member to move an amendment ?

The CHAIRMAN.—Provided it is in order.

COLONEL NOLAN.—I have also an amendment to propose, but as I cannot move an amendment upon an amendment, I presume I would not be in order. Before any action is taken on this resolution, I hope, Mr. Chairman, you will receive other amendments.

MR. ABRAHAM.—Would I be in order in moving this resolution ?—" That, acting upon an imperative sense of our duty to our country, we the members of the Irish party do declare that Mr. Parnell's tenure of the chairmanship of this party is hereby terminated."

The CHAIRMAN.—I decide that that is not an amendment.

Mr. JOHN BARRY.—It seems to me we can go on to some practical step by my withdrawing my resolution, and for these reasons. My resolution was for a full meeting of the party. That is met by the full meeting of the party assembled here now, and the second reason is that the resolution, having asked that you should get more time to reconsider your position ——

The CHAIRMAN.—Are you speaking now on a point of order or asking for leave that you should be permitted to withdraw your resolution? Because you must limit yourself. If you wish to withdraw it, you must ask the leave of the party. You will not be allowed to make a second speech.

Mr. BARRY.—All that I am asking for is to make a single word of explanation in asking permission to withdraw my resolution.

The CHAIRMAN.—You are perfectly entitled to explain it. I only wish to draw your attention as to the necessity for some limitation as to the nature and extent of your speech.

Mr. BARRY.—My second reason, as stated in my resolution, that time be given to Mr. Parnell to reconsider his position, and that he has reconsidered his position by issuing his manifesto ——

The CHAIRMAN.—You cannot go into the question of the manifesto, because if you do I shall have to go into a great many other questions, and we will be kept here a long time.

Mr. BARRY.—I now wish to withdraw my resolution.

The CHAIRMAN.—With regard to the request that this resolution be permitted to be withdrawn, I shall require and decide that it cannot be withdrawn without unanimous consent of the meeting. ("Hear, hear," and cries of "Oh.") I am following the precedent of the House of Commons, which has always been carried out at our meetings. (Hear, hear.)

Dr. TANNER.—Might I ask to have the resolution read once more? (Cries of "Oh.")

The CHAIRMAN.—Come here and read it yourself if you like.

Mr. BARRY.—I wish to know—are the standing orders of the House of Commons to be carried out here?

The CHAIRMAN.—Those rules have always regulated the proceedings at the meetings of our party, and if you wish to form special rules and regulations you will have to do so. (Hear, hear.)

Mr. A. O'CONNOR.—It is desirable, at any rate, that we should como to some amicable, some quiet, and some decisive decision. (Hear, hear.) The motion now before the chair is that a meeting be held on a certain Friday in order to enable you, Mr. Parnell, to reconsider your position.

The Chairman.—What ·question are you addressing yourself to now ?

Mr. A. O'Connor.—To the question of the admissibility of the amendment.

The Chairman.—There is no such question before me at present. The question is that the withdrawal of this resolution be permitted. It can only be withdrawn by the unanimous permission of the meeting

Mr. A. O'Connor.—I would ask, as a matter of order, whether it is not competent for a member to move, as an amendment, that the resolution which is so retained for the meeting ——

The Chairman.—You can only move an amendment to this resolution when the motion for leave to withdraw it has been withdrawn.

Mr. A. O'Connor.—I thought that leave to withdraw it had been refused.

The Chairman.—I have not so ruled. I have ruled it must be with the unanimous decision of the meeting. That question has not been put. The only question that can be put is whether it is your pleasure that the resolution be withdrawn, and there can be no further debate until that question is decided. I now put it to the meeting—Is it your pleasure that the resolution be withdrawn ? (Loud cries of " Hear, hear," and " No, no.")

Mr. Sexton.—Divide.

The Chairman.—There can be no division on such a question. Mr. Sexton knows that perfectly well.

Mr. A. O'Connor.—I wish to ask a question on a point of order. Now that we have the resolution retained, is it not competent for any member to move an amendment to the resolution embodying any proposition which relates to the subject matter of that resolution ?

The Chairman.—If you will show me your amendment I will tell you whether it is in order or not.

Colonel Nolan.—I claim priority for my amendment. (" Hear, hear," and " No, no.")

MR. ABRAHAM.—Mr. Chairman, I beg to hand you my amendment.

COLONEL NOLAN.—And I beg to hand you my amendment also.

MR. CONDON.—I beg leave to second Mr. Abraham's amendment.

COLONEL NOLAN.—On a point of order, I claim that my amendment shall come first. My amendment is a hostile one and one of a character that is usually received first.

MR. T. M. HEALY.—That is not a point of order.

MR. A. O'CONNOR.—I submit that the motion—the terms of which I cannot exactly remember—handed in by Mr. Abraham is perfectly pertinent to the subject matter of the original resolution, and in no way infringing any of the rules of the House of Commons as bearing upon the question of the amendment. I submit, Sir, that Mr. Abraham's amendment is perfectly in order.

The CHAIRMAN.—I decide that Mr. Abraham's amendment is entirely out of order (" Hear, hear," and cries of " Oh ")—that it is in direct contradiction to the amendment itself. Colonel Nolan's amendment is perfectly in order.

At this announcement there was some applause, followed by an outburst of laughter.

The CHAIRMAN (warmly).—I hope we shall avoid those expressions of opinion amongst ourselves, and I believe if we do not that there is sufficient public spirit in this meeting and sufficient determination amongst the members at this meeting to support the chair in preserving order. (Loud cheers.)

MR. A. O'CONNOR.—On a point of order, will you hear me ? The amendment proposed a certain adjournment, to enable you, Sir, to consider your position as leader of the party. The amendment is perfectly absurd in its terms, no doubt, but I would submit there is nothing in it which prevents its being accepted as a perfectly admissible amendment.

The CHAIRMAN.—I have carefully examined your amendment, and I can only give my judgment. No chairman of any public meeting would accept this as an amendment. (Hear, hear.)

MR. T. M. HEALY.—Divide, divide.

The CHAIRMAN.—You cannot divide on a point of order.

MR. T. M. HEALY.—I presume I shall be allowed an expression of opinion here as well as in the House of Commons.

The CHAIRMAN.—Probably a much fuller expression of opinion. (Hear, hear.)

DR. TANNER.—I wish, Sir, to make a few observations. I wish to speak before you, Sir, and my colleagues, as I am always prepared to speak before you and the country, and I say with the greatest respect, with profoundest respect and regret, that you, Sir, as a leader of our party, as a gentleman that I always honoured and respected during my connexion with politics—I was not a politician bred and born (" Hear, hear," and laughter)—I wish to say that in addressing the meeting at the present time my feelings will perhaps interrupt my utterances. I say it with profoundest regret, that last Tuesday, when you, Sir, were re-elected as our leader during the present Session, had I not been misled by reports that apparently came from an authoritative source, that you were going to resign the chair after being voted to it as a mark of our respect—had I not believed that you would have withdrawn after the vote of confidence was passed in you for all your past services—I should have felt it my duty to have voted against you as leader of the party during the present Session. (Hear, hear.) I wish it to be perfectly understood, notably now that the Press is present, that I at any rate voted for your continued leadership, hoping that you would not have continued, but would have accepted the position. I regret to have to say now—and it is one of the most painful duties of my life to have to say—I must unhesitatingly and unflinchingly vote against your continued leadership, and may God protect the right. (Cheers.)

MR. T. M. HEALY.—I wish to give my reasons for voting against the resolution of my friend Mr. Barry. Chronologically, I believe that resolution is now an absurdity. (Hear, hear.) That resolution was moved upon Wednesday last, requesting you by the Friday following—meaning last Friday—requesting that a meeting be called for that day, and that you were to have an opportunity in the interval of reconsidering your position. Upon that, as I understand, not having been able to be present at either Tuesday's or Wednesday's meeting, it was considered advisable by some of the more immediate supporters of the chair to require an adjournment until Monday, and that request, being a most rational and proper one, was unanimously agreed to by the meeting. Therefore, without wishing for one moment to quarrel with the ruling of the chair, I say that to my mind the resolution has been placed out of date by the acceptance of the subsequent amendment, carrying the adjournment over the further date appointed for consideration in the original resolution.

The CHAIRMAN.—You will see, Mr. Healy, that no casting back can now be allowed. You are in reality combating the decision of the chair, and though your argument might have been relevant to the question at the time, it is not relevant to the question before the chair now. (Hear, hear.)

MR. T. M. HEALY.—I hope that I may be allowed to give the reasons which occur to me for asking those who would have supported Mr. Barry on Wednesday last to vote against him now. However, I bow to your ruling, Sir, and the further point I wish to put is this. I am debarred by the ruling that has just been given from giving the real reasons that influence my judgment. We have now arrived at half-past 2, after having sat here since 12 o'clock, with a considerable adjournment for luncheon. I consider, if *technique* or any other consideration be allowed to be interposed between the judgment of this meeting and its decision, unfortunate consequences might arise. And while everybody would be naturally anxious, upon the first resolution being put from the chair, to express their opinions, in the sense that Dr. Tanner has done or otherwise, yet at the same time I think it will be in accordance with good policy if those who take the view that I have had the honour to express would allow that resolution to be put from the chair as speedily as possible, and vote against it, and then consider Mr. Abraham's resolution as the one upon which they shall desire to express their opinions. (Hear, hear.)

MR. RICHARD POWER.—Which amendment comes first, Mr. Abraham's or Colonel Nolan's ?

The CHAIRMAN.—Clearly Colonel Nolan's comes first.

MR. SHEEHY.—Might I ask, Mr. Chairman, what is the amendment ?

The CHAIRMAN (reading).—" That the question touching the chairmanship of the Irish Parliamentary party be postponed until members have had an opportunity of personally ascertaining the views of their constituents and until the party can meet in Dublin." (Hear, hear.)

COLONEL NOLAN.—That amendment, I may say, was drawn up without consultation with any one. (Cheers.)

MR. M. HEALY.—On a point of order I submit that Colonel

Nolan, having already spoken on the resolution, cannot speak again. (Cries of " Oh !")

The CHAIRMAN.—As the Press are here now, we cannot have the same rules as regulated our private meetings. I decide now that it will be open to every member of the party to speak again. (Cheers.)

COLONEL NOLAN.—Mr. Chairman, I consider that my resolution is one of first-rate importance, and that it is really the most important question before this meeting, whether we shall decide exclusively on our own initiative or whether we shall do so on this solemn occasion after having consulted our constituents (cheers), and possibly other people who have got the right to speak on the matter. I should greatly deplore any serious division in this party. (Cheers.) I sincerely hope and trust that this discussion will be conducted in public as it has been conducted hitherto, without one word of acrimony being dropped from the lips of any member which could embitter the situation, and we all know that embittering the situation would eventually weaken the Irish party and the Irish representation, and weaken the whole Liberal cause and the prospects of Home Rule. (Cheers.) I hope we shall argue this debate in public as we have already done in private, in such a fashion that we may all eventually be able to agree and again work together as we have done before for the cause of Ireland. (Cheers.) I believe my amendment tends entirely in that direction. I believe, now that we are after the first rush, when we were under the cynosure of the eyes of the political world, when we now have time to hear what our constituents have to say (cheers), to hear their views, that if my amendment is adopted we shall have no division at all. You may ask me, if my amendment is carried, how long would it take to ascertain the views of our constituents ? I can only answer by telling you what the *minimum* time would be and what the *maximum* time would be. The *minimum* time, I should say, would be eight days, and the *maximum* time would be about three weeks. That would enable us to discuss this matter fully and thoroughly, enlightened by the opinions of all parties in Ireland. I shall exclude no party, and I believe we shall all agree. That is the first reason I give. You may say that what I suggest is a dangerous precedent, and that this party cannot always be asking for the advice of their constituents. I quite admit that. It may be said we are running the risk of undoing ten or 11 years of hard work ; we do not know how we may unsettle the votes of the Irish voters in England. If we settle this matter to-day, we do not know how it will be received in Ireland. (Hear, hear.) Every one who has spoken on this subject has been obliged to acknowledge the surpassing services of Mr. Parnell. Every member also has spoken with respect of Mr. Gladstone. On reading the papers on Tuesday I find they tried to put one of these men against the other. What could be more foolish ? When we go to Ireland things will be put in a different way. Our constituents will use persuasion with us and will try to make us unanimous on this point. I now come to the second part of the resolution. I do not think it matters very much whether we meet in Dublin or in London to decide the matter, but at the same time I think, in a matter affecting Home Rule so much, we ought to pay some tribute to our own capital. (Hear, hear.) There is no doubt that when we meet here we are influenced by surroundings. (Hear, hear.) I say the people at home, while we meet here, will not expect the same independence from us as if we met in Dublin and chose our chairman in Dublin. I do not think we should be open to the accusation of having taken a panic vote, or that we were influenced by the greatest statesman of modern times. If we are to throw over Mr. Parnell, I say we should first go to our constituents (cheers), and be in the position as if we had an Irish *plébiscite*. I hope there will be no argument used about the delay that may take place, such as that we have been annoying the Liberal party. I believe that our attitude towards the Liberal party will not be changed during the interval, while we will have the unquestionable advantage of deciding for the whole of Ireland, without there being any suspicion of pressure being brought to bear upon us as to what we ought to do in this supreme crisis. (Cheers.) I beg to move my amendment.

SIR JOSEPH M'KENNA seconded the amendment.

MR. SEXTON.—Mr. Parnell, Sir, I deeply regret that I find it impossible to vote for Colonel Nolan's amendment. I am extremely anxious to treat this grave case with every consideration (hear, hear), and to allow any time that may be judged necessary for arriving at a just decision. But according to my judgment the case is urgent, and it admits of no delay. (Hear, hear.) I felt on Wednesday last that in adjourning until Monday we were incurring a serious risk, and I submit to this meeting that, from the reports which we receive from day to day, the refusals of Liberal members, of English Liberal members, to meet their constituents, the determination of Liberal candidates to retire from the field, and the reports from Liberal agents as a result of their investigations in all parts of the country, if we postpone this question till the end of the present Session, or for a month, or even for a week, we may substantially be guilty of one of the most terribly criminal acts that ever were committed by a body of public men in the course of the history of the world, and that act would be the breaking up of an alliance in which you have led the people to hope, the breaking up of an alliance in which they have fondly hoped for the last four years, of an alliance built up by the unimaginable labours and pains of the past 11 years, an alliance between the people of Ireland and the only friends from whom we have any reasonable hope—I mean the Liberal democracy of Great Britain—an alliance firm, affectionate, progressive, and destined, tried no matter by what test, to succeed and to endure. (Cheers.) I cannot, for one, accept the risk of breaking up the alliance, and it is as well to secure it as to fulfil another duty ; and it is to relieve this country and our own from the torture of anxiety and suspense (hear, hear) that I plead urgency for the grave case now before us. (Hear, hear.) I share in the hope of Colonel Nolan that passion will be absent from our debate. (Hear, hear.) The case is not one for passionate declamation. (Cheers.) We are a body of representative men who are trained to judge of the bearings of public questions. The case is one for the calm and firm exercise of an independent judgment. We have laboured together hard and long in the sacred cause of Ireland, and it would cause me deep and lasting grief if anything avoidable were said to-day to render it impossible for us to labour together in the good cause hereafter. (Cheers.) It is needless for Colonel Nolan and for any man to call to my mind the services of Mr. Parnell to Ireland. I am well aware of them ; I have good cause to know them. (Hear, hear.) I stood beside him in the original struggle for the formation of his party ; I stood beside him in the State trial of 1880 ; I shared his imprisonment in Kilmainham ; I am one of those who have stood immediately by his side during the past 11 years in the House of Commons ; I have humbly shared his labours. (Hear, hear.) I have done my best to render them effectual, as Mr. Parnell well knows, and I say of myself, what is also true of my colleagues here—that it is unnecessary for any Irishman to remind us now or hereafter of the labours and the services that were our glory and our pride. (Cheers.) Nothing that can happen here can obliterate the services of Mr. Parnell from the heart of the country or from the history of his time. (Hear, hear.) But gentleman, no service by any leader entitles him to ruin his cause (cheers), and, indeed, the greater the services that he has rendered, the greater the capacity and the genius that he has shown, the greater cause have we and the greater right to look to him and to expect him, for such time as may be needed, to sacrifice his personal feeling, and even some part of his personal prestige, for the supreme interest of his country. (Cheers.) I have spoken of the necessity of guarding by prompt action—action, prompt, decided, and unmistakable—the alliance between Ireland and the Liberal party, which is our only hope. What will become of that alliance if we delay ? I have it on the best authority that the Irish Press Agency, our propagandist department in this country, has ceased to have any useful existence. Its literature is not being sought for ; its speakers are no longer wanted ; and if the present uncertainty is allowed to remain and the growing passion to develop, is not that one sign sufficient token that before we have time to meet in Dublin and elsewhere the alliance, which has already been strained to the point of sundering by the excitement caused by Mr. Gladstone's declaration, may be broken off, and broken off for ever ? (Hear, hear.) I do not dwell upon the point that we ought to meet in Dublin. I wish we had oftener met in Dublin. (Loud cheers.) It is no fault of mine, no fault of my friends that we have not ; and if a meeting had been called in Dublin at the opening of every Session I should have been one of those who would have been found present. (Hear, hear.) It has been suggested to us that we ought to consult our constituents. (Hear, hear.) I deny that this question is one upon which we are bound to resort to an appeal to the country. (Hear, hear.) We are engaged upon a question of the organization of our party. We are engaged upon a question of the tenure of the chair, and is it to be argued that upon such a question, upon a question of the removal or appointment of chairman—which is a party emergency such as it may easily be supposed might arise for decision any day, and

which would be decided in an instant—that we are bound to resort
to an appeal to the country ? I submit to you that in this grave
matter, as in every other case of public duty, we are bound first
to act upon our judgment, and then to account to our constituents. (Hear, hear.) The dictate of my judgment is quite clear ;
even my constituents could not alter it. (Hear, hear.) There is
no power on earth that could alter it, for it is the *fiat* of my conscience. (Hear, hear.) But so far as concerns my constituents,
I have not the slightest reason to doubt that they concur with me.
They are aware of my intention ; they have had ample notice of
it ; no word has reached me to dissuade me from my course. I
am entitled to assume their assent, and I do most absolutely
assume it. (Hear, hear.) I am under no need to resort to them
or consult them, but if hereafter it should appear that my action
to-day is unsatisfactory to them, I shall not wait to be called upon
to retire, but I shall facilitate them by instantly restoring to their
hands the public trust I have kept unstained. (Cheers.) So much
upon the question of appeal. I find an urgent case before me ;
I claim to act on my conscience. I say there is no human
power, whatever it be, that could alter my decision. If my constituents support me I shall be proud of their confidence. If they
dissent from me I shall accept the penalty. (Hear, hear.) There
is excellent reason to believe that the unfortunate conjuncture of
affairs that has arisen invites the Government that is now oppres-
sing Ireland to resort to dissolution. How if a dissolution finds
us with the question undetermined (cheers), with England excited,
with large classes of persons enraged by the present condition of
affairs, with our own country torn into wars and factions ? We
should be thrown at the mercy of the enemy. (Cheers and counter-
cheers.)

Mr. PARNELL.—At the mercy of the unrivalled coercionist of
the Irish race. (Cheers and counter-cheers.)

Mr. SEXTON.—And I therefore regard it as a main point of
political policy, and a necessary matter of prudence, that, before
a Tory Government have an opportunity of resorting to a dissolution, this unfortunate and lamentable question which engages us
to-day shall be determined one way or the other. (Hear, hear.)
An intolerable evil would be suspense, a supreme danger would
be lack of determination and decision. I have one other reason,
gentlemen, for claiming at your hands, as a matter of patriotic

duty, an immediate decision upon this question. Whilst for the sake of my country I hope that the decision will call upon Mr. Parnell to retire, yet if it should happen that the decision should be the other way, I for my part will be happy to quit public life with a grateful sense of the services that he has rendered, and blot out of my mind for the rest of my life any thought of bitterness and wish him success in the rest of his career. (Cheers.) But there is one other reason for emergency which is demanded by self-respect. Mr. Parnell in his manifesto has declared of the men who besought him to retire that their integrity and independence have been sapped and destroyed by the wirepullers of the Liberal party. I do not ask him if he believes it.

MR. W. A. MACDONALD.—I believe it.

MR. SEXTON (continuing).—I ask Mr. Parnell if he believes any of his supporters gives credit to that statement—I ask him if he believes that Ireland will believe it ? (Cheers and counter-cheers.) I believe to be true of every man who stands by me in this conflict what I know to be true of myself, and what I cannot but think that Mr. Parnell knew also, and that is that no wirepuller of any English party dared approach any man of us with any proposal to corrupt or cajole (cheers), and that if he ventured it—from Mr. Gladstone down to the humblest hanger-on of politics—he would have reason to remember it and regret it to the last day of his life. (Cheers.) Against what men, Mr. Parnell, have you levelled this imputation ?

MR. PARNELL.—You have got first to substantiate that I have levelled it against any man. You had better heed what you are talking of.

MR. SEXTON.—It is the opening sentence of your manifesto.

MR. PARNELL.—Will you read it ?

MR. SEXTON.—I have no need to read it. I know it—it has burnt itself on my mind.

MR. PARNELL.—Read it.

MR. SEXTON.—" That the integrity and independence of a section of the Irish party " ——

MR. PARNELL (with emphasis).—"Of a section."

MR. SEXTON.—What section ?

MR. PARNELL (rising).—The section who are in treaty with Mr. Labouchere and Professor Stuart—the section of the party with whom you and other men inside this party, who ought to know better, have arranged to put me out of my position in this party. (Cheers and counter-cheers.) In every hole and corner of this House this conspiracy has been going on for days, and I would have issued no manifesto to the Irish people if I had not felt that the time was come for me to let them know what was going on behind their backs, and to recall the self-respect of the party. (Cheers and counter-cheers.)

Mr. SEXTON.—I have to declare, Mr. Parnell, with all the calmness I can command, that the statement you have made, so far as it concerns me or any member of the party of whom I have any knowledge, is absolutely and utterly unfounded. (Cheers and counter-cheers.) I have never entered into any treaty with any member. (Cheers.) My first knowledge of the circumstances which led to this painful position was the letter Mr. Gladstone addressed to Mr. Morley, of which I only knew a few moments before the assembly of a number of the members of this party and this party alone, and it was upon the impulse and patriotic feeling of the members of this party and this party alone, gathered together without a suggestion from, or without connexion with, any other party whatever, that the movement arose which has led to this meeting to-day. (Cheers.) I have been faithful and my friends have been faithful in our fealty to this party, and I challenge any man to offer a proof, or attempt to offer a shadow of proof, that I or any friend of mine has ever consulted with any English member against the leader of this party. The imputation must be levelled, if it is levelled against any friend of mine, against the men who, acting upon a sense of duty, have besought you to retire. Who are they? They are the men who stood beside you in the original fight by which this party was founded. They are the men who shared your imprisonment in Kilmainham and endured many imprisonments besides. They are the men who endured with you the ordeal of the Special Commission ; they are your own chosen lieutenants in the strife of Parliament.

Mr. JOHN O'CONNOR.—Not all.

Mr. SEXTON.—The exception proves the rule.

Mr. PARNELL.—All I have to say with regard to choosing representatives is that I have not chosen eight members of the Parliamentary party. Everybody has chosen my colleagues except myself.

Mr. SEXTON.—The point I was endeavouring to urge was that

D

amongst the men who from public duty besought you to retire are to be found the men who have stood immediately around you during the past 11 years, who have borne the brunt of the Parliamentary fight—the men whose advice you continually sought, and the men whose advice in moments of emergency you liked to have—and, let me add, the men who now find themselves confronted by this imputation are the very men who created the integrity and vindicated the independence of this party under circumstances which would not have made it strange if the independence and integrity of any party had been sapped and destroyed. (Cheers.) I refer to the men who for weeks and for months and for years back have had to guard and guide this party at times when you were not in their midst, and when they had no opportunity of referring to you, and strengthening themselves by your wise counsel and advice. And if these circumstances, Mr. Parnell, in your judgment, should not have intervened, I believe that in the judgment of Ireland and the civilized world they will effectually intervene between your followers and the imputation which in a moment of personal emergency you have ventured to cast upon them. (Cheers.) Integrity is not unconditional acceptance of the views of any man ; independence is not submission to the will of any man. We are your colleagues, Mr. Parnell, but we are not your slaves.

MR. PARNELL.—Hear, hear. (Cheers.)

MR. SEXTON.—I claim in the face of the world, and I claim in the presence of the Most High, that the integrity of the Irish party is unstained, and that its independence is absolute. (Cheers.) The question, the urgent question, is between the leader whom we have loved—whom we can never forget, and whoso useful tenure of his position circumstances have made impossible —the question is between him and the cause to which our fealty is due. If the leader is retained, in my judgment the cause is lost ; if the cause is to be won, it is essential that the leader should retire. (Cheers and counter-cheers.) I am acting, I solemnly declare, against my natural will and against the whole strong current of my disposition. Be my time in politics long or short—and I shall be happy to be relieved of the obligation of public life—but be my time in politics long or short, I assure you, Mr. Parnell, and I beg you to give me credit for sincerity in this declaration, I assure you I never can have a leader whom I can love and regard as I have loved and regarded you. (Cheers.) I am obliged to do violence to my own desire, I am obliged to overcome my natural inclination, acting upon the stern compulsion of duty, and if it were the last act of my life—the act by which I would ask my friends to remember me and the country to judge me—I am obliged to vote that the retirement of our leader, for a period at least, is urgent, and that to accept Colonel Nolan's motion would be to create a public danger, because I believe that every day's delay in determining this situation is filled with the most dangerous risk. (Cheers.)

Mr. JOHN REDMOND.—Sir, the speech to which we have just listened seems to me, in its tone at any rate, to be a strong argument for a delay of this question (hear, hear), and I have risen for the purpose of supporting the amendment moved by my hon. and gallant friend Colonel Nolan. One of the earlier declarations made by Mr. Sexton is one which bodes ill for any useful purpose from a debate of this question in this room. I allude to his statement that no power on earth can change his mind upon the matter. (Hear, hear.) If that be so I ask myself what earthly use is debate or discussion on the matter, if men's minds are closed to argument and to reason? If that be so would it not be better for us at once and without delay of even half an hour to give our votes, without reason or argument or discussion, upon this mere matter of party organization (hear, hear), which when looked more closely into involves the deposition of the leader of the Irish race?

Mr. SEXTON.—Mr. Redmond will allow me to say that when I spoke of power I meant, of course, compulsion.

Mr. REDMOND.—I understood Mr. Sexton to say that his mind was irrevocably made up upon this question. (Hear, hear.) If that be so there is no relevance in his interrupting me. I claim to speak here with just as much authority as Mr. Sexton. (Hear, hear.)

Mr. SEXTON.—Hear, hear.

Mr. REDMOND.—Do not let me be misunderstood. I do not claim the same authority from attainments or services, but I do claim the same authority as he has claimed for himself to speak here on behalf of the men who stood by your side, Mr. Parnell, when, almost alone, you created this movement. (Hear, hear.) I claim the right to speak as one of those who, during the ten years that have elapsed, both in Parliament and in the country and in America and Australia and throughout the world, have freely given the best years perhaps of my life in sustainment of the cause which Mr. Sexton served and you led. And there was one portion of Mr. Sexton's speech which found a responsive echo in my heart, where he deprecated any heated expression from members of this party which might lead to bitterness and animosities, which probably, if not checked, might last for a lifetime. I echo that; but in echoing that I am bound, as an honest man, to say that that consideration did not have the effect of modifying many of the expressions used and almost the whole of the tone adopted by Mr. Sexton in his speech. This is a question, gentlemen, whether you will come to a decision now on the question of the retirement of the leader of the party or whether you will adjourn it for further consideration. One of the arguments used by my hon. and gallant friend Colonel Nolan is that we ought to meet for this purpose in the metropolis of our country. That may seem a matter more of sentiment than of practical importance, but I am bound to say that in this matter it is impossible, in my opinion, for the representatives of the Irish nation to place sentiment entirely out of their mind. (Hear, hear.) It was in the capital of the Irish nation that you were called formally to that chair that you occupy, and I do say that if you are to be deposed from that chair the proper place to do it is in the capital of the Irish nation and in the face of the Irish people. (Loud cheers.) Mr. Sexton has said that he denies that this is a question that he feels bound to appeal to his constituents upon. That seems to me to be an unanswerable argument of his. If he is true to his description of these proceedings, that it is a matter merely of party organization, then I admit that this party meeting anywhere at very short notice might deal with it. But let us not shuffle with the real situation. This is not a mere question of party organization. (Cheers.) This is a question as to whether the man who is not merely the leader of this party, but who has, by his services, earned for himself the position of leader of the Irish race throughout the world, is to be deposed from the position by a vote of the representatives of the Irish people; and it does seem to me a heartbreaking circumstance that any consideration of danger to party alliance in England or any other matters should have such an effect upon the minds of the national representatives of the Irish people as to induce men like Mr. Sexton to deprecate in this matter a short delay, that the Irish members may make sure that in this matter they are acting in accordance with the full wishes and opinions of the Irish race at home and abroad.   Mr. Sexton used a very strong argument, if this was a small matter such as he described, in saying that a dissolution of Parliament may take place, as I understood, within the eight days for which my friend Colonel Nolan asks for an adjournment ; or, to take the other extreme limit which my hon. and gallant friend suggested— three weeks—that a dissolution of Parliament may find us, if it takes place during that time, if an adjournment is granted, in a disorganized and disunited position.   Is there any man in this room sanguine enough to say that if to-day by your vote you depose from that chair the leader of the Irish race, in eight days the result of that action will have so disappeared that the Irish race will present to the enemy an unbroken and united front ? (Loud cheers.)   My position on this matter is a very plain one. I have been, as you know, Mr. Parnell, a faithful and loyal colleague and follower of yours ; I have as you, gentlemen, know —those of you at any rate who have been for years in this party with me know—that I have been a faithful colleague.   I owe loyalty to the leader of this party, and I also owe loyalty to the party ; and I think—although this is not perhaps the main issue, I do think—the sooner we make our position clear the better. (Hear, hear.)   I intend to vote and to use every exertion in my power for the leadership of this party and the Irish people by Mr. Parnell, but at the same time I recognize the duty I owe to this party, and I recognize the obligation and the pledge which I took when in 1885 I was elected a member of this party—that if this party comes to a decision hostile to my view, then before taking any steps to support Mr. Parnell, if he chooses to go further, I will resign my seat and consult the wishes of my constituents. It seems to me that this amendment raises matters of the gravest importance.   Mr. Sexton has based his refusal of a delay upon this ground—namely, that this matter is urgent.   And why is it urgent ?   Because you will say that the continued leadership for eight days means the utter destruction of the Liberal alliance. (" Hear, hear," and laughter.)   Now, the danger of an alliance between the Irish party and an English party at this moment is no doubt a matter of concern and importance, but in deciding a question of this kind, where we are asked to sell our leader (loud cheers) to preserve an alliance, it seems to me that we are bound to inquire what we are getting for the price that we are paying. (Renewed cheers.)

The CHAIRMAN.—Don't sell me for nothing. If you get my value, you may change me to-morrow. (Renewed cheers.)

Mr. REDMOND (resuming).—The first thing, Mr. Parnell, that I desire to make plain is my view on this point. It seems to me that in selling our leader in order to preserve the Liberal alliance, we are selling absolutely and irrevocably the independence of the Irish party. (Loud cheers.) This party has been powerful only because it has been independent. Every Irish party that ever existed in this House fell in the same way—through the independence of the party being bartered away ; and I believe in my heart that if we sacrifice you to preserve this alliance that the days in our generation of the independence of the Irish party are at an end. What, I would like to know, would be the position of this party if you were sacrificed, and if a portion of the party held together—I am supposing a number of things—and if the Liberal party came back to power and a Home Rule Bill were proposed—what position, I want to know, would the Irish party under such circumstances be in if they went to Mr. Gladstone and demanded from him a full measure of our national rights ? Why, Mr. Gladstone would be absolutely unfettered, and he would have the Irish party, so to speak, in the hollow of his hand. The independence of the party would be gone, and it would be—and this is one of the most urgent reasons for the course I am taking—a discredited and powerless tool of the Liberal party. (Hear, hear.) Mr. Parnell and gentlemen, in estimating the value of a Liberal alliance, we are bound to take into account the statements made by you in the manifesto which you have issued. Now, you have made certain statements with reference to the provisions of the Home Rule Bill which Mr. Gladstone says he will introduce if he comes back to power. You have given a description of that Bill, which I challenge contradiction from any Nationalist in this room when I say it reduces that Bill to a sham and a fraud on the Nationalist aspirations (loud cheers), and if that description given by you be true, then all the sacrifices made to obtain that Bill would be thrown away, and we would bo sacrificing you for what would bo regarded by the Irish race throughout tho world as a compromiso of our principles and a betrayal of our cause. But Mr. Gladstone has made a denial. He has denied your recollection of what ho said on the four points mentioned by you, upon tho vital point of tho control by the Irish Executive of the Irish police, upon tho equally vital point of tho power to deal with tho land question being given to tho Irish Parliament. He says his recollection differs from yours, and ho denies your version of the provisions of the Bill. But Mr. Gladstone abstains absolutely from giving to the public or tho Irish nation anything in the shape of a definite or clear statement as to what he proposes (cheers), and if it comes to a question of recollection—in this I speak only for myself—if it comes to a question of recollection, of veracity, I have no hesitation in saying that I am prepared to tako your word before his. (Hear, hear.) But what I want to point out is this. This party is probably aware—if it is not awaro of it, I will ask you, Sir, to confirm what I say, and I will appeal to Mr. Justin M'Carthy, also, to confirm it—this party is probably aware that on Saturday last you made a proposal to Mr. Gladstone of such a character as I venture to say stamps tho wholo of your conduct in this matter as highly patriotic and self-sacrificing.

The CHAIRMAN.—Tho proposal was made by Mr. M'Carthy to Mr. Gladstone.

MR. T. M. HEALY.—On his own account?

MR. REDMOND.—Well, now, wo will deal with that afterwards. I have said that I will ask Mr. Parnell and Mr. M'Carthy to confirm what I am saying. That proposal as I understood it—I speak subject to tho correction of theso gentlemen—as I understand it was this—that if Mr. Parnell's recollection of what took place at that interview were wrong, then let Mr. Gladstone givo definite and clear assurances——

Tho CHAIRMAN.—To Mr. M'Carthy privately.

MR. REDMOND.—To give power to a Parliament in Dublin to deal with tho land question and to give to that Parliament control over the police—that then under these circumstances you were willing, having gained that for the Irish nation, to sacrifice every personal consideration and retire from public life. (Loud cheers.) And, Mr. Parnell, as I understand tho situation, that overturo to Mr. Gladstone has been fruitless, and, for ono reason

or another, as to which others must speak, Mr. Gladstone declined to give the assurances required. I mention these things
for two reasons. First of all—and God knows it seems a heartbreaking thing for an Irish Nationalist member to have to say it—
I use this argument because I think it seems your conduct is
honourable, patriotic, and self-sacrificing. I allude to it, also,
because it shows the measure of the value of this Liberal alliance
for which we are sacrificing you. (Cheers.) This Liberal alliance
means this—that if we consent to sacrifice you the Liberals will,
forsooth, make some little endeavour in the country to act up to
their solemn pledges of supporting Home Rule, not for love of us
or of you, but because it was a just cause. They will, if we
sacrifice you, continue to advocate Home Rule as a just cause,
and they hope—a very delusive hope, as it seems to me—that
under those circumstances they may be able to obtain a majority
at the English polls. Very well, and that will mean the introduction by Mr. Gladstone of a Home Rule Bill. You have challenged that Home Rule Bill as a fraud upon the national hopes,
and you have told Mr. Gladstone that if he says he will introduce provisions making it a genuine Home Rule Bill you will
retire, and I say that you can appeal with confidence to the Irish
race to decide between you. (Loud cheers.) If this be the
measure of the benefit to be gained by Ireland by the preservation
of the Home Rule alliance, I do not believe the Home Rule
alliance is worth preservation, at the enormous, at the terrible
cost of sacrificing you. (Cheers.) Mr. Parnell, I was one of
those who, in common with a large number of gentlemen in this
room, freely spoke our mind in Dublin of your political position
immediately after the newspapers had told us the details of the
recent trial. I was not present at your re-election on Tuesday,
but, as I understand it, the party unanimously re-elected you
as chairman (hear, hear), with the full knowledge, of course,
of the proceedings to which I have alluded. The alteration in the attitude of the party only came about when
Mr. Gladstone issued his ukase that, forsooth, you should
be trampled under foot. (Cheers.) I say that attitude taken
by Mr. Gladstone was unworthy of a great man. I say that
in my belief the attitude taken by him was not the attitude,
and up to this moment is not the attitude, of an honest
man. My belief is that if he were a great man he would not be

so precipitate in writing that letter. If he were an honest man
and he were true in his denials of your manifesto, he would now,
even at the eleventh hour, give such assurances as would ease
the political situation. No. It seems to me, however, that his
desire is that you should be trampled to the ground, and whoever
tramples you I will not take part in the transaction. (Cheers.)
As to your retention being a danger to the Irish cause and the
Home Rule cause, I do not believe that that is a real danger, and
these are the reasons why I do not believe my friend Mr. Sexton's
argument is a sound one when he says that this matter is urgent,
because this alliance would be broken up if you are retained.
There is one other matter to which I want to allude, and that is
a matter which has not been directly mentioned in this room,
excepting some communications read from the chair, but which
has formed, both in your manifesto and outside, a considerable
ground of argument and discussion—viz., the question of evicted
tenants in Ireland. Now, I am speaking in the presence of my
friends Mr. Condon, Mr. Sheehy, Mr. John Roche, and other
men who have been specially connected with this question, and
I claim from them the concession of this position to me—that I
have been identified during the whole of this Campaign movement in Ireland as much as they have been identified with these
tenants. I am as much pledged to those tenants as my friends
Mr. Condon or Mr. Sheehy. When Mr. Dillon and Mr. O'Brien
were leaving this country they did me the honour of asking me to
take some share, with one or two of my friends, in the manage-
ment of the affairs on these estates ; and, therefore, I think I
can speak as one who has had some responsibility in the matter
and as one who, by his action, has shown he is full of sympathy
for these tenants, and I say here that I would sooner cut off my
right hand than do anything which would have the effect of
destroying the hopes of these men and leaving them to starvation.
But, Sir, I take a different view altogether with reference to this
matter from that taken by my friends. I fear that if this party,
yielding to English clamour, yielding to the dictation of English
statesmen, sacrifices you, that the source of the supply on which
these tenants have been depending for so long—the generosity of
the Irish people in America—will be diverted from these tenants
in a way which could not be possible under any other conceivable
circumstances. (Hear, hear.) Any man who has been in

America, as I have, and knows America as intimately as I do, must be aware of the fact that your dethronement will rend the Irish people in America in twain (cheers) ; and I say, in the face of such a calamity as that, in America it will be impossible to rely on the source of the generosity of the people which has been sufficient to sustain these tenants in the past. I have to say more than that. I believe that in the pledge you have given that you will stand by those tenants those tenants have the most complete assurance that they will in the future be dealt with ; that the portion of your demands on the Home Rule Bill in reference to the power to be given to the Irish Parliament to deal with the land question is a direct demand on your part for power to restore those tenants to their homes. (Cheers.) I believe that these tenants would unanimously reprobate the idea that you are to be sacrificed for them. (Hear, hear.) I believe that if these Campaign tenants were polled to-morrow they would have sufficient manliness and patriotism to say to their representatives here, " Your first duty is Ireland—your first duty is to the loyalty you owe to the independence of your party and your leader ; and you are not to allow your position or your interests in the remotest degree to interfere with the discharge of that duty." I will say nothing about my motive in this matter ; I disdain to do it. (Cheers.) My public record, without any boasting, I should say entitles me to the belief (loud cheers), entitles me to entertain the belief that, whatever course I take, the Irish people will believe that I am actuated by the highest motives of patriotism. (Loud cheers.) It is true that I have a feeling of personal loyalty to you. I have said elsewhere, and I say here, that you have been my friend, and I think this is no time in which a man who has been once your friend should turn against you. (Hear, hear.) But I most solemnly think that while you remain my friend and my personal attachment is the same to you as it always was, I declare most solemnly, and I know I will be believed—I am entitled to be believed—that in this consideration I am not allowing my personal attachment to you to weigh in the balance. I would sacrifice my liberty, I would sacrifice my life, I would sacrifice the liberty and life of the truest and best friend I have in the world for the sake of the independence of my country. (Cheers.) It is not a personal motive that animates me ; it is because

I believe your maintenance is necessary to the success of our cause. (Hear, hear.) It is because I believe that your overthrow will be an instance of ingratitude such as has been shown in no other country in the world, perhaps, and such as will stamp the Irish people as unworthy of those rights which you and all of us have been working for. For this reason, and with the full sense of my responsibility, I am here to support your leadership, and I hope it will not be considered irreverent of me if I say that I hope the God of our fathers will direct the heart and conscience of every man in this room to come to a just decision ; and I consider that, whatever arguments may sway the minds of men, their main reason for supporting you, or even opposing you, will be a desire for the welfare of their country (hear, hear), and, expressing my hope, with which I will conclude, that this terrible crisis in the history of Ireland and in the history of our party may not be allowed, shall not be allowed, to bring once more upon our people the terrible curse of disunion —second only to the terrible curse of want of independence to which in the past we have owed most of the miseries and misfortune of our country—I invite you, gentlemen, to give your votes for Ireland. (Loud and prolonged cheers.) I invite you to give your votes for the independence and honour of Ireland's representatives (renewed cheers), and from my point of view you cannot give your vote for Ireland or the independence of our party or the cause of our freedom unless you give it in support of the man who has brought us to our present position, and who, in spite of all, in my humble judgment, is destined to lead us to the fulfilment of all the hopes and traditions of our race. (Loud cheers.)

Mr. T. M. HEALY.—I am very glad indeed that my friend Mr. Redmond has so eloquently and truly stated that there is no necessity on the part of any man here present by his vote to vindicate the motives with regard to which he is influenced in casting it. I heartily and cordially declare that in the bitter days that have gone by I have never found greater occasion to admire and respect my colleague, and I will say this—that, whatever vote may be given to him to-day, I have the fullest assurance that this party will remain united and unbroken (hear, hear), and I no more challenge the rectitude of purpose of any man opposed to my own views (hear, hear) than I would permit any man to challenge the rectitude of my purpose. (Cheers.) Therefore it was that I regretted that in the very opening observations of my friend Mr. Sexton he should have been interrupted with the statement that he was to be found in the lobbies and corridors of the House of Commons taking treasonable counsel with the opponents of Mr. Parnell to eject him from his position in order practically to better his country ; and I am amazed that my friend Mr. Redmond, seeing the patience with which that insult was borne, should have complained that Mr. Sexton's reply was harsh or imported anything of a bitter feeling. I must say for myself that I do not think I possess sufficient self-command, if such accusations were hurled at my face, to deal with them with the moderation that he did. Now I pass from that subject and I address myself to the argumentative portion of my friend Mr. Redmond's address. The amendment of Colonel Nolan before the chair is that we shall delay our decision and meet in Dublin. We are, I presume, as much in possession to-day of Mr. Parnell's views through his manifesto as we shall be were we to meet in Dublin. I do not think he could very well add anything to what he has said in that manifesto. For it is unlikely that he would have omitted therefrom any argument that could be used to affect opinion in the position in which he was placed. Therefore, as the statement of the case is put forward on Mr. Parnell's behalf by the best authority—namely, himself—we ought to be in full possession of his side of the argument. I do not see, therefore, where would be the gain to him in this delay. As for the place of meeting being Dublin, I honour the motive of my friend Colonel Nolan, but, really, poor Dublin has been so passed over in meetings of this party in the past that it is a somewhat novel proposal to make now that judgment should be given in a particular locality. I next come to the statement of Mr. Redmond with regard to yielding to English clamour and to English statesmen. Our demand from the English people is such a measure of Home Rule as we can honourably accept for our country. We abated many of our demands when we accepted the Home Rule Bill of 1886. (The CHAIRMAN.—Hear, hear.) The abatement of those demands was made by the members of our party who had been sentenced to be hanged, drawn, and quartered in endeavouring to achieve a greater measure of self-government for Ireland. Why was that abatement made ? To conciliate English opinion. (The

CHAIRMAN.—Hear, hear.) And is English opinion now only to be described as clamour when we have to sacrifice all the historic claims of our country handed down to us for generations ? We believe that the Home Rule Bill outlined in Mr. Parnell's manifesto is not one the Irish people could accept. I cordially join in that sentiment. (Loud cheers.) I pledge myself to accept no such measure. (Renewed cheers.) But let me mention this strange circumstance—that the two matters in that Home Rule Bill of 1886 were the very matters that Mr. Parnell declared horrified him at Hawarden in 1889. As I apprehend—I speak subject to correction—in the Home Rule Bill of 1886 we did not regain or obtain the immediate control of the constabulary. In the Home Rule Bill of 1886 we did not regain or obtain the immediate control of the judiciary, and, with all that, the entire body of Irish members, not 32, but 103, were to be excluded from the Imperial Parliament. Now the objection is put forward, as I understand, that we are only to have 32 members. I am assuming now as the basis of my argument the Hawarden interview upon Mr. Parnell's lines.

The CHAIRMAN.—You are assuming Michael Davitt's account, not mine. (Hear, hear.)

MR. HEALY.—I do not know anything about Mr. Michael Davitt. I am afraid he would not allow me on any occasion to become his spokesman. I certainly shall not allow ·myself to be made his spokesman to-day. I therefore say, in so far as those two arguments go, that we came to an agreement—an agreement solemnly ratified by Mr. Parnell—to accept the Home Rule Bill of 1886, and I say that no measure smaller than the Home Rule Bill of 1886 will satisfy us. (Hear, hear.) But Mr. Parnell says I have accepted Mr. Davitt's account of the interview. Quitting Hawarden, almost immediately Mr. Parnell made his way to a public meeting in Liverpool, and the suggestion has been put forward in the manifesto that for nine months he retained the terrible secrets intrusted to him at Hawarden, kept his colleagues in ignorance, allowed some of them to go to Australia, others to America, and all to spend their time and their intellects on English platforms, while he was persuaded at that interview, to use the expression, that "we were at the mercy of the unrivalled coercionist of the Irish race."

The CHAIRMAN.—It was an expression that I used at Wexford three days before I was arrested.

MR. HEALY.—Why did not Mr. Parnell say three days after he left Hawarden ? (Loud cheers.)

The CHAIRMAN.—I told you that I did not say them.

MR. HEALY.—You will have the difficulty of summing up to this jury, you being at the same time the judge and the defendant. (Cheers and cries of " Oh " and " Shame.") Here are the expressions used at Liverpool after the Hawarden interview—on the very day of the Hawarden interview. The Hawarden interview was on December 19, and on that very day Mr. Parnell found himself speaking at Liverpool,—" We trust that not only in Liverpool, but in the great county of Lancashire, we shall be able materially to assist in increasing the forces of Liberalism which will rally at the next general election to the assistance of our grand old leader." (Laughter.) And at a subsequent meeting, upon the same day, Mr. Parnell said,—" The great Liberal party has come to the help and the rescue of Ireland. My countrymen recognize, and join with me in recognizing, that we are on the safe path to our legitimate freedom and future prosperity. They will accompany me and continue both until you have helped your great leader to win this bounty which I trust we are on the eve of entering upon." Was that misleading the Irish people ? Was that misleading the English people ? Has there been any subsequent interview, and, if so, why was it not stated in the manifesto, in which Mr. Gladstone abandoned the position that he took up in the Home Rule Bill of 1886 ? And why, if the Hawarden interview be the capital matter on which Mr. Parnell bases himself in his manifesto, why, I say, were these false words uttered at Liverpool ? Either Mr. Parnell at Liverpool was false or his manifesto was false. (" Hear, hear," " No, no," and " Shame.")

The CHAIRMAN.—I will not stand an accusation of falsehood from Timothy Healy, and I call upon him to withdraw his expressions.

MR. HEALY.—Out of respect to the chair I will withdraw the accusation. (Hear, hear.) I say this—that, so far as public utterances went, the position in which the Irish people were left was the position at Liverpool on the day of the Harwarden interview. Which is likely to be the more correct kind—that deliveranco, fresh and straight, with no suggestion of personal motive or personal opposition that could be levelled, or the position assumed on the occasion of this manifesto ? Is the Irish party so bankrupt in its confidence that Mr. Parnell says, as his manifesto declares, that there was not one single member of his colleagues to whom he could have intrusted these vital secrets ? (Hear, hear.) So much in reference to that point. I then come to the suggestion that in the action we are taking we are taking it in conjunction with Mr. Labouchere and Professor Stuart.

The CHAIRMAN.—Hear, hear.

MR. HEALY.—William O'Brien and John Dillon are in Chicago.

MR. DALTON.—Four thousand miles away. They do not know what is going on.

MR. HEALY.—Precisely. They are 4,000 miles away from Mr. Labouchere and Professor Stuart.

DR. KENNY.—What communications were sent to them ?

MR. HEALY.—The long despatch of our delegates in America was ruled out upon a technicality, though no man questions, or could question, its genuineness.

The CHAIRMAN.—It is not to hand yet.

MR. HEALY.—We have all read it, and I therefore say that the suggestion need not be levelled at my friend Mr. Sexton, or any other man, that he has arrived at any conclusion adverse to Mr. Parnell because of interviews and colloquies in the corridors or lobbies. It is so unfounded as to be almost absurd. These men have come to their conclusions surrounded by that free America which Mr. Redmond threatened us will have its sympathies dried up. We are appealed to by Mr. Redmond on the ground that America will be adverse to our action and that he has travelled in America, and that no more will the evicted tenants be supported from the United States, because he knows the feeling in that great Republic. Who knows it best, John Redmond or John Dillon—the men who are there now, and who, from their place in America, surrounded by tens of thousands of Irishmen, and, ay, of Irish regiments with bayonets and arms in their hands—which are more likely to give in to the clamour, and to English clamour alone ? I say this—that to void the action of the Irish party, or any section of that party, upon the accusation of personal motive is a proceeding which recoils upon its author. It is unfounded, and the retort that, on my part, it will receive is that what personal motives influenced us influenced our leader. I will assume that no personal motive animated anybody, and when Mr. Redmond reminds us of declarations made in Dublin, I say that the declaration which I shall have the most reason to look back to with satisfaction in my life was the declaration I felt able to make for Mr. Parnell in the Leinster Hall (hear, hear), and if he had any glimmerings of the honesty and patriotism in the breasts of those who opposed him he would have seen in that declaration the greatest evidence of the sacrifice that we were prepared to make for him in the cause of Ireland. (Hear, hear.) Yes, I went to the Leinster Hall meeting and pronounced for Mr. Parnell in the face of English clamour. Aye, we stood up for Mr. Parnell against the Bulls of the Pope of Rome. (Cheers.) It was not likely we would allow ourselves to be influenced by the declarations of a single Wesleyan pulpit. Therefore, until it was made manifest to me that, for reasons into which I shall not enter, he had alienated the bulk, I may say the entirety, of that body of opinion which we were bound in this matter to defer to, until it was shown that he had left himself no foothold upon which he could help Ireland through the medium of the English people, it was then, and then only, that I felt driven to the position which I occupy to-day. And let me remind him that I was not alone in that declaration. He refers to Mr. Labouchere, I notice, as the name of the person with whom we have been colloguing. I notice that Mr. Labouchere took up an exactly similar position, and that Professor Stuart, through the columns of the *Star*, of which he is a director and editor, in as far as he could stem the torrent of English opinion, endeavoured to prevent the calamity of dissension and disunion among the friends of Ireland by recommending the retention of Mr. Parnell. So far, then, for the personal matter. Why do I defer to English opinion? Why did we defer to it in the settlement of 1886? (Hear, hear.) Why then were we willing, when passion and hatred animated many members of our race—why were we willing to endeavour to commence an apostolate of friendship with the English people? We were willing to do so because we were led by Charles Stewart Parnell, and he was able so to abate that passion and that recollection of wrong and of centuries of suffering on the part of Ireland as to insure this acceptance, almost without an exception, by every body of representatives of the Irish nation. Ireland possessed neither armies nor fleets. Having neither armies nor fleets we are bound to rely upon constitutional and Parliamentary methods. There was no hope for Ireland until Mr. Parnell succeeded in obtaining the promise of a Home Rule settlement. (Hear, hear.) He did it in consultation with English opinion, abating many of our demands, forgetting much of our wrongs and sufferings, and when we to-day calculate from that expression of English opinion that, not in units, or in tens, or in thousands, but in millions, the voters of the Liberal party have declared themselves against Mr. Parnell, and declared that the result of the mischief which will result to Ireland by his continuance in the leadership must be fatal to the hopes of our country, I found myself upon the hard necessities of the case ; and while I would rather, if I could, prevent this cataclysm in the party, while I would rather, if I could, prevent the possibility of dissension, or of division, or of difference among our scattered people, I say that the necessities of Ireland are paramount. I tell our chairman this —if he consults freely the opinions of his supporters here to-day he will conclude from them that the best thing he could have done for Ireland would have been to have on Tuesday last retired from his position. There may be, of course, individuals amongst our friends of a contrary opinion, but I speak of the volume of opinion of the party and of the volume of opinion amongst his own friends—namely, that if he could have seen his way to have sacrificed his personal feelings upon Tuesday last, and not have been paid, in the events that occurred, the overwhelming and un-paralleled compliment of re-election—if he had been able to say, " Yes, I have served Ireland truly and well ; my services are not denied, they are acknowledged ; but now I have been in-formed by Mr. Gladstone, or I collect from English opinion, that my presence as your leader may present a difficulty in the future ; and, acting upon that feeling of self-sacrifice which has always animated me, I will temporarily withdraw from a scene where I am no longer of the same advantage and value to my country," it would have been better. That was not the course taken by our chairman. Why was it that on Tuesday last, on the occasion of his re-election, knowing, as he did, what was the feeling of Mr. Gladstone with regard to his position, why did he not there and then take his party into his confidence—(hear,

E

hear), and, having taken it into his confidence, why did he not then reveal to them the explanation of Mr. Gladstone's attitude that he has inserted in his manifesto of Saturday? Why was the Irish party allowed on Tuesday and on Wednesday to meet with distracted counsels, without knowing that the secrets of the manifesto were soon to be revealed to the world? Why was not, then, some communication made to my friends Mr. Sexton or Mr. M'Carthy? Why were they not told—"Ah! there is a bitter plot against the liberties of Ireland. I am to be driven out. The integrity of the Irish party has been sapped, and I am here to warn you and advise you upon it." Why was Tuesday allowed to pass, Wednesday allowed to pass, and Thursday allowed to pass, and then not the party, but the entire world, learn of this event for the first time? On this ground I oppose the resolution of Colonel Nolan; but I do so, also, upon this further ground. We have been maintaining Mr. Parnell for years and years, not only on account of his Parliamentary services and his capacity for further service, but because of the great value of his name as a magnet and centre for Irish patriotism. Under that name the scattered units of our race have been collected; around that name many great historic associations must for ever linger; but let us retain Mr. Parnell as our leader, and of what value is that name to us? It will be maintained under these circumstances that Mr. Parnell, having been declared against by the body and volume of English opinion, purchased his place at the head of our party by driving out of our cause and out of the ranks of political service the first great English statesman who has held out the hand of help and fellowship to Ireland. (Cheers.) Might not that consideration give him pause? Might he not consider that at least there is a possibility of dissension, as to whether he should go or stay, amongst these scattered units of the Gael? Would we be able in future to conjure with that name which had been used as a battering ram to drive Mr. Gladstone out of the possibility of further service to Ireland? We have a distracted public opinion in Ireland. That at least will be conceded. Let the proposal of my friend Colonel Nolan or of my friend Mr. Redmond be carried, and let us maintain Mr. Parnell in his position; can we doubt that there will be dissension and distraction amongst our countrymen? Can we doubt that we would no longer be able to magnetize our people by that name, when it is known that we have only agreed in rallying round him against the better judgment of all the more important members of our party—of Dillon, O'Brien, T. D. Sullivan, of Justin M'Carthy, of Sexton, of Arthur O'Connor, and of so many honoured names amongst our people? And if we were now, on the appeal of Mr. Redmond, to close our ranks once more round the name of Parnell and to determine to exorcise Mr. Gladstone from English politics as if he were the evil spirit, " the unrivalled coercionist of the Irish race," if we were to drive him out from his capacity for service to the Irish people by muttering incantations of unity and of friendship, when there can be neither the one or the other, our unity as a party is gone. Our friendship—where is it in the face of accusations that our integrity is sapped and that we are engaged in treasonable cabals around the corridors against our country's greatest friend? Freedom, unity! I say to Mr. Parnell his power is gone. He derived that power from the people. We are the representatives of the people. (Loud and prolonged cheers.) Place an iron bar in a coil and electrize that coil and the iron bar becomes magnetic. This party was that electric action. There (pointing to the chairman) stood the iron bar. The electricity is gone, and the magnetism with it, when our support has passed away. If my words appear to some of my friends to be too strong or too bitter, I say this—that I speak in this arraignment fully conscious that we, upon our side, must confine ourselves to the irreducible *minimum* of statement ; and that, upon the other side, every argument, every appeal, every artifice (cries of " Oh ")—I withdraw the word if it is offensive—every sentiment that passion or friendship can arouse may be safely and generously appealed to. We have nothing before us but stern realities. (Hear, hear.) We cannot found our position upon sentiment, upon the claims of friendship, upon anything except the awful necessities that surround us in the presence of a trembling Irish cause. (Hear, hear.) I say, then, and declare, that my vote shall be for the deposition of the chairman of this party. I will not give that vote without regret. We are not all cold and passionless. I give it under what I conceive to be the solemnest obligations of duty and of patriotism. (Hear, hear.) If we could have maintained Mr. Parnell in that position we would have done so. Did we leave one stone unturned or effort unmade, one meeting unaddressed or unappealed to, to maintain

him where he was ? I examine my conscience in regard to my
duty towards Mr. Parnell in this crisis. I find therein no prick
of conscience. I say, then, that, having regard to the distractions to our country if he remains, and to the knowledge I possess of the patriotism of my colleagues who will support him,
and the patriotism and sense of unity of the Irish race, that I
believe if he remains his party and his country will be distracted. That being the case, as all men are ephemeral, and as
nothing is eternal save the Irish cause founded upon a basis of
right and judgment (cheers), I know that those who support him
most strongly to-day will, once the vote of the majority is recorded, rally round the position which he now occupies, and
which will then become the heart and centre of Irish authority
and patriotism. I know that my country similarly and its people
will rally round that position. Men pass away and causes
remain, and the Irish cause will march through these dissensions and these distractions purified and eternal. (Cheers.) I
tell Mr. Parnell that if he has a sacrifice to make upon the altar
of his country there is yet time. He can still hand down to his
countrymen a name upon which no fleck of even bitterest malice
can be cast if he takes counsel with those who are as patriotic as
himself, who are as single-minded and as single-purposed as
himself, but who are resolved here, defying every consideration
except the consideration of country, who are determined here to
cast their votes for that country, and to cast their votes for it
believing that they are doing an act which will yet hew a path-
way to freedom. (Loud cheers.)

Mr. PARNELL, who was greeted with loud cheers, said,—I
think that the time has come, on this second day of silence on
my part, that I should intervene in a debate which has not been
provoked by me and in reference to an opposition that has not
been made by me—an opposition created, on the day on which
this House met, by the letter of Mr. Gladstone. We shall have,
and those who will be responsible for the decision of this party
will have, to deal with first causes in this matter. In apportion-
ing the responsibility, you will have to consider your own responsibility and what it was from the first. The movers and
seconders of this resolution—the men whose ability has not been
so conspicuously exercised as that of Mr. Healy and Mr.
Sexton—will have to bear their responsibility in all this. And who

can doubt it ? Mr. Healy has been trained in this warfare, and who trained him ? Who saw his genius ? Who telegraphed to him from America to come to him ? Who gave him his first opportunity and chance ? Who afterwards got his seat in Parliament for him, rebuking and restraining and going past the prior right of my friend Jack Redmond in Wexford ? That Mr. Healy should be here to-day to destroy me is due to myself. But I am glad he is here to-day to destroy me, if he understands the meaning and effect of his own proceedings. If he does, he is responsible and I am not. Mr. Healy has reminded us that he attended the meeting in Dublin. He reminded me of his services. He has not been slow to remind me of his services to me and the party. He reminded us that he attended that meeting in Dublin. (Mr. Healy.—I reminded Mr. Redmond.) I understand that Mr. Healy attended this meeting in Dublin and seconded the resolution calling on me not to retire from the leadership. (Loud cheers.) Who asked him to do that ? Did I ? (Renewed cheering.) Who asked Mr. Justin M'Carthy to travel to Dublin and to say that he could give secret information to throw a different complexion on hidden events ? Did I ? (Loud cheers.) Where was Mr. Sexton at this meeting ? (Renewed cheering.) When his counsel might have been of importance in preventing the ravelling of a false situation, where was he ? Where were you all ? Why did you encourage me to come forward and maintain my leadership in the face of the world if you were not going to stand by me ? Why did my officers en_ courage me to come forward and take my position on the bridge and at the wheel if they were going to act as traitors and to hand me over to the other commander-in-chief ? (Renewed cheering.) I did not ask them to do that. I did not ask them for this certificate of character, of which so much was made at the Dublin meeting. I did not give Mr. Justin M'Carthy any information. I did not ask that that meeting should be held. And you talk of the position that has been created and why it has been created. I will show you before I sit down why it has been created, and that the blame for its creation does not rest with me. Of the man that has been put up—I was going to say the leader-killer (laughter and cheers)—the leader-killer who sharpens his poniard to stab me as he stabbed the old lion, Isaac Butt, in the days gone by—I remember well, and it will be a recollection which will always be a comfort to me, that though Isaac Butt " reneged " me, I never in word or deed counselled the attacks made on him, and although the times were times of crisis, such as we did pass through and may again—although the times were times of stress—I allowed that old man to go down honoured to his grave rather than that I should seek to step into the shoes of a politician who, however many his faults, had created a great movement, and had given to me, and to many others, the power of participating and taking part in it. (Loud cheers.) Now, what is to be said about my temporary retirement ? Was that request as honest as the one Mr. Sexton made me when he asked me to resume the leadership ? (Ironical cheers.) He who had refused to come to the Dublin meeting comes to the London one. He asks me to take the leadership with one voice, and ten minutes afterwards he announced, to my astonishment, that when he made me that request he believed that I would reject it. (Laughter and cheers.) Oh, yes ! It is easy enough to talk about honesty in politics. It is easy enough to talk about speeches in seeming contradiction one with the other. I am asked about going to Hawarden. I go to Hawarden. I receive this communi-cation from Mr. Gladstone. I am told that this communication is not to be divulged to any of my colleagues—that it is an important communication. Mr. Healy expects me to go on the Liverpool platform, and, on the strength of this Hawarden decla-ration, to denounce Mr. Gladstone, and say he is not a Grand Old Man, and because, gentlemen, forsooth, within an hour after receiving this Hawarden communication, I failed to do anything, well, then I am held up to public odium as deceiving the good citizens of Liverpool and deceiving this statesman, who I hoped then would have done something for the cause of Ireland. My responsibility was enormous. Was I, at a single stroke, without either giving any time or opportunity to Mr. Gladstone to recon-sider his position, to denounce him on account of a half-com-pleted programme ? Surely the absurdity of this must be patent to every one. It does not require any words to show Mr. Healy how ridiculous the proposal is (hear, hear), that I, at Hawarden, having received this communication, should at once go on the platform and denounce this old man on the strength that he was not going to carry out his Irish proposals. Remember, I had only just received those proposals. I was not allowed to bring them before my colleagues. I was told that none of them were to be taken as definite or final, and that the chief proposal of all—the proposal that refers to the retention of 30 members—was the proposal which might be subject to further revision. In any case it was not a question of drafting a private Bill. It was a question of dealing with a gentleman much my senior to whom I was bound to pay every reverence and courtesy within limit. But as to appealing to a meeting which contained some of his own supporters, that is a very poor ground for asking you to vote for my deposition. Now, then, I want to ask Mr. Healy a further question, but perhaps I ought not to be too personal—I want to ask you all a further question. I want to ask you, before you vote my deposition, to be sure that you are getting value for it. (Cheers.) On Saturday night I made a proposal to Mr. Justin M'Carthy. I was anxious to keep this proposal from the newspapers. I do not know now that I ought to give it to the newspapers, but I do not see how it is to be prevented.

MR. JOHN O'CONNOR.—It was in the papers on Sunday morning.

MR. JOHN REDMOND.—It was in the papers the next morning, however it got there.

MR. PARNELL.—The proposal was this. There is a difference of recollection between Mr. Gladstone and myself with regard to the statements that were made in this Hawarden conversation. You all admit—and this is the misery of it—we are all agreed that you will not have this Bill. (Mr. Condon.—"Hear, hear," and loud cheers.) There has not been a man to say a word in favour of this Bill. But are you sure that you will be able to get anything better? Can Mr. Healy say you will be able to get anything better? Can Mr. Justin M'Carthy say it? Can Mr. Sexton say it? If they can say it, for God's sake let them say it, and I will not stand for a moment in the way. (Loud cheers.) What was the proposal that was made? Will Mr. Gladstone, Sir William Harcourt, and Mr. Morley give to Mr. M'Carthy letters declaring that, in the event of the return of the Liberal party to power, a Home Rule Bill be proposed under which the control of the Irish constabulary will be vested in an Irish executive responsible to an Irish Parliament, and will they also include in the same measure power to deal with and settle the Irish land question, and that these provisions will be regarded as vital to the

Bill? Now Mr. M'Carthy went to Mr. Gladstone with these pro-posals. I stated, before he went, that I would not communicate with Mr. Gladstone; that Mr. Morley had pointed out to me, through Mr. M'Carthy, that Mr. M'Carthy was the channel through which all further communications were to be made from the party to him. That was the last communication I had from Mr. Morley; if there were any further communications they were to come through Mr. M'Carthy. I said, " Very well, then." On Saturday night I said to Mr. M'Carthy, " Will you take these communications to Mr. Gladstone—not from me, but from the party, or from a section of the party, or from yourself, and as a matter for his consideration before this question comes up again for decision? And I assured Mr. M'Carthy that, although it was not a matter that I desired to be put before Mr. Gladstone, yet that if these two concessions were made I should retire from public life as a matter of course. This was done on Saturday, and Mr. Gladstone has replied that he will not hold any com-munication with me as leader of the party.

MR. M'CARTHY.— No, no.

MR. PARNELL.—He is perfectly welcome to that. The com-munications were also put before Sir William Harcourt, and his reply, as I understand it, was that under no circumstances will he give any promise whatever, either now or hereafter, to any Irish party: and Sir William Harcourt, remember, is the man whom you will have as your leader when Mr. Gladstone dies.

MR. CONDON.—Not our leader.

MR. PARNELL.—Won't you? Mr. Morley will not deny that this great man, Sir William Harcourt, whose chain you are going to put about your necks, is the man who has the reversion of the Liberal leadership; is the man who has declared that his limits and ideas about Home Rule are Mr. Chamberlain's scheme of local government, and if Sir William Harcourt ever comes into power he will give you local government and plenty of coercion. (" Hear hear " from Mr. Parnell's supporters.) That is not from Mr. Morley, but it is from myself. I know very well what Sir William Harcourt will do for you, I know what Mr. Gladstone will do for you, I know what Mr. Morley will do for you, and I know that there is not a single one of the lot to be trusted unless you trust yourselves. (Loud cheers.)

" To thine own self be true ;
" And it must follow, as the night the day,
" Thou canst not then be false to any man."

That is what I have to say to the Irish party. If I am to leave
you to-night, I should like to leave you in security. I should
like—and it is not an unfair thing for me to ask—that I should
come within sight of this " promised land." (Loud and enthusiastic cheers.)

MR. JUSTIN M'CARTHY said,—I do not intend to make any
lengthened speech on the general and main question before
you. I do not propose to endeavour to add to the arguments and
emotion which have been developed on the one side or on the other.
I only wish to make some statements of what went on within my
own knowledge, and which may make the situation a little more
clear to you, and that is in reference to what occurred on Saturday and Sunday, as far as I am concerned. On Saturday, at
a hastily-summoned meeting of some friends of our chairman
—amongst whom I was glad and pleased and proud to be
reckoned—I had unexpectedly the office thrust on me of going
to Mr. Gladstone and endeavouring to reopen the negotiations
that had been going on. I shall tell you—and Mr. Parnell will
bear me out in this—that I myself strongly and repeatedly
objected to undertake any mission. I said that I did not think
it good under any circumstances or under any conditions, and
I told them I considered it was not wise and in any event not
worthy of the Irish party to send any letter to any English statesman whatever to get from him any promise that involved the
resignation of the chairman of the party. I told Mr. Parnell and
the meeting that I would be strongly opposed to bearing a message
of that kind to Mr. Gladstone, or to any English statesman whatever, if it involved the resignation, not of Mr. Parnell but even of
the youngest and most obscure member of the Irish Parliamentary
party. I urged that our quarrels amongst ourselves were for ourselves and for our own party and our own nation, and that we
ought not to place ourselves at the feet of any English statesman,
however great or however well-meaning towards us. (Loud cheers.)
I think I was wrong now in yielding to the strong pressure brought
to bear on me by friends in that room. There was one strong
appeal made to me by a respected colleague, who said, in earnest
tones, that he believed that I would be deserting my duty if I left

the least stone unturned in the way of reconciliation by going to Mr. Gladstone. Under that pressure I consented to go. I shall tell you in the briefest form what occurred. The names of three men were mentioned—Mr. Gladstone, Sir William Harcourt, and Mr. Morley. I did not succeed in seeing Mr. Morley. I saw Mr. Gladstone and Sir William Harcourt. Mr. Gladstone had talked to me before and talked to me since about the difference of recollection between himself and Mr. Parnell as to points of agreement and disagreement at Hawarden. He still adhered to his declaration that Mr. Parnell's impression of what he (Mr. Gladstone) said on that occasion was absolutely mistaken. On those two or three important points mentioned by Mr. Parnell Mr. Gladstone adheres to the declaration that Mr. Parnell is absolutely mistaken. He adheres to his declaration that Mr. Parnell and he parted in general agreement as to the basis of a Home Rule measure, and that there was not one word more of difference between them than there would be between two of the closest colleagues in planning out a measure as to which they had not agreed about the details. We now come to the offers I was pressed by my friends and pressed by Mr. Parnell to make to Mr. Gladstone. It is perfectly true that Mr. Parnell told me that he would not enter into any communication himself with Mr. Gladstone.

Mr. PARNELL.—I did not say that on account of any personal feeling or hurt on my own part, but I did so after the statement in the *Daily News* that Mr. Gladstone communicated with you, and that he had declined to see me.

Mr. M'CARTHY.—That is a question of pure misunderstanding. I never heard that Mr. Gladstone refused to see you.

Mr. PARNELL.—You came down with Mr. Sexton to the smoke room, and he said, " Won't you see Mr. Gladstone to-night ?"

Mr. M'CARTHY.—I never saw Mr. Gladstone myself at that time.

Mr. SEXTON.—It was a mere suggestion on my part, thinking it might lead to a healing measure.

Mr. PARNELL.—I thought you would not ask me to see Mr. Gladstone except you were directed to do so.

Mr. SEXTON.—It was a mere suggestion on my part. I merely said, " Would it not be well to see Mr. Gladstone ?"

Mr. M'CARTHY.—I went down to the smoke room with Mr.

Sexton, but till Mr. Parnell mentioned this, I never heard a word about Mr. Gladstone refusing to see him. We come now to what Mr. Gladstone said about this document. He said, in the first instance, that he did not feel himself entitled to interfere in any way in any discussions of the Irish party. For him Ireland was represented by the Irish party, the Irish party was represented by the elected leader of the party, and for him there was, therefore, no one but the elected leader of the Irish party with whom he could feel himself entitled to negotiate. He regretted the condition of things that made us disorganized for the time, but he said he could not regard me as representing in any sense the Irish party. I had, in fact, told him that, apart from our communication, I did not represent the party ; that I could not profess to represent the party ; that I came from no meeting of the party, but that I came from a number of friends, hastily assembled, who thought it would be a good thing for the country if I made this statement to Mr. Gladstone. Under these conditions Mr. Gladstone said he could offer no suggestion, sign no document, and give no message for me to convey to the Irish party ; but he furthermore added that in any case, and supposing it were possible for him to enter into any such arrangement, he could not sign that document and give it to me with any certainty that it might not be used in print by any of those concerned in it.

MR. PARNELL.—I did not even want to see the document. I merely wanted your assurance that it had been given.

MR. M'CARTHY.—I never understood I was to get a document, and that Mr. Parnell was to know nothing about it, or that Mr. Parnell was not to make up his mind about resigning before he knew what came from Mr. Gladstone.

MR. PARNELL.—I only wanted your word.

MR. M'CARTHY.—Does any one believe I would undertake that responsibility, that I would go to Mr. Gladstone and procure a document, that I would go to Mr. Parnell and say " the document is all right," and that on my mere word Mr. Parnell would resign his leadership ; that I would go to the party and say, " I have received a telegram from Mr. Gladstone, the contents of which I could not tell Mr. Parnell, but which induced Mr. Parnell to resign " ? If any member thinks I would do that, then he puts little store on my experience, on my common sense or friendly feelings to Mr. Parnell, and on my patriotism. (Cheers.) As to Sir William Harcourt, he did not say and did not suggest that he would not make any promise of any kind to any Irish member. He said that, under the condition of the manifesto issued by Mr. Parnell, which he said he believed to be a conversation to be kept in the most absolute secrecy, he would not give me or anybody else any assurance in writing or by word of mouth that was to be brought in any way under the notice of Mr. Parnell. He said almost nothing about the general question, but he said not a word to me that meant to convey that he would not enter into any arrangement with any Irish party or any member whatever. That is my story about these negotiations—I cannot help calling them the unfortunate negotiations, which I undertook most reluctantly— and only undertook when a last appeal was made to me not to neglect my duty by leaving any stone unturned that might lead to a settlement of this terrible question. Now as to the general question. I do think that Mr. Parnell has made too little of the error committed by keeping private till now the conversation between him and Mr. Gladstone at Hawarden.

Mr. PARNELL.—I am perfectly willing to admit that I was to blame in that, but I am glad I have told it all now before the mischief was done. (Cheers.)

Mr. M'CARTHY.—I only give my view now as to what I think an Irish leader should have done. You possessed a secret almost vital to the cause of your country. Supposing it were so, you go about the world with this secret at your heart, and see your party and your country sliding down to this precipice, and, because you had taken a pledge of privacy, you say you could not disclose it. That is a pledge I could not have accepted on any condition whatsoever. But suppose I had accepted it, and was bound in that terrible silence, I was not bound to go on the platform and commend Mr. Gladstone. (Cheers.) I was not bound to allow my countrymen here, and in Scotland, and in Ireland, as well as in America and Australia, to go about glorifying Mr. Gladstone while I know in my heart of hearts that Mr. Gladstone's purpose was, if he could, to betray the Irish cause and the Irish people. (Cheers.) But, supposing I had felt that terrible bond of silence, that seal as rigid as the seal of the confessional itself, pressing on me, would I have broken that seal of confession for the sake of publishing a manifesto under any conceivable condition of public

affairs ? (Cheers.) If that agreement was ever to be known, the
time of making it known was when it might have been of great
service by warning Irishmen against false friends, and not at a
moment when, after concealing it so long from the party, a manifesto was sprung upon the party and country. Speaking for myself, the whole transaction seems to me to have betrayed from
the beginning a vital error of judgment. (Mr. Parnell, " Hear,
hear.") Many of the remarks made about small inconsistencies
are not worth serious and solemn consideration ; but I think that
was an inconsistency which, in my mind, imperilled, and must
always imperil, your leadership and your capacity for leadership
and work. (Cheers.) I think some of us should have known
something about it. That secret, borne about so long and revealed
at the wrong time, does so weaken one's confidence in the judgment of our leader that I cannot see any hope, if the present
arrangement of the party should last, that the cause of the country
is to be served and saved.

MR. JOHN O'CONNOR.—Mr. Chairman, I have listened with
very great attention, as the case demanded, to the speeches
which have been delivered by your opponents. Those speeches
appear to me to place your supporters at this meeting in a false
light before the world. (Cries of " Hear, hear," and " No, no.")
It has been held up to this meeting that, if we vote for you, we
vote against the country. I entirely deny the accuracy of that
statement. (Cheers.) I think I may claim for those who will
vote for your leadership to-day as strong a desire to act in
accordance with the interests of the country as the other side
claim for themselves, and as I am willing to accord to them.
I think that the reading of those resolutions at the early stage
of our meeting, which came from Irishmen assembled in Ireland,
England, and Scotland, show that those who support your
leadership to-day are in accord with the country in this matter.
Almost all the telegrams and letters conveying to us the opinions
of our fellow-countrymen at home and abroad in meeting
assembled have, with two or three exceptions, called upon this
meeting to support your leadership. (Cheers.) Our people at
home act upon the principle initiated by Mr. Healy at the
Leinster Hall, when he said, " We gained our present position
by independence, and by independence and independence alone
we can maintain it." (Cheers and counter cheers.) The young

men of Ireland met in Young Ireland's Society, and in the organization you, Sir, have created, have sent their message here to this meeting in tones almost unanimous in support of you, and those who will vote for your leadership. They know well what the condition was in the past. The young men of Ireland know that you have reconciled the conflicting elements in which you found Irish politics when you became our guide and our leader, and they feel that, once your guiding hand is removed, once your cementing genius is withdrawn, Irish politics will resolve themselves again into those conflicting elements. (Hear, hear.) We are asked to vote you, Sir, out of the leadership of this party and nation on the ground that there is danger to the alliance between the Liberal party of England and the Irish people. I entirely traverse that opinion. I believe there is no fear for that alliance, and I have reason to believe it. I have been upon many platforms in England since the verdict was given in the case that was the origin of all our trouble, and local leaders upon those platforms, addressing meetings variously composed—some composed entirely of working men, and some of people living in the suburbs of great cities—have stated that no matter what any man might do, no matter what might occur to any man in the future, they had been working and striving for Home Rule for the Irish people, and they would continue to do so, and that nothing in the world would alter their opinions in that respect. That was the expression given from local leaders—men who in their own localities were considered saints and leaders and guides—and these expressions of opinion were applauded to the echo by the audiences to whom they were addressed. That, Sir, is my experience. I have read the speech of Earl Spencer wherein he in unmistakable terms stated what he wished you to do in order to solve this problem. He stated he personally wished that you, Sir, might retire from the leadership of the Irish party. He added that in the event of your retaining the leadership their plain and simple duty as leaders was to stick to the principle of Home Rule. (Cheers.) That statement was made at a large meeting and was applauded to the echo, and if the Liberal newspapers of this country and the Liberal leaders of this country had only the backbone of Earl Spencer the English people would have remained true to that opinion. (Hear, hear.) Let us remember that this alliance that has been spoken of was formed at a time when you, Sir, were charged with conniving at murder, and when every man here was charged with some crime in connexion with the agitation in Ireland, and these accusations were not considered a bar to that alliance. (Hear, hear.) I have no hesitation in saying that, if we show that independence which the Irish people have unmistakably shown, there is no danger to that alliance, and that it will be stronger if in this great and important crisis the Irish people and their representatives remain true to the independent principles that have guided them in the past. What are we asked to do to-day ? We are asked to go back upon the past history and traditions of the Irish people, to step down from the proud position of an ancient nation and become the mere tail of an English party, to be wagged by the will of its head. (Laughter and " Hear, hear.") When you, Sir, asked me to join this party, I joined it as an Irish Nationalist, and I shall continue to belong to this party only so long as it is an Irish Nationalist party. (Loud cheers.) I shall cease to be a member of it when it becomes a mere tail of an English party. (Renewed cheering.) These are the reasons which will guide me in supporting you in that position from which you have taught the Irish people to respect themselves, from which you have taught the world to wonder at and admire you. These are the reasons for which I vote that you retain that position to-day.

Mr. T. O'HANLON supported the amendment, and claimed that all the Irish members should have time to consult their constituents, as they ought to be guided by them in voting on this matter. He believed that those men who were about to vote for their leader's destruction were those whom Mr. Parnell had brought from obscurity and placed in the position which they now occupied. (Cheers.)

Mr. W. REDMOND also supported the amendment. He alluded to Mr. Parnell's great services to the Irish cause in the past, and argued that among the Liberals of England and Scotland there was not the outcry for Mr. Parnell's expulsion which some parties were anxious to represent. He himself had addressed a large number of meetings in England, and he believed he was right in saying that the circumstances which had led up to the meeting would only prove a mere temporary check to the Irish cause (cheers), and that those men who at present were impressed with the justice of Ireland's claims would now put them aside simply because of a personal matter affecting one man. He maintained that Mr. Gladstone would never have brought forward a Home Rule Bill, only that he had been forced to do so by Mr. Parnell, and in conclusion he earnestly asked them to postpone this important question until the proposition which had been made by Mr. Parnell to Mr. Gladstone had been either accepted or rejected.

Mr. PIERCE MAHONY said a great deal of capital had been made out of that portion of Mr. Parnell's manifesto referring to the Hawarden interview. He (Mr. Mahony) did not hold with those who said there was a breach of confidence involved in making public that interview. He was glad that there was a unanimous feeling at the meeting that the Home Rule Bill shadowed forth in that interview would not be accepted by the Irish party.

Dr. KENNY thought the delegates in America, had they listened to Mr. Parnell's touching appeal, would not have joined in any cry of "*A la lanterne*." He was convinced that had they known of the offer made to Mr. Gladstone which now placed on his back the burden, they would have entertained a different opinion. Mr. Parnell was reproached with two things. One was that he held his peace when the bond of secrecy was placed on his lips and that he did not go forthwith to the nearest platform and proclaim the terms of the Home Rule Bill. On the other hand he was reproached that, when this miserable ghost of a Bill was being dangled before the eyes of Ireland to win votes from him, he then under the stress of circumstances declared the terms of that Bill. They were now discussing the *dictum* of a statesman who said to them, "Throw away your leader or you will take the consequences" It was a hypocritical cry and clamour got up by the old women of both sexes in this country to "bulldose" the Liberal party and Ireland. He urged a further delay and time for consideration. Precipitancy had landed them into that morass and precipitancy would not get them out of it. By delay they could communicate more fully with the delegates in America.

Dr. TANNER.- Read their letter.

The CHAIRMAN.—Order. Who is interrupting.

Dr. Tanner.—I spoke, Sir; I wish their communication to be read.

The Chairman.—I must ask you to resume your seat, Dr. Tanner.

Dr. Tanner.—I have done so.

Dr. Kenny, continuing, said that if they were guilty of such a suicidal act as to get rid of their leader they would have nothing but uncertainty before them.

Mr. J. Nolan spoke next, and declared that the question could not be settled by the prominent men of the party, nor by the people in Ireland, but it was one to be settled by the Irish race. He referred to the number of votes of confidence that had been passed in Mr. Parnell since the recent case, and he referred to the speech made by Mr. Healy in the Leinster Hall, which concluded with the impressive words in reference to Mr. Parnell, " Don't speak to the man at the wheel." (Cheers.)

Mr. Edward Harrington, interrupting, said,—No; but cut his throat. (Hear, hear.)

Mr. J. Nolan, continuing, said that at the meeting of the party on Tuesday last Mr. Sexton had declared that Mr. Parnell's leadership was essential to the existence of the party.

Mr. Sexton.—I said it appeared to me at that time that course was best calculated to preserve the unity of the party. On the following day I thought, however, the question of the cause of Ireland came in.

Mr. J. Nolan said he accepted the correction, but he thought Mr. Sexton had said that in obedience to self-preservation, the first law of nature, they should elect Mr. Parnell.

The Chairman.—I think Mr. Sexton said I was the only man fitted to lead the party.

Mr. Sexton.—I said I thought Mr. Parnell more likely to conserve the unity of the party than any individual or group of individuals.

Colonel Nolan.—I think Mr. Sexton said nearly everything possible, because I know he left me nothing to say. (Laughter.)

Mr. J. Nolan said it had been boasted there that the Irish people supported Mr. Parnell even in opposition to the Pope. Were they now going to resign him at the crack of the Gladstonian whip ? (Cheers.) He would support Mr. Parnell.

Mr. J. C. Flynn declared that though the members of the

F

party had rallied round Mr. Parnell at the last meeting they would now rally round their country as between Mr. Parnell and Mr. Gladstone. He would support Mr. Parnell against a thousand Gladstones ; he would not support him against his country or what he believed to be the interests of his country. Some of them had been spoken of as catspaws, but he claimed for those on his side of the question, who differed with the greatest regret from their beloved chief, that they were no more catspaws than those who supported him. But he would now suggest that there had been enough debate. ("Hear, hear," and "No, no.")

MR. JOHN REDMOND.—Closure, closure ! We have had no debate at all.

MR. FLYNN said he did not intend to move the closure, but he only intended to bring forward an argument. The discussion which had taken place had put them in possession of the facts of the case.

SIR JOSEPH M'KENNA supported the amendment, and expressed his strong approval of Mr. Parnell's continued leadership.

MR. E. HARRINGTON alluded to what he described as a conspiracy of silence on the part of those who were anxious that Mr. Parnell should be deposed, and ascribed their silence to the fact that they were anxious to decapitate their chief that very night. He was aware that many members present were pledged to their Liberal friends, who were in the corridor outside waiting for the "Noes" from their friends inside, who were determined to have their leader out dead or alive.

MR. SHEEHY spoke strongly in favour of Mr. Parnell's retirement. He accused Mr. Parnell of having acted unfaithfully towards the evicted tenants by not divulging what he knew of the Hawarden interview for such a long time. Why did he not divulge it 12 months ago, when a good deal of the sacrifices that had since been made would not have been necessary. It was only recently that any effort was made to help those tenants.

MR. PARNELL (warmly).—Who made the plan ? Whose brain planned it ? Who got the hundred thousand pounds last year for the Irish tenants, and devised the plan by which it was obtained ?

MR. SEXTON.—As Mr. Parnell asks the question, I may say it was I who suggested the plan to him. (Cheers.)

Mr. PARNELL denied that statement.

Mr. PINKERTON expressed himself as against Mr. Parnell's continued leadership, the manifesto having caused him to come to that opinion.

Mr. CONWAY denied that any harm could be done to Home Rule by Mr. Parnell's continued leadership. He referred to a statement which, he said, Mr. Sexton made on the journey from Dublin to London prior to the opening of Parliament, to the effect that Mr. Gladstone was about to issue a manifesto that he should retire from public life unless Mr. Parnell was thrown over.

Mr. SEXTON (interrupting) declared upon his solemn word of honour that he never made such a statement.

Mr. CONWAY repeated that the statement was made in the presence of himself and other members of the party, and that this was one of the circumstances which showed the conspiracy which was on foot against their leader. He made a strong attack upon Mr. T. M. Healy for his inconsistency in supporting Mr. Parnell in Dublin a fortnight ago and now seeking to hunt him from public life. Why did not Mr. Healy support him now ?

Mr. T. M. HEALY.—Because he is useless for any purpose. (Cries of " Oh.")

Mr. CONWAY.—There is life in the old dog yet. (Loud cheers.) He concluded his speech by appealing to his colleagues not to suborn themselves to any English party.

Mr. KNOX said he did not think that under the circumstances they could complain of the issue of Mr. Gladstone's letter. Mr. Gladstone might have been in the past a coercionist, but he had at heart the Irish cause. He was an old man now, and knowing he could not be spared for many years he felt that if Mr. Parnell refused to retire all his latter days would be useless.

Dr. FITZGERALD strongly supported Mr. Parnell's leadership.

Mr. J. H. M'CARTHY said he came into Parliament under the leadership of Mr. Parnell six years ago, and during that time to the best of his ability he had helped Mr. Parnell. Ireland during that time had passed through a course of serious difficulties conducted by Mr. Parnell, who had shown them that he could carry them through the present difficulty, and under these circumstances he (Mr. M'Carthy) had made up his mind that his only course was to give his vote to Mr. Parnell.

Mr. LEAMY said that Mr. Sexton, in the course of his speech, stated that Ireland was distracted, and that if some issue was provided it in the matter in dispute, it would bring some chance of joy to the nation. He asked whether there was any man in the assembly who would stand up and declare that if the result of their deliberations was that Mr. Parnell were ousted from the leadership the result would be received with joy in Ireland. (Cheers.)

Mr. WEBB urged that the Irish party were not actuated by personal motives. He should vote for the discontinuance of Mr. Parnell's leadership, and he did so in the interests of Ireland.

Mr. CHANCE, in expressing the same intention, remarked that he was not a prominent member of the party or one of its great debating members.

Mr. CAMPBELL.—You are a dishonest one.

Mr. HEALY rose to order.

Mr. CAMPBELL.—I know that he is a dishonest man for this reason, he has been intriguing and wire-pulling, Mr. Parnell, against your leadership in Kilkenny for the last three or four days.

Mr. PARNELL. —I think, Mr. Campbell, you should withdraw the expression.

Mr. CAMPBELL.—I will not withdraw.

Several members asked Mr. Campbell to withdraw the remark, and he then consented to do so in obedience to the general views of his friends.

Mr. BLANE pointed out that they had been sitting for 11 hours, and he therefore, he said, would move an adjournment.

Mr. PARNELL.—The question is " That this debate do now adjourn." As many as are of that opinion say "Ay." (Cries of " Ay.") I declare that the "Ayes" have it.

Mr. HEALY complained that the other side had not been asked whether they agreed.

Mr. PARNELL (rising).—The adjournment has been carried.

Mr. T. HEALY.—I move that Mr. M'Carthy take the chair. (Loud cheers.)

Mr. PARNELL.—I have not left the chair yet.

Mr. HEALY.—Then put the question, Mr. Parnell.

Mr. PARNELL.—I have put the question.

Mr. HEALY.—You have not.

Mr. PARNELL.—I am not going to have my ruling challenged by Mr. Healy.

After some other remarks Mr. Parnell again put the question, when the majority appeared to be in favour of continuing the debate, and therefore Mr. Parnell said that the discussion must proceed.

Mr. HEALY said that a division should be taken, as one had been challenged.

Mr. CONDON and Mr. SEXTON said it was not necessary.

Mr. E. HARRINGTON and Mr. JOHN REDMOND said that at such an advanced hour it was almost physically and mentally impossible to continue the debate, and they suggested an adjournment till the following day.

MESSRS. CLANCY, O'KELLY, and BYRNE proposed the adjournment of the debate.

Mr. T. HEALY said he would agree to an adjournment on the understanding that the debate would terminate the next day.

Mr. PARNELL.—Do not have any understanding with him.

Mr. T. HEALY.—It is very hard to have any understanding with Mr. Parnell.

Mr. PARNELL.—Do not be dictating terms to me.

Mr. HEALY said he wanted to have an understanding that the next day another adjournment would not be asked for.

At this point Mr. SEXTON interposed, asking that in the interests of unity and good feeling the adjournment should be agreed to.

The meeting was ultimately adjourned until 12 o'clock on the following day, Tuesday, December 2.

MEETING OF THE IRISH PARTY—FOURTH DAY—DIVISION.

The meeting of the Irish Parliamentary party, which adjourned at 10 minutes to 12 on the night of Monday, December 1, was resumed at noon on Tuesday, December 2. Mr. Parnell was the first to arrive, just before noon, and he was soon followed by the whole of the members who were present on Monday. The following account of the proceedings has been officially supplied :—

Mr. Parnell took the chair, and at the outset a number of letters and telegrams, addressed to Mr. Parnell and members of the party, were read. This occupied a considerable time.

At 20 minutes to 1 Mr. J. F. X. O'BRIEN moved that business be proceeded with.

MR. PARNELL.—We will read first the telegrams that have been received in the meantime. If any members have received telegrams from public bodies in Ireland, they should be read. I noticed that a great many telegrams had come in. The members who received them should hand them in to the chair to be read.

MR. BARRY.—I move that the communication from our colleagues in America be read. (Hear, hear.)

MR. PARNELL.—Yes, as soon as I receive it. If you wish to have it read I shall have it read. I do not think I have even read it myself.

MR. JOHN O'CONNOR.—I have not read it either.

MR. SEXTON.—It will be found, Mr. Parnell, in any of the morning papers.

MR. PARNELL.—Have you been able to find this communication yet, Mr. Barry ?

MR. BARRY.—It is in the morning papers.

MR. T. M. HEALY.—I understand that yesterday you ruled, when Mr. Sexton wished to read a communication from the Bishop of Sligo, that the debate should not be interrupted. I object to the debate being interrupted now for anything except the American delegates' telegram.

MR. JOHN O'CONNOR.—Surely you are not afraid of Irish opinion. (Cheers.)

MR. T. M. HEALY.—We want definite rulings, and those rulings adhered to.

MR. PARNELL.—I have made no rulings to-day contrary to my rulings yesterday. You might as well have said that prayers should not be read before the meetings of the House during an interrupted debate.

MR. HENRY CAMPBELL then read the American delegates' message from one of the morning papers.

MR. PARNELL.—There is a passage in this that I ought to refer to now. They say, "So painfully alive were we to all that might be involved in the loss of such a leader, that we eagerly co-operated with our colleagues in every effort to retain his influence in our councils." I wish to know whether that refers to communications made to them since the issue of Mr. Gladstone's demand for my resignation, or before it. There have been statements made, I know not on what authority, that communications have been made to Mr. Dillon—more than one communication—and communications independently of those sanctioned by the meeting of the party, and I think we ought to have all these communications before us. (Cheers.) If it be true that any communications have been made to Messrs. Dillon and O'Brien, except the communication which was sanctioned by the party since its first meeting on the Tuesday, then I think we should have those communications before us and know by whom they were made, whether by individual members, the chairman of the party, or other persons. The only communication of which I had a knowledge was a telegram, or rather two telegrams, one sanctioned by the party, from Mr. Richard Power, giving the division and a statement as to my view of the responsibility of my position, and another one, which I sent them myself, asking them to refrain from expressing any opinion until they had seen my manifesto. But I think, before we can come to any judgment as to the weight to be attached to this announcement, that we ought to know what communications were made to them by members of the party. (Cheers.)

DR. KENNY.—I beg to say, Sir, I sent a wire from Dublin exclusively on my own account, carefully guarding myself against giving any expression but my own individual opinion on the *status quo*. I used the words "individual opinion," so that there could be no misconception. I do not think there was any violation of any rule in doing that. I thought I was perfectly justified in doing it, as I think any member of the party would be. I cannot trust my memory to repeat the words, but the message ran this way :—"My individual opinion is that our salvation is retention of Mr. Parnell in the chair." I carefully guarded myself by saying that I expressed no other opinion but my own. If I did wrong I regret it, but at the same time I think that it was a legitimate thing to do, and that I have nothing to be ashamed of.

MR. JUSTIN M'CARTHY.—I rise to say one word, in consequence of an absurd statement in several papers to-day, that I telegraphed to John Dillon conveying him some message. I have not telegraphed to any of our friends in America ever since this discussion began, on any matter whatever. (Hear, hear.) The statement is so absurd that I should hardly have spoken, but to allow even so ridiculous a rumour at this time to go forth would be to create a prejudice. I know of no communications made to our friends in

America, except those officially published and the one I have just heard of from Dr. Kenny. (Hear, hear.)

Mr. BARRY.—I shall be in the recollection of the meeting that on Wednesday last it was resolved that the Whips of the party should send an official message to our colleagues in America, and Dr. Commins and myself, the mover and seconder, should see the telegram before it was sent. When the meeting was over I went to Mr. Richard Power, and I said, "What about the telegram?" He replied, "Oh, we will send it to-morrow." I said it was a grave matter of importance, and that the telegram should be sent immediately, and I asked Mr. Power to be kind enough to draft the telegram. He drafted the telegram, which I hold in my hand. He then handed me the telegram and asked me how it would do. It read :—"Meeting adjourned till Monday."

Mr. PARNELL —I have seen it.

Mr. BARRY.—Let me read it :—"Meeting adjourned till Monday. Sexton, M'Carthy, Arthur O'Connor, Barry, Commins, Sheehy, Dickson, Webb, Flynn, spoke in favour of Parnell reconsidering position. Colonel Nolan, Blane, Conway, W. Macdonald, Huntly M'Carthy, and Dr. Kenny supported Parnell." Mr. Power left me with the message in the lobby, and went, I thought, into the House. I thought he had left me only for a moment. I waited in the lobby for an hour, but as Mr. Power did not return I felt there was some misunderstanding. Mr. Power did not say anything to me about sending the telegram, but he simply placed it in my hands. I waited for fully an hour, and everybody had left the lobby of the House. I then proceeded to the telegraph office and forwarded this telegram to Mr. Gill, Fifth Avenue Hotel, New York. I have since ascertained Mr. Power sent a second telegram with your knowledge and sanction.

Mr. PARNELL.—And at my request.

Mr. BARRY.—I submit that it was understood and arranged by the party that any telegram sent in an official sense by the party should be submitted to the mover and seconder of the resolution, and I protest against any other course being adopted in regard to the second telegram.

Mr. PARNELL.—You had better hear what the telegram is.

Mr. BARRY.—I say here was an arrangement arrived at by the party, and surely the party is entitled to some consideration, and it was a reasonable proposal that the mover and seconder should see any telegram that was sent.

MR. CAMPBELL.—Only one Whip sent it ; the other was not consulted.

MR. PARNELL.—I think it is rather comical your objecting to Mr. Power sending a telegram containing an addition to your telegram, when you had framed this telegram behind my back and sent it on your own authority admittedly, without the authority of the Whip. (Cheers, and cries of " No, no.")

MR. BARRY.—Let us have this matter set right.

MR. PARNELL.—It appears it was not the Whip of the party who sent the telegram, but you ; and it was sent before I had an opportunity of seeing it. I say that mere ordinary courtesy should have dictated to Mr. Barry's mind the necessity of showing the telegram before it was sent.

MR. BARRY then explained that Mr. Power framed the telegram and asked him to send it ; but a second official telegram was sent by Mr. Power, which he himself thought ought to have been submitted to the mover and seconder of the resolution.

MR. PARNELL.—We explained why the second telegram was sent, which has caused such wrath on the part of Mr. Barry.

MR. RICHARD POWER.—Mr. Barry has made rather too much about these telegrams, and I will briefly state exactly what did occur. When I left the room here I met Mr. Deasy, and I said to him that we should consult together about this telegram. Mr. Deasy said he would be satisfied with any telegram I would send. That was as regards the second telegram. As regards the first telegram, I say I perfectly agree with Mr. Barry. I must say I objected to putting the names in, but Mr. Barry objected to taking them out, and said it would be very unfair if the names were not put in. He was supported in that view by two other gentlemen, whose names I do not remember. I betrayed a little weakness, and very wrongly sent it without seeing Mr. Parnell, who had left the House. As regards the second telegram, I met Mr. Parnell in the lobby, and he said he wanted to speak to me.

MR. BARRY.—Excuse me, you intended I should send the telegram.

MR. R. POWER.—Certainly, but I protested against the names being put in.

MR. BARRY.—You finally agreed to the names going in.

Mr. E. Harrington.—My name was left out.

Mr. R. Power.—For the sake of harmony and peace I agreed to that, and told Mr. Barry that he might send the telegram if he liked, and I left him there in the hall. As regards the second telegram, Mr. Parnell asked me had I sent the telegram ? I said I had, and he said, very properly, that I had no right to send it without showing it to him. I had no right to send it ; I take all the responsibility. But Mr. Parnell said " You should now send the following telegram ; it is only fair to me you should state exactly what occurred at the meeting." The second telegram was, " Mr. Parnell refuses to reconsider his determination," and, I think, " refuses to retire," as well as I remember. That is all we sent, and if there was any member of the party in the House at the time Mr. Parnell can correct me. I said, " I will go and see if there is any member in the House I can show the telegram to." I could not see any one except Mr. Deasy, and he said, " I will agree to anything that you and Mr. Parnell agree to." I could not find any member in the House at that time, but I found afterwards they were engaged at a meeting at their own conference room, to which I was not invited or Mr. Parnell. (Cries of " Nor I," and cheers.) These are briefly the circumstances of the case. I do not think I have violated my duty. The only mistake I made —and I admit it was a mistake—was that I ought to have shown the telegram to Mr. Parnell.

Mr. John O'Connor, as one of those who felt aggrieved on the occasion, desired to say that he felt that in the sending of such a telegram an injustice was done to those who were supporting Mr. Parnell's leadership, and the sending of the names to America was calculated to mislead their friends. It was well known that he himself supported Mr. Parnell, yet his name was not contained in the telegram. This business was not being conducted according to the principles of fair play. (Loud cheers.) He was glad this matter had been brought up, that there was an opportunity of exposing to the Irish people at home and abroad the dastardly attempts that had been made to mislead the public as to the position of many men at the meeting, who were as honest and patriotic as those who were determined to put Mr. Parnell down. (Cheers.)

Mr. Campbell.—Sir, I rise to strongly support the argument put forward by my hon. friend, in exposing these infamous proceedings on the part of the caucus in the corner. (Cheers and cries of "Oh.")

MR. BARRY.—I rise to order.

The CHAIRMAN.—What is your point of order ?

MR. BARRY.—Mr. Campbell pointed his hand to this part of the House and spoke of the infamous caucus in the corner. I respectfully submit that is not in order.

The CHAIRMAN.—The country will have to decide as to your proceedings. (Cheers.) I shall confirm Mr. Campbell's word if necessary. (Cheers.)

MR. BARRY.—More shame for you.

MR. CAMPBELL.—I look upon it as the most infamous thing that has ever happened before the Irish people, that your colleagues, who ought to have supported you and stood by you and shown you fair play in a fair fight, that they should have gone behind your back and wirepulled, telegraphed, done everything that was infamous, to mislead our colleagues in America as to the position which you still hold in this party. If I had known for one moment that that telegram was about to be despatched, I should have insisted upon rising at this board to tell the people whom I represent and to tell the Irish people the world over that I was with you, so that my colleagues in America, humble though I be, might know that I had not deserted the Irish cause. That is the position I would have let my colleagues know in America, if I had had an opportunity of speaking on that day. I had not that opportunity, and I brand as infamous the action of colleagues who would thus go behind your back and try to cut your throat before the Irish people. (Cheers.)

MR. SEXTON.—I think no contentious reference need be made to any meetings of sections of the party, because if I am speaking of sections in connexion with this unhappy dispute, undoubtedly meetings of both sections have been held. ("Hear, hear," and cheers.)

The CHAIRMAN.—Not after Saturday.

MR. SEXTON.—There was an important meeting held by Mr. Parnell on Saturday at the Westminster Palace Hotel.

The CHAIRMAN.—After many other meetings held on your side.

MR SEXTON.—It is impossible, unreasonable, it is fatuous, to suppose that with men holding strong opinions in matters of great importance it would be possible to restrain their conversation with one another. You cannot reduce men to the condition of individual isolation. They must take such opportunities as offer for consultation with each other. But I am not aware of any gathering of members from which any member of the party was excluded.

Mr. R. POWER.—While the meeting was taking place Mr. Parnell and myself were in the House, and we know nothing about the matter.

Mr. SEXTON.—I am aware that a meeting was held on Saturday evening at the Westminster Palace Hotel, attended by a body of members of the party who support Mr. Parnell in this business, and that I and some other members were not invited.

Mr. JOHN REDMOND.—I may mention that Mr. Abraham, who, I understand, is to be your spokesman when the main question of your deposition comes on, was present at that meeting. (Hear, hear.)

Mr. SEXTON.—The statement of Mr. Redmond does not at all affect my statement. I hope we shall not have an angry wrangle on a question of this kind. (Hear, hear.) We all know that Mr. Parnell summoned meetings to which all the members of the party were not invited.

Mr. PARNELL.—I followed your example. (Hear, hear.)

Mr. SEXTON.—It would be thought absurd of us if we refrained from any consultation which we could have with one another. Mr. John O'Connor has said that the business is being worked. Undoubtedly it is being worked. (Cheers and counter-cheers.) The view of my friends was that this was eminently a case for the decision of the party.

Mr. PARNELL.—Hear, hear. Why don't you leave it to the party ? (Hear, hear.)

Mr. SEXTON.—I left it to the party, recognizing that we, who had the fullest knowledge of the facts—that we, who had political training necessary to enable us to appreciate the question before us—we were best able to judge of our grave and terrible responsibility. I therefore told my friends last week that it was desirable no attempt should be made to affect the deliberations of the party. I may say that I received a telegram from the Corporation of Dublin, of which I am a member, announcing that a special meeting was to be held to express confidence in Mr. Parnell, but I refrained from sending any reply (hear, hear), because I was determined that by no act of mine could it be said that I attempted, in this grave crisis of our country's cause, to influence in the least degree, by any outside appeal, the deliberations of this party. (Hear, hear.)

MR. JOHN O'CONNOR.—Can anybody explain who is responsible for the placarding of the city of Cork with copies of the American delegates' cablegram ? (Hear, hear.)

MR. SEXTON.—I know nothing about the matter. The arrangement of the party in reference to the telegrams to America was that no communication should be initiated on behalf of the party with the body of delegates in America unless through the Whips of the party, who should submit their telegrams, for the satisfaction of both sides in this dispute, to the mover and seconder of the resolution.

DR. FITZGERALD.—Only to the Whips.

MR. SEXTON.—Mr. Power wrote one telegram, and he submitted it to the mover of the resolution, and the mover is blamed for having sent it. Mr. Power admits that the telegram should be sent, and therefore I think Mr. Parnell will not maintain the reproach which he directed against Mr. Barry a moment ago.

MR. PARNELL.—Most certainly I do.

MR. SEXTON.—I think the original arrangement entitled Mr. Barry to send that telegram, and that Mr. Barry, in despatching the messages, was simply carrying out the purpose of the Whips. But we have it also before us that a second message was sent on behalf of the party which did not conform to the conditions agreed upon.

MR. JOHN REDMOND.—Was there anything unfair in it ? (Hear, hear.)

MR. SEXTON.—That is not the question. The question is whether the arrangement agreed upon has been carried out. I became aware at the end of the week that a number of messages were being received from the delegates in America.

MR. PARNELL.—Hear, hear. Where are they ? (Hear, hear.)

MR. SEXTON (continuing).—From individual delegates addressed to individual members of the party.

MR. PARNELL.—Where are these cablegrams ?

MR. JOHN REDMOND.—Name, name. (Hear, hear.)

MR. SEXTON.—I cannot give the names, but I am informed they

were individual messages. I received a telegram of inquiry from one of the delegates in America.

MR. PARNELL.—Where is it ?

MR. SEXTON.—I have not got it here, but I can state the substance of it. It was a message from Mr. T. P. O'Connor, in which he requested me to give him my views on the situation. That demand by him to me was a demand which I felt obliged to respect. (Hear, hear) I did not feel that the distance of Mr. T. P. O'Connor from me entitled me to refuse him the knowledge which I would give him if he were here. I did send a message informing him that, in my opinion, the majority of the party were of opinion that the retirement of Mr. Parnell would be—I think I said—necessary for the welfare of the Home Rule cause, and also for the security of the evicted tenants. (Cheers and counter-cheers.) I have stated that view in my public speeches here. I do not wish to conceal it now, and I further added that, if the envoys saw their way to support the majority of the party, I had a hope that substantial unanimity would be secured. I believe that in sending that message I discharged my duty. I have not a copy of that reply ; but if it be thought that that reply should be laid before the party I have no objection that it should be done.

COLONEL NOLAN.—I really think now that Mr. Sexton in some public way should withdraw the expression of opinion contained in that telegram, because I believe he made a mistake. It is so important, such an important expression of opinion, that I hold that the telegram from America is probably founded on it. (Hear, hear.) Mr. Sexton said that substantial unanimity would be obtained in the party provided the delegates voted for the retirement of Mr. Parnell. He must now see that that statement is totally devoid of foundation (cheers), and I hope he will withdraw it.

MR. JAMES O'KELLY.—I think it right to say that I also received a telegram from Mr. T. P. O'Connor asking my views, and I thought it my duty to reply that, if Mr. Parnell were overthrown, it would cause dissension in the party, which would lead to civil strife in Ireland. (Cheers.)

MR. LEAMY.—I ask the meeting to come back to the origin of this present discussion. The adjournment from Friday to Monday was granted by the party for the specific purpose of enabling the delegates in America to offer their opinions on the situation. I think they were not entitled to get any information of what occurred in this room at that meeting. Now, what has been the effect of sending on the telegram that a number of members spoke for the motion and a number against? Unquestionably a false impression was caused at home and abroad. (Hear, hear.) I have been a victim of that false impression. I learned only this morning that I was set down in the newspapers as neutral in the matter. I have got letters asking me, " Is it possible that on an occasion of this kind you are standing neutral ?" That, of course, was because I had not had the opportunity of expressing my opinion at the meeting of the party. I therefore think it was not fair to send out telegrams that certain members were opposed to Mr. Parnell and certain members for him.

MR. T. M. HEALY.—I rise to a point of order. I ask if the chairman will be good enough to inform me what is the question before the meeting.

MR. E. HARRINGTON. No, no. You were out.

MR. PARNELL.—A discussion has been opened by Mr. Barry on the question of communications with the delegates in America, and that discussion will have to proceed to its end.

MR. T. M. HEALY.—Another piece of pure obstruction ! (Cheers.)

MR. PARNELL (vehemently).—I think that a most insolent and impertinent observation (counter cheering)—a most insolent and impertinent observation. (Renewed cheering.)

MR. BARRY.—I rise ——

MR. PARNELL.—Sit down, Mr. Barry, please.

MR. BARRY.—Allow me ——

MR. PARNELL.—I will not allow you, Sir. Mr. Leamy is in possession. Let him go on.

MR. LEAMY.—What I say is that a false impression was produced by the telegrams to America implying that a majority— and among them the leading members of the party— were going in one direction. Now, the reason why the speaking at the meeting on Friday was all in that one direction was because we thought it only fair and reasonable that our opponents should be allowed to give their reasons for their extraordinary change of front. (Hear, hear)

MR. W. REDMOND.—My position is this. I think, if any names

were sent to the delegates in America, all the names of all the men on each side should have been given. (Hear, hear.) I feel it my duty in connexion with this matter to draw attention to a statement which has appeared in some of the newspapers. It was said that the cablegram from our friends in America was received by certain members of the party with cheers. (Hear, hear.)

MR. PARNELL.—Where ?

MR. W. REDMOND.—In an English club. (Loud cheers.) I say that that statement ought to be contradicted by our opponents in this matter (hear, hear), for I acquit every one of my colleagues here of participation in that proceeding, believing as I do that the decision of our colleagues in America gave our opponents as much regret and pain as it has given us. (Hear, hear.) I say, if Mr. Parnell is to be deposed by a majority, in God's name let the majority depose him; and if it be a matter for cheering, it is not a matter for cheering in any English club. (Cheers.)

A number of members here rose together, and from them Mr. Parnell called Mr. Barry.

MR. T. M. HEALY.—I thought you had ruled he had spoken.

MR. PARNELL.—I will allow him to have another try.

MR. BARRY.—I wish to say that I am perfectly satisfied with the explanation of Mr. Richard Power (hear, hear), and after that explanation, in which he has stated that he gave me the telegram and asked me to send it, I ask you, Sir, to relieve me from the imputation you threw out, in, I am sure, a moment of heat, that I was guilty of treachery in sending this telegram to America behind your back. (Hear, hear.)

MR. T. HEALY.—I ask my friends on our side not to continue this discussion. It is evident and patent to every man who will apply his mind to this question, and not allow himself to be influenced by this kind of red herring which has been drawn across our path, that Mr. Parnell asked the delegates to suspend their judgment pending the issue of his manifesto, and that then, having that manifesto before them, they came to the conclusion upon that manifesto and upon the merits of the case put forward therein by Mr. Parnell. (Hear, hear.) Now we are in a position, as I understand, of having our proceedings on this occasion conducted strictly on Parliamentary lines. That was laid down yesterday from the chair in the most formal manner, and the chairman ruled in every sense, so far as he could, in a formal strictly Parliamentary manner.   I would appeal to the chirman not to depart from that position.   I entertain, if Mr. Parnell will allow me to say so, the highest personal respect for him, and I have expressed privately—that is to say, I have not run to the newspapers with it, but to every one who has come to me;I have declared my sense of the dignity with which Mr. Parnell conducted our proceedings, and the gentlemanly character of his whole temper and bearing yesterday, notwithstanding the very painful position in which he found himself.   (Hear, hear.)   If any one wants to go to where those opinions were expressed he can go to the quarter where some of our political opponents are so fond of foregathering—the National Liberal Club.   (Hear, hear.) Now, I appeal to Mr. Parnell on the present occasion to adhere to strict Parliamentary ruling.   (Hear, hear.)   Then I complain that Mr. Parnell should have allowed Mr. Barry to speak twice. I complain that Mr. Parnell has allowed this debate to be interposed between the question before the House ; and, whatever opinion anybody may have of Mr. Parnell, they must all regard him as a man of enormous Parliamentary ability and reputation. Therefore, I would say to him for his own sake, as he is in the chair, exercising the enormous influence which his chairmanship gives him, and as it is his own personal position and conduct which are under debate, I invite him to be even more rigid in his Parliamentary decisions than he would be if it were the conduct of one of his humblest colleagues that was under discussion. (Hear.)

MR. DEASY said that, with regard to the cablegrams alluded to by Mr. Barry and Mr. Power, though he remained in the room until the last moment, he was unaware that any duty was cast upon him to wire to their colleagues the same night.   He thought it should be done the next day.   When about to go to his hotel he met Mr. Power, who said that Mr. Barry and himself had drafted a cablegram, and that Mr. Barry was waiting for him (the speaker) to see it.   He returned to the Lobby, and, not seeing Mr. Barry, concluded the cablegram had been sent.   He saw Mr. Campbell in the Lobby next day and said it was extremely unfortunate that any names had been sent, and that unless the entire names were sent none should have been sent.   Furthermore, he said he thought it hardly right to send any names at all, because at a large gathering of men such as they had those who gave their opinion first might be the leading men of the party or they might be the rank and file, and a wrong complexion might be given because of the way the debate turned. He expressed the same opinion to Mr. Richard Power, Mr. Barry, and several of his colleagues, and Mr. Power said he regretted his weakness in allowing the names to be sent. Mr. Power asked what he should do, remarking that Mr. Parnell was angry, and he advised him to see Mr. Parnell. He also told Mr. Power that he might affix his own name if Mr. Parnell and Mr. Power sent a telegram, even if he did not see it. He had the same respect for the honour of Mr. Parnell and Mr. Power then as he had now, and he felt that neither of those gentlemen would put anything on paper that he would be ashamed to put his name to. (Hear, hear.)

MR. PARNELL.—Mr. Healy has raised a point of order that this discussion ought to terminate.

MR. MURPHY.—I rise, but not with the view of carrying on this discussion.

MR. PARNELL.—If it is carrying on the discussion we must proceed with the reading of the telegrams. I am perfectly willing to carry on the discussion, but it will be my turn to say something.

MR. MURPHY.—I do not wish to say anything further than to point out that the paragraph that gave rise to the discussion—

MR. PARNELL.—But this is precisely the matter you want to carry on. You must see you cannot do both things—namely, ask me to stop it and to go on with it.

MR. JOHN REDMOND said he understood Mr. Parnell invited from members present information concerning the sending of cablegrams to America. He himself sent a cablegram to Mr. Gill, suggesting from himself that the best way to settle the difference would be if by any possibility the delegates could come home and meet the party. (Cheers.) He did not think there was any importance to be attached to it; but if he suppressed the fact importance might be attached to it hereafter. (Hear, hear.)

MR. JOSEPH NOLAN.—A complaint has been made—

The CHAIRMAN.—I think we had better go now to the reading of the telegrams.

Mr. Condon.—I wish to speak on the subject of the cablegrams. (Interruption.)

The Chairman.—If we are going on to the subject of the cablegrams, all I can say is ——

Mr. Condon.—Very well, if the meeting does not wish to hear me (cries of "Order") ——

Mr. Joseph Nolan.—A complaint has been made that you decided yesterday and to-day that the proceedings should be carried on according to the rules of Parliamentary procedure.

Mr. Healy.—I beg pardon; I did not say that Mr. Parnell decided to do so to-day.

Mr. Nolan.—I do not think that Mr. Healy should have made use of the expression that a red herring was being drawn across the trail.

Dr. Fitzgerald rose to speak, but was inaudible, amid cries of "Spoke" and "Chair."

The meeting adjourned at 2 o'clock.

At a quarter to 3 proceedings were resumed.

Mr. Healy.—Can we not make some progress, Mr. Chairman?

The Chairman.—Before we go from the subject which was occupying our attention before the adjournment, I think I am entitled to say that I suppose no other communications were made to the American delegates, except those which have been mentioned to me.

Mr. Condon.—No, Mr. Parnell. On Saturday afternoon, having read the manifesto, I met Messrs. Sheehy, Lane, Roche, and Kilbride, and we discussed that part of the manifesto in reference to the evicted tenants, and we then considered it our duty to cable to Mr. O'Brien and Mr. Dillon our views with regard to the effect that part of the manifesto would have upon the tenants in Ireland, and, though I cannot give you the exact words of the cablegram, I can give you the substance, which was to the effect that in our opinion that part of the manifesto would have a weakening if not a disastrous effect upon the Campaign tenants in Ireland. Mr. Sheehy and the other gentlemen are here and can bear me out in this. I have nothing to hide in the matter. (Hear, hear.)

Mr. Sheehy.—I concur in the statement Mr. Condon has made. I do not think it would have been honourable of me, having sent it, if I did not avow it. (Hear, hear.)

The CHAIRMAN.—Then I suppose I am to assume that no other member of the party has made any communication ?

MR. KILBRIDE.—I also was a party to the sending of the cablegram.

MR. SHEEHY.—The gentlemen whose names have been mentioned attached their names to the cablegram.

The CHAIRMAN.—That refers only to one cable. Then I assume that no other member of the party made any communication with the delegates ?

MR. JOHN REDMOND.—I think I have some reason to complain that, when a communication was sent to the delegates in America on behalf of a number of gentlemen professing to speak on behalf of the Campaign tenants, no communication was made to me. I am in this position—that, in conjunction with my friends Mr. Sheehy and Dr. Kenny, I was left in Ireland by Mr. Dillon and Mr. O'Brien specially charged with looking after the interests of these tenants.

MR. SHEEHY.—As a matter of explanation, neither Mr. Condon, Mr. Kilbride, Mr. Lane, nor myself ventured to express the opinion of anybody but ourselves. (Hear, hear.)

MR. CLANCY.—I do not know whether it is necessary for me to say, but perhaps it is, that on Wednesday morning last, before the meeting of the party took place, Dr. Kenny and myself sent a cablegram to America to this effect:—" Wire views of Dillon and O'Brien on Mr. Gladstone's letter, which was not before meeting of party yesterday. This message from selves alone."

The CHAIRMAN.—I think we may assume that these are all the communications that have been made. Mr. Campbell will go on with the reading of messages.

MR. CAMPBELL then read a number of telegrams and letters. MR. HEALY and MR. FLYNN objected to some of them being read, as being personal letters ; they had received a number of such letters.

MR. CAMPBELL.—I have 2,000 or 3,000 telegrams in your support, which have been put on one side.

MR. M. HEALY asked that a telegram from Canon O'Mahony, of Cork, should be read.

The CHAIRMAN.—Certainly ; I think it ought to be read.

MR. JOHN O'CONNOR.—I have received telegrams from Father

Sheehy and others, and I have not read them, as being personal telegrams.

Mr. M. HEALY.—Wait until you hear it read.

Mr. CAMPBELL then read the telegram.

The CHAIRMAN.—I know when I was elected I had only one priest supporting me out of the whole of the Cork priests.

MR. T. HEALY.—And that priest was Canon O'Mahony.

The CHAIRMAN.—And that was the reason I allowed his letter to be read.

MR. JOHN O'CONNOR.—I, of course, do not object to its being read.

MR. JAMES O'KELLY, who was received with cheers, said he supported Colonel Nolan's amendment for the adjournment of the meeting to Dublin for two reasons. The first was that before they took a decision upon the question they should have some opportunity of gauging the real opinion of Ireland. From the telegrams which had been read it was evident that there was a vast body of opinion running counter to the action which they knew the majority of the party intended to take. Another reason why he supported the amendment was because their proceedings were in part judicial proceedings. They were at once the judges and jury, and the atmosphere in which they were sitting was not a judicial atmosphere. (Cheers.) The people of Ireland would be scandalized if they were to see the proceedings that followed the meetings of that party. Would any honest man stand up and say that when the doors of the House were thrown open and when they went into the lobbies, scenes would not be witnessed such as were witnessed as late as the previous night ? (Cheers.) What would be said of a jury which went into conference with men who were known to be hostile, and bitterly hostile, and demanding the destruction of the man upon whom the Irish party were sitting in judgment ? (Cheers.) Whatever the decision of the party, it was felt on both sides that the business would not end in that House or in that room. (Cheers.) When Mr. T. P. O'Connor asked him his views he said that if they were to drive Mr. Parnell from the party they would be beginning a civil war. (Cheers.)

MR. T. M. HEALY.—What about the party pledge ?

MR. O'KELLY said that as for the party pledge, if he were beaten at home he should resign his seat. (Cheers.) From the inception of the party it had been their boast that whatever they did was done in obedience to the will of: the people. What about the pledges they had given over and over again to the people of Ireland to do only that which they approved of? The adoption of Colonel Nolan's proposition would give them time to think, and it would give the country time to think. The incident that occurred the other night at the National Liberal Club had been mentioned there. He would not refer to it otherwise, because it was too shocking to his mind that any body of Irishmen should have stood up in that English club and rejoiced over the fall of their chief and the disunion of their country. (Loud cheers.) Why were they in such a hurry to forestall the opinion of Ireland? If time were given, and if the decision of the country was clearly against them, he would submit absolutely, and would be no party to resistance to the will of the country. (Cheers.) But he would not submit to a decision which was forced along by the intrigues and pressure of an English party and an English statesman. (Cheers, and cries of " No, no.") That was the view he took, and it was the view he believed the country would take. He asked them to argue from the decision of the Dublin Corporation that the opinion of Ireland had not been changed from its friendliness to Mr. Parnell by anything that had happened. (Hear, hear.) Let them convince him that the throwing over of Mr. Parnell would give them a measure of Home Rule which they themselves would accept, and he would vote with them. (Cheers.) But what was the fact? They had the account given by Mr. Parnell showing the kind of Home Rule Mr. Gladstone proposed to give them. (Hear, hear.) They had such contradiction as Mr. Gladstone had made, and what was the value of it? Would any man, knowing Mr. Gladstone's intellectual subtlety, get up and say there was anything like real or valuable contradiction of anything that Mr. Parnell had said in that letter of Mr. Gladstone? There was nothing they could hold on to. (Cheers.) If Mr. Gladstone and the Liberal party wanted to·settle this question they had got the chance. (Hear, hear.) The challenge had been thrown down to them. (Cheers.) It was said that to give an answer might spoil the Home Rule Bill, but some day that Bill would come to the front, and the sooner the better. (Cheers.) There was one point which seemed to be lost sight of in this discussion—the _statement that Mr. Gladstone had of himself with his party the power to grant Home Rule. Now, he denied that the Liberal party had the power to give Home Rule. Their power to do anything was strictly limited by the power of the House of Lords to deny them when the Bill went to the Upper House, and that power of the House of Lords was an unenfranchisable barrier to all progress unless it was backed by the fear of revolution. He held that that fear was absent in the case of Ireland (hear, hear), and they would never see a revolution in England based upon any Irish claim. (Cheers.) Coming to the question of Mr. Gladstone's letter, he said Mr. M'Carthy was almost too honest for political life, and seemed to think that the mere assurance that was given by Mr. Gladstone, Mr. Morley, and other men in the Liberal party favourable to them was a sufficient guarantee ; but he would call to Mr. M'Carthy's recollection a little scene which took place in the House some years ago, when a similar question of relying on the honour of English statesmen arose. It was on the night on which they threw Mr. Gladstone out of power. A small committee of the Irish party was holding a meeting, their chief being present, when communications were made to them from the Conservative party. There were certain promises given to them on the faith of English gentlemen and on the faith of English statesmen. He himself wished those promises to be put in writing, but Mr. M'Carthy said it would be impossible, and it was against the habits and etiquette of English life. Mr. M'Carthy trusted those men implicitly. Did he not know that in a few months those men came up and lied themselves out of the situation ? (Cheers.) They not only betrayed the Irish party, but denied that the thing had ever happened. (Cheers.) He himself followed Mr. Parnell from the Council-room, and saw him go direct to Mr. Winn, the Conservative Whip, and in half an hour afterwards Mr. Gladstone's Government was thrown out. They then gave themselves away on the honour of these men, and notwithstanding that experience Mr. M'Carthy was now prepared to give himself away to the other party on their honour. (Hear, hear.) The situation was a very slippery one for the men who represented Ireland to put themselves in. If they were going to give up their chief, they should at least give the people something in exchange for him. (Hear, hear.) He asked them not to go with empty hands and shadowy promises, with the experience they had had of Parliament, and of the confidence which could be placed in the words of English gentlemen and English statesmen. (Hear, hear.) The deception was not merely historical ; they had had it within their own experience. And if they had recovered from that position, how had they recovered ? By the unity of the party, by the unity of the race, by fighting like one man. (Cheers.) The moment they gave away their chief they laid down a rule by which the political life of the next man who led them was rendered insecure. (Hear, hear.) What man would trust them afterwards ? (Cheers.) Would the English trust them ? (" No, no.") Trust was based upon general respect. (Cheers.) The third point upon which they based their action was the unity of the cause, the unity of the people, and he held that that unity must include the unity of the Irish race. It was not enough to be united in that room. Five of the most respected of their men were in America, and they had issued their manifesto. What, it the Press were to be trusted, had been the result ? It had killed their action in America, or, at least, their action would be hampered. He had had communications from America, both of them absolutely unsought ; one from their old friend Devoy—the one which he himself had published —and the other the one they had read there that day. These men represented not themselves alone, but a volume of opinion of some importance. He did not come to a decision hastily, but waited to hear what the men who differed from him had to say. It seemed to him that the supreme question was the question of holding their own cause and the people together, whatever temporary evil might result from that action. The really important thing was to keep the Irish race united under their leader. (Cheers.) He was the standard round which the whole Irish race was ranged. Pull down that standard and they would find their battalions dispersing in more than one direction. (Cheers.) If Mr. Parnell fell, in his fall the statue of Irish liberty risked being smashed to pieces. (Loud cheers.)

At this point Mr. Parnell left the room temporarily, and during his absence Mr. Justin M'Carthy took the chair.

MR. A. O'CONNOR said one of the things which pained him most was to find himself differing for once from his friend James O'Kelly. This might be the last occasion possibly on which he himself would address either this party or any other Irish Parliamentary party. He believed that his own independence and in-

tegrity had been beyond question until now. (Cheers.) He declared to them that no wirepulling of any English party had ever
affected him, and at this moment his independence and integrity
were intact before the leader and the country. (Cheers.) On
that black and dismal day within the last three weeks when the
result of the proceedings in the Probate Division was made
known, he felt that for himself at least and for Ireland the con-
tinuation of Mr. Parnell as chairman of that party was impossible.
(Hear, hear.)

DEC. 2.

MR. E. HARRINGTON.—Why didn't you say so at the time ?

MR. A. O'CONNOR.—I speak for myself, and I say that from
that moment I felt that Mr. Parnell was an impossible leader, and
I believe now that Mr. Parnell is an impossible leader, for the
people of my race. (Hear, hear.) When, on Tuesday, on entering this room, I found a resolution in course of preparation I was,
I admit, ashamed, overwhelmed, and confused. (Cries of "Oh!")
I arrived at the conclusion that it must have been through some
misunderstanding or another. I considered myself then in the
position of one of the Old Guard of Napoleon giving a parting
salute.

MR. E. HARRINGTON.—You won't ride off on that plea here.

MR. A. O'CONNOR.—I have not interrupted any one (cheers),
and I promise to avoid any language which would give reasonable offence to any one. After that meeting, when I found myself
in consultation with other members of the party, I did declare
without hesitation or compromise or qualification that I considered the vote of the afternoon should be reconsidered ; and
before I knew of Mr. Gladstone's letter, before I believe any
member of this party knew of Mr. Gladstone's letter, I had
already urged upon some of my colleagues the necessity of taking
immediate action, so that the character and dignity of this party
might be preserved, and that we might not be influenced by the
opinion of any English statesman or party. (Hear, hear.) When
Mr. Gladstone's letter appeared it added to my previous conviction. I regarded that letter as the effect of a cause. I hold
myself independent of English public opinion. I have not
courted English public opinion ; but I look to the opinion of my
own countrymen and to the approbation of my own conscience.
But if there had been room for doubt before the publication of the
manifesto, that would of itself have removed it. I can, I think,

through the lines of the manifesto, trace the nature of the consultation which it recalls, and in that consultation, whatever may have been Mr. Parnell's impression at that time or since, I believe when the whole matter is known nothing that can fairly be made ground of complaint against Mr. Gladstone will be forthcoming. A great many questions have been raised in the course of this debate which are beside the real point. The real issue before us is simple. It may be read in the delicate wording of the resolution such as Mr. Barry proposed on Saturday, on which the meeting stood adjourned. It may be shelved for a time, as is admitted by the amendment of Colonel Nolan, and it may be easily stated, as in the amendment of Mr. Abraham, and rejected, I am sorry to say, by the chair ; but the issue is clear and distinct. We all understand it. There is no shirking it.

MR. JOHN REDMOND.—No one wants to shirk it.

MR. A. O'CONNOR, continuing, said he was willing to believe that no one wanted to shirk it ; but the issue was the question of the chairmanship of Mr. Parnell. No man in the room had appreciated more thoroughly than he the transcendent services of that statesman ; for he was a great statesman. He himself was fully aware of the disadvantages which must attend the Irish cause if Mr. Parnell's leadership was brought to an end. The decision must be damaging ; but if it was a mere question of policy that was to guide them, however great the disadvantages of Mr. Parnell's retirement might be, the disadvantages of his retaining office were incomparably greater. (Hear, hear.) It was proposed to adjourn the decision until the opinion of the Irish people was ascertained, though they were not told how that opinion was to be ascertained and how they were to act upon it. Upon that proposal his decision was clear. They owed it to themselves as self-respecting men of independence and integrity ; they owed it to the party and to their convulsed and distracted country to settle this question at once definitely and permanently. The country had left to them the responsibility of choosing their chairman, and they must decide. (Cheers.) The situation was distressing and heartrending in the extreme ; its prolongation was intolerable.

COLONEL NOLAN.—Yes, for you.

MR. O'CONNOR.—Yes, I admit I am speaking for myself.

Mr. Campbell (ironically).—Give me the dagger ; I will do the deed. (Cries of " Order.")

· Mr. O'Connor appealed to the meeting to come to a definite decision on the real issue. Whatever motion was put from the chair, he should so vote as to show that in his opinion the chairmanship of Mr. Parnell should be determined. If the decision of the party was adverse to what he considered it should be, he should at once surrender to his constituents the trust they had committed to him and surrender it uncompromised and unstained, with full confidence that he had honestly done what he believed was his duty. (Hear, hear.)

Mr. W. A. Macdonald, referring to the speeches delivered by Mr. Sexton and Mr. Healy, asked whether these gentlemen had always maintained the position they now took up. They had told them that Mr. Parnell's leadership was impossible. Mr. Sexton did not go to the Leinster Hall meeting, but on the first day of the Session he came down to the House and told the members of the party that Mr. Parnell's leadership ought to be continued. (Cheers.) In 24 hours afterwards Mr. Sexton was a most powerful advocate for the directly contrary view. (Laughter and " Hear, hear.") He wanted to know what had changed Mr. Sexton in the interval. (Hear, hear.) After criticising the course which Mr. Healy had taken, the speaker warmly supported Mr. Parnell's leadership, and contended that the voice of the Irish nation was with him, and that without him the Irish party would become discredited and disorganized. He hoped that Ireland would speak decisively, and that in the interests of Ireland, which Mr. Parnell had served so long, and in the interests of the colleagues who were standing by him, Mr. Parnell would not for one moment relinquish his claim to be the chairman of the party and the leader of the Irish people, until the Irish people, by an unequivocal vote, had dethroned him from that position. (Cheers.)

Mr. William Corbett said Mr. Parnell had brought Ireland out of bondage. He had sacrificed his health and everything for her. Were they now to cashier him in deference to the cry of an English party ? He did not envy the people who could lightly take that view. Mr. Healy was a lawyer by profession, and could always make black white.

Mr. T. M. Healy.—What is Mr. John Redmond's profession ? You have more lawyers on your side than we have. (Laughter.)

Mr. J. Redmond.—But you have more attorneys.

Mr. Campbell.—All the Healy family are attorneys and lawyers. (Laughter.)

Sir Thomas Esmonde paid a high tribute to Mr. Parnell's services to Ireland, but said that he came into politics, not to bind matters to any man, but to serve his country. He believed that a change in the Irish leadership was necessary.

Mr. Richard Power supported Mr. Parnell's leadership, and deplored the sudden and extreme change of opinion that had taken place on the other side. Men who now wanted to depose Mr. Parnell were, three days ago, his warmest supporters. He believed the cause of Ireland could only be saved by Mr. Parnell's leadership. In the course of further remarks, the speaker referred to Sir Thomas Esmonde, and said he did not tell them why he had now changed his mind upon this question. (Hear, hear.) He told them that he had changed his mind on Tuesday. He (the speaker) challenged him to deny this—that on Wednesday evening at the National Liberal Club he declared himself in favour of Mr. Parnell. (Hear, hear.)

Sir Thomas Esmonde.—I have not the least recollection of having said anything of the sort.

Dr. Kenny.—But I am the member who first gave to Mr. Power the information he has just used. I ask Sir Thomas Esmonde whether he did not leave me at the National Liberal Club on Wednesday evening, before going to Ireland, in perfect accord with me as to the leadership.

Mr. Healy.—"Question, question."

Sir Thomas Esmonde.—I have not the least recollection of what my friend Dr. Kenny says. If I did make any remarks on the subject, he must have misunderstood the purport of them.

Dr. Kenny (who rose amid cries of "Order" and "Sit down") said he wrote to Sir Thomas Esmonde from Dublin, and, if the letter were produced, and a certain passage in it read, it would show that he (Dr. Kenny) was right.

Mr. Healy.—You have no right to talk that way. (Cries of "Order.")

Mr. E. Harrington.—It is a question of honour, Healy ; leave him to himself. (Renewed cries of "Order.")

SIR THOMAS ESMONDE said he would produce the letter to-morrow if he could find it.

MR. R. POWER (continuing) said he would pass ·from that matter, and ask Sir Thomas Esmonde another question—if, upon a certain occasion, he sent a wire to Mr. Parnell saying that he and others would issue a manifesto in support of him, and two hours after, the same evening, came to his colleagues and withdrew his name from that manifesto ?

MR. Healy here went over and spoke to Sir Thomas Esmonde.

MR. E. HARRINGTON.—Look at his legal adviser. If he is an honourable man, he wants no legal adviser.

MR. R. POWER.—I am not surprised that Mr. Healy is anxious to give assistance to his friend on this occasion.

MR. HEALY.—On the contrary, I told him to hold his tongue and not assist this obstruction.

MR. POWER.—Then you gave him excellent advice, and I am only sorry he did not follow it. Mr. Power went on to say that they were responsible to the people who had sent them there, and the people who sent them to Parliament were the people who ought to have a voice in this matter, and not be shut out from the deliberations which were now going on. (Cheers.) Referring to a remark of Sir Thomas Esmonde's, that there was no objection previously for the Irish party to be the tail of the Liberal party, Mr. Power said he agreed with him that there was no objection before, but the tail at that time had a head, and now they wanted to take them without a head and have nothing at the tail. (Cheers.) He firmly believed that the Irish people in America and Australia would not have given them the support which they had if they had not believed that the party was animated by a spirit of inde-pendence. There was no disguising the fact that they had now come to a fierce and, he regretted to say, a bitter fight between two sec-tions of the Irish party. It was a fight, but let it be said openly that it was a fight between Mr. Sexton and Mr. Parnell. (Cheers.)

MR. BARRY.—Between Mr. Parnell and Ireland. (Cheers.)

MR. E. HARRINGTON.—Between John Barry and Ireland. (Cheers.)

MR. POWER asked why, if it was a question between Mr. Par-nell and Ireland, they did not go over to Dublin and settle it ? (Cheers.)

MR. W. REDMOND.—Henry Grattan would have gone to Dublin.

MR. POWER said it was not a question between Mr. Parnell and Ireland, but a question whether they would remain a solid and independent party in the House of Commons, led by the only man who could lead the Irish party, or whether they would throw themselves helpless and hopeless into the hands of the Liberal party to-day. In conclusion, he expressed his determination to stand by Mr. Parnell. (Cheers.)

MR. CRILLY, after a few personal explanations, said that up to Tuesday he had been of opinion that the outcry against Mr. Parnell in England was only that of a few fanatics; but he was now satisfied that the situation had been vitally and fundamentally altered by two facts. These two facts were the issue of Mr. Gladstone's letter and Mr. Parnell's own manifesto. (Cheers.) If this fight for Ireland were worth fighting within the Constitution, it could only be won, to his mind, by an honourable and manly self-respecting alliance with the British democracy, and, because he believed that Mr. Parnell's action had not only imperilled and jeopardized any possibility of such an honourable and upright alliance but had utterly destroyed any such possibility, he intended to vote dead against the continued leadership by Mr. Parnell of the Irish party. (Cheers.) He had come to this conclusion with intense pain, sorrow, and agony (hear, hear), and he was prepared to abide by the consequences. Mr. Parnell had done him the honour of bringing him into the party, but he was willing to face the consequences if it involved his retirement, because he should carry with him the conviction that in this terrible crisis he had done what he thought was best for Ireland. It was almost breaking his heart-strings to give the vote he was going to give. He came into the party animated by the one ambition to serve the cause of Ireland, and to serve it until he died. (Cheers.) Although he should vote against Mr. Parnell that night, he was voting for the liberty of Ireland. (Cheers.)

MR. M. J. KENNY said they were told they must consult with the people of Ireland. He was prepared to consult with them and to abide by their decision; but he contended that they must not shirk their duty at that meeting. If the decision of that meeting was not to be abided by, and the minority intended to appeal to the people of Ireland afterwards, they would be disregarding the fundamental rule of the Irish party, that the minority should be bound by the decision of the majority, and he believed, under such circumstances, it would be useless to continue the discussion. The main question that concerned them was whether they should vote for the destruction of the alliance with the English Liberal party or whether they should vote for Mr. Parnell's retirement. In such an alternative there was but one choice. They were reminded of the efforts of the past 16 years. What had been those efforts, and what were they intended to lead up to ? (Cheers.) If they were not the gratification of personal ambition, they were to lead up to self-government for Ireland. (Cheers.) How was self-government for Ireland to be attained ? Could they obtain it as a separate and independent party ? They were bound to enter into an alliance with some English party before they could ever obtain Home Rule for Ireland. (Cheers.) The Tory party never betrayed them. They entered into an alliance with them, and, at a certain moment, when they became useless for the party, they (the Nationalists) entered into an alliance with the Liberal party. The moment they broke that alliance they would be cast back into the position they occupied ten or 11 years ago. (Hear, hear.) The Liberal party would become useless, and they would have to start over again. Suppose they did ? What was it to lead up to but another alliance in the future ? Were they, then, to be at the mercy of one man, who, at a critical moment, might fall as Mr. Parnell had fallen ; and were they to be cast into the melting-pot again ? (Cheers.) The people of Ireland might be committed to one eternal round of political agitation leading nowhere. He refused to subordinate the interests of Ireland to the accidental chance of the integrity of some particular man ten or 20 years hence. They had been asked who was responsible for the present situation. He said it was Mr. Parnell. Let there be no shirking of the point. He contended that Mr. Parnell had led his friends into a certain position, and when he found that he could not remain where they placed him, his duty was to have withdrawn. When the party met last Wednesday Mr. Parnell was offered on behalf of the majority of the party a most honourable and just compromise.

Mr. Parnell.—What was it ?

Mr. Kenny, continuing, said it was suggested that Mr. Parnell should retire from the chair for a time, they undertaking not to fill it up in the meantime. In June last Mr. Parnell had expressed implicit belief in the *bona fides* of the Liberal party. Why was it that he did not produce this conversation until an issue personal to himself was raised? (Cheers.) The inference which Mr. Parnell wished them to draw from the Hawarden conversation was that he could not trust the Liberal party—(MR. PARNELL.—Hear, hear)—and that they were bound to betray them if Mr. Parnell ceased to be their leader. If he (Mr. Kenny) thought that the Irish party was so stupid and ignorant or so helpless that, without Mr. Parnell's lead, they would be at the mercy of the chicanery of any English statesman he would have no hope in the future for the Irish party or Parliament. (Cheers.) But the Irish people looked to their representatives, and not to the chairman of those representatives, for the ultimate salvation of their country ("Hear, hear," and cries of " No, no "); and he believed that if Mr. Parnell had been really desirous of saving the situation he would have withdrawn. He would then still have been a great force, and would have been of great service to Ireland ; but by obstinately retaining a position which was untenable, by appealing to Ireland and distracting the people there on the eve of a general election, he might be the means of rendering Home Rule absolutely impossible. Under the circumstances it was impossible that the interests of Ireland could be safeguarded otherwise than by Mr. Parnell's compulsory retirement from the chairmanship of the party.

MR. J. F. X. O'BRIEN said Mr. O'Kelly told them that they had nothing to hope from the Liberal party. Then what was the meaning of their alliance with that party for the last five years? Was it a sham? Mr. O'Kelly also said that they gave themselves away some years ago to the Tory party. Under whose leadership did they do that? It was also said that they gave themselves away to the Liberals ; but under whose leadership did they do that? (Hear, hear.) Mr. O'Kelly also referred to the waning influence of the Irish in America, and Mr. Eugene O'Kelly, of New York, said that commenced after the proceedings in the Divorce Court.

MR. PARNELL.—He said nothing of the sort.

MR. O'BRIEN.—Then, if he did not, it would be a very becoming thing for him to say. (Laughter and cheers.)

MR. PARNELL.—Why did'nt you say that on Tuesday, Sir ? (Cheers.)

MR. O'BRIEN.—On the question of leadership I wish to say we have had very little leadership of any kind from Mr. Parnell during the last few years. (Hear, hear.) As for me, after the Divorce Court *exposé*, I came to the conclusion that your continued leadership was intolerable and a disgrace. (Interruption, and cries of " Order.")

MR. E. HARRINGTON.—Why did'nt you say so on Tuesday ? We cannot allow this to go on. Our own side ought not to allow it.

MR. PARNELL.—Let him go on. Order for Mr. O'Brien, please.

MR. O'BRIEN.—On Tuesday last before going to the meeting I was assured by Mr. Barry that you had decided to retire, if re-elected. (Cries of " Oh.")

MR. BARRY.—I was informed so by Mr. Lane. (Renewed cries of " Oh, oh.")

MR. PARNELL.—Another Cork member.

MR. LANE.—It is not a lie, Mr. Parnell.

MR. PARNELL.—I did not say it was a lie. I said it was another Cork member to whom we were indebted for that.

MR. LANE. —Well, Mr. Parnell, I am not ashamed of being a Cork member. (Loud cheers.) As to the statement that you would retire if re-elected, I was told so by Mr. Tuohy.

MR. PARNELL.—You have misunderstood me, Mr. Lane.

MR. LANE.—I am very sorry, Mr. Parnell, if I have.

MR. PARNELL.—I did not say it was a lie, or impute false-hood to you, or cast any reflection on the Cork members. Mr. O'Brien is in possession of the Chair, and cannot be interrupted.

MR. J. F. X. O'BRIEN.—In re-electing you last Tuesday we were only paying you a compliment, for we thought you intended to resign. (Laughter.) As to the Hawarden meeting, I do not think the people of Ireland will be satisfied with your explana-tion. You said you knew then that Mr. Gladstone had become false to us.

MR. PARNELL.—I did not say he had become false to you. (Hear, hear.)

MR. O'BRIEN.—I will allow the people of Ireland to think about that for themselves, Mr. Parnell. (Cheers and counter-cheers.) You kept silence on that treachery, and left your colleagues under the impression that all was safe, and went about the country praising Mr. Gladstone. I leave you, Mr. Parnell, to convince the people of Ireland of the honesty of your part in that grave matter. This is the most wretched moment of my life, for I see, shattered by you, who brought us to our splendid position, all the hopes of Ireland.

At this stage an hour's adjournment for dinner took place.

On the resumption of the meeting,

Mr. PARNELL said,—I wanted, in regard to a question of disputed recollection between Mr. Lane and Mr. Barry a short time ago ——

Mr. T. HEALY.—I rise to a point of order. I understood you had called upon Mr. Garrett Byrne.

Mr. PARNELL.—Yes ; but it is a matter which, I think, the meeting ought to have in their possession.

Mr. HEALY.—I respectfully submit to you that you cannot occupy the position of chairman in conducting our debates, and at the same time continue the position of counsel to yourself. (Cheers and counter cheers.) This is a matter which has got to be met now, and I will meet it. (Cheers and counter cheers.)

Mr. PARNELL.—What is it you want to meet ?

Mr. HEALY.—I want to meet the fact that the debates are not being conducted by the Chair in accordance with the position laid down yesterday—viz., in accordance with the rules to which you referred.

Mr. Parnell here rose from the chair.

Mr. HEALY.—Am I in possession or not ?

Mr. PARNELL.—At present I am in possession, and I wish to have a matter cleared up with regard to a statement made in reference to the Cork members, and to Mr. Lane in particular, just before we adjourned.

Mr. HEALY.—Will strangers be requested to withdraw in the meantime ?

Mr. PARNELL.—No ; this is a matter which comes within the competency of the meeting, and it should be within the competency of the reporters. The Press were present.

Mr. HEALY.—I don't refer to the reporters.

Mr. PARNELL.—Who are the strangers ?

Mr. HEALY.—I see one behind me, Mr. J. M. Tuohy.

Mr. LEAMY.—Why, Mr. Tuohy is chief of the *Freeman* staff.

Mr. Parnell.—This is Mr. Tuohy who is wanted in this matter. Mr. Lane was under the impression I stated to the meeting that he had received from Mr. Tuohy a statement, which he communicated to Mr. Barry, that, prior to the meeting on Tuesday, I had expressed my intention of resigning in case I was re-elected to the chairmanship of the party, and that this information, so communicated by Mr. Tuohy, produced a powerful impression on his mind, and also on Mr. Barry's, with reference to the subsequent proceedings. Now, I have asked Mr. Tuohy to state to you ——

Mr. Lane.—If you will allow me one moment ——

Mr. Healy.—I have raised a point of order.

Mr. Parnell.—What is it ?

Mr. Healy.—I will state it.

Mr. Parnell.—Very well.

Mr. Healy.—I am waiting for you to sit down.

Mr. Sexton.—I will ask my friend Mr. Healy not to strain the discussion. (Loud cheers.) My friend has often deferred to me in the midst of difficulty, and I would ask him not to strain a point of order in this matter in which Mr. Parnell is so deeply concerned, but, on the contrary, to allow the utmost latitude. (Cheers.)

Mr. Healy.—Mr. Chairman, may I make an observation ?

Mr. Parnell.—Certainly.

Mr. Healy, proceeding, said that, the chairman having initiated the discussion, he would say, on the other hand, he differed from their friends who took the opposite view, that they should not allow extraneous matter to be introduced.

Mr. J. Redmond, alluding to the point of order, appealed to his friend Mr. Healy not to interpose an obstacle.

Thereupon,

Mr. Conway rose to order.

Mr. Healy acceded to the suggestion made by his friend Mr. Redmond, but said that what he would point out was that when an accusation was made yesterday of the most terrible kind against his friend Mr. Sexton and when four members rose in succession to give their testimony for Mr. Sexton they were ruled out.

Mr. Parnell.—They all spoke.

Mr. Sexton.—No ; you refused to hear any one of them.

Mr. Parnell.—I did not allow them to interrupt the debate.

MR. HEALY now appealed to the chairman, whose fairness he would like to acknowledge, to endeavour, as far as his personal position enabled him, to give them the same liberty of appreciation as they were most happy to accord to him. (Hear, hear.)

MR. W. REDMOND wished to ask the chairman if there was anything whatever to prevent the four gentlemen who wished to corroborate Mr. Sexton from rising in their places in the ordinary course of debate. (Cheers, and cries of " No, no.")

MR. LANE.—I did not state at any time that I heard you say you were about to retire, and I distinctly denied on last Wednesday that I myself was in any way influenced by that statement which Mr. Tuohy made to me in the vote which I gave for your re-election. I stated distinctly when I came into this room that I was determined, if you presented yourself for re-election, to support you.

MR. PARNELL thought that Mr. Lane had misunderstood his reference to him. It was not in any way intended to be offensive.

MR. LANE said he had explained the way the matter took place. He felt the tone of Mr. Parnell's ejaculation very deeply ; so did his colleagues for the city and county of Cork.

MR. PARNELL.—I am a Cork member myself. (Cheers.)

After further conversation, MR. TUOHY, at the invitation of the chairman, said he saw Mr. Campbell at his office on the Saturday before the House met, and had a conversation with him about the position of Mr. Parnell. They were discussing the matter, and Mr. Campbell stated, as his own opinion, and expressly excluded himself from giving it as Mr. Parnell's opinion or intention, that, in certain contingencies, he thought Mr. Parnell might retire. When he met Mr. Lane in the Lobby, he stated to Mr. Lane, in the first instance, that Mr. Campbell had given this entirely as his own opinion, and that it was not given as Mr. Parnell's intention at all.

MR. LANE.—Quite so.

MR. TUOHY added that he had not the least recollection of being asked any question by Mr. Lane afterwards, nor of his having spoken to him from that time to this.

MR. LANE wished to remind Mr. Tuohy of a statement he made to him before the meeting that Mr. Parnell was about to retire, without any qualification.

MR. TUOHY.—No.

Mr. Lane said that after the meeting was over Mr. Tuohy told him that he made the statement upon the best authority possible, that of Mr. Campbell.

Mr. Tuohy said that he had not the least recollection of having met Mr. Lane in the way stated.

Mr. J. Huntly M'Carthy said that he had no knowledge of what Mr. Tuohy said to Mr. Lane, but in a conversation which he had with Mr. Tuohy, he distinctly understood from him that his impression was that Mr. Parnell would not resign. (Cheers.)

Mr. Campbell denied that he ever told Mr. Tuohy that he knew Mr. Parnell was going to resign, or that Mr. Parnell told him that he was going to resign.

Mr. M. J. Kenny said that on Tuesday Mr. Campbell told him that it was Mr. Parnell's intention to hold on to the leadership.

Mr. G. M. Byrne also said that Mr. Campbell on Tuesday stated that Mr. Parnell was going to accept the chairmanship.

Some discussion then took place with reference to a statement made by Mr. Conway as to a conversation between Mr. Sexton and others in reference to the leadership.

Mr. G. M. Byrne contended that there should be no unseemly haste in arriving at a division on the subject before them, and declared his intention of supporting the chosen leader of the Irish party.

While Mr. Byrne was speaking, a messenger from the House announced that a division was about to be taken on the Land Purchase Bill, and a suggestion was made that members should take part in the division, but this was met with loud cries of " No, no," while Mr. Leamy said, amid cheers,—" This is the Irish Parliament. Don't mind the English Parliament."

Mr. G. M. Byrne proceeded with his remarks, and said he was surprised to hear from Mr. Sexton that without Mr. Gladstone they could expect no hope. If Mr. Sexton and Mr. Healy were so frightened or panic-stricken, he was not panic-stricken. (Hear, hear.) He asserted that the letter written by Mr. Gladstone was a great piece of dictation, and he hoped that when the Bishops of Ireland met that week they would see that it was a piece of dictation, and would not allow themselves to be dictated to by anybody. The object of the letter was to intimidate Mr. Parnell and to intimidate the Irish party, and prevent them from electing Mr.

Parnell. (Hear, hear.) They ought not, he contended, lightly to get rid of Mr. Parnell's leadership. (Cheers.)

Mr. DALTON spoke in favour of Mr. Parnell's retaining the leadership, stating that he would not vote for " selling " the Irish leader to an English party for any price whatever. With regard to Mr. Parnell's version of what occurred at Hawarden, he believed the Irishman rather than the Englishman when it came to a question of accuracy between them. As to the danger to the alliance with the Liberal party, he believed the Liberals would stick to Ireland as long as it served themselves and no longer.

Mr. HARRISON addressed the meeting in support of Mr. Parnell's retention of the leadership. In face of the position taken up by Mr. Gladstone, it would be madness and folly to abandon the best leader the Irish people ever had for vain and illusory pledges from which it was perfectly easy for Mr. Gladstone to escape. He expressed the view that at the next general election they would be in a better position with Mr. Parnell as their leader, with 85 followers behind him, than they could be without him. He would probably hold the balance of power and be able to extort from the Liberal party a measure of Home Rule, to which they were every one pledged.

Mr. TUITE said he had arrived at the decision to vote against Mr. Parnell's leadership with the greatest pain. The present occasion demanded that every man should do his duty according to his conscience, and it was the Irish people that weighed on his heart. He did not care what were the consequences to himself.

Mr. T. A. DICKSON said the reason which would influence his vote was solely a moral one, and if he voted for Mr. Parnell's leadership he would be false to every religious conviction he ever held during his life.

Mr. HAYDEN, speaking in support of Mr. Parnell, believed that the retention of the member for Cork as leader would not for one single hour stand in the way of Home Rule.

Mr. P. J. O'BRIEN said the vote that he would give would be wrung from him by the deepest sorrow that the situation should compel him to cast it against the leader whom he had so loved and respected.

Mr. BLANE said after the Special Commission he refused to believe that the witnesses of British hire ceased at the Divorce

Court. Hence it was that he appealed to his colleagues not to recognize any decree from that Court.

MR. JORDAN said that Mr. Parnell in his speech yesterday asked who created this position, and he replied that it was not he. (Hear, hear.) If not, who did create the position ?

A voice.—Mr. Gladstone.

MR. JORDAN.—Not we.

MR. E. HARRINGTON.—All except yourself.

MR. JORDAN.—And I surely say not the Liberal leader, nor the Liberal party. I say plainly and boldly that it was Mr. Parnell himself, the leader of the party. Continuing, the speaker said he resented the charge of conspiracy. He was a Nonconformist, but he was prepared to admit that where genuine coin was, there also would be the spurious, and there was a certain amount of canting in all societies and amongst all parties. (Cheers.)

MR. E. HARRINGTON.— And recanting.

MR. JORDAN said that he, at any rate, had never recanted. (Cheers.) Whether his constituents approved or disapproved what he did, he had made up his mind, and if they demanded his retirement he should have the greatest pleasure in giving up his trust to the constituency from whom he had received the greatest possible kindness.

MR. PARNELL.—I shall now put the amendment :—" That all questions touching the chairmanship of the Irish party be postponed until the members have had an opportunity of personally ascertaining the views of their constituents, and until the party can meet in Dublin."

The division was taken as follows :—

FOR THE AMENDMENT OF COLONEL NOLAN.—29.

Blanc, A.	Hayden, L. P.	O'Connor, J.
Byrne, G. M.	Kenny, Dr. J. E.	O'Hanlon, T.
Campbell, H.	Leamy, E.	O'Kelly, J. J.
Clancy, J. J.	M'Carthy, J. H.	Parnell, C. S.
Conway, M.	Macdonald, W. A.	Power, R.
Corbet, W. J.	M'Kenna, Sir J.	Quinn, T.
Dalton, J.	Maguire, J. R.	Redmond, J.
Fitzgerald, J. G.	Mahony, P.	Redmond, W.
Harrington, E.	Nolan, Colonel	Sheil, E.
Harrison, H.	Nolan, J.	

DEC. 2.

AGAINST.—44

Abraham, W.
Barry, J.
Chance, P. A.
Commins, A.
Condon, T. J.
Cox, J. R.
Crilly, D.
Deasy, J.
Dickson, T. A.
Esmonde, Sir T. J.
Finucane, J.
Flynn, J. C.
Foley, P. J.
Fox, Dr. J.
Healy, M.

Healy, T.
Jordan, J.
Kenny, M. J.
Kilbride, D.
Knox, H. V.
Lane, W. J.
M'Cartan, M.
M'Carthy, Justin
M'Donald, P.
MacNeill, J. G. S.
Molloy, B. C.
Morrogh, J.
Murphy, W.
O'Brien, J. F. X.
O'Brien, P. J.

O'Connor, A.
O'Keeffe, F. A.
Pinkerton, J.
Power, P. J.
Reynolds, W. J.
Roche, J.
Sexton, T.
Sheehan, P.
Sheehy, D.
Stack, J.
Sullivan, D.
Tanner, Dr. C.
Tuite, J.
Webb, A.

ABSENT.—12.

Carew, J. L.
Dillon, J.
Gilhooly, J.
Gill, T. P.

Harrington, T.
Lalor, R.
Leahy, J.
O'Brien, P.

O'Brien, W.
O'Connor, T. P.
O'Gorman Mahon, The
Sullivan, T. D.

Mr. PARNELL said,—I find that the noes are 44 and the ayes 29, so I declare the noes have it by a majority of 15.

There was no demonstration at the announcement of the numbers.

On the motion of Mr. CLANCY, the debate was adjourned till 2 o'clock on the following day, Wednesday, December 3.

A letter from Sir William Harcourt to the Editor of *The Times*, and also a joint letter from Mr. Henry Labouchere, M.P., and Professor Stuart, M.P., contradicting statements made by Mr. Parnell, were issued on December 2. They were as follows :—

"To THE EDITOR OF THE TIMES.

" Sir,—Mr. Parnell has made a statement with reference to me which I think it necessary to contradict, though it has already been declared to be untrue by Mr. Justin M'Carthy, from whom alone Mr. Parnell could have derived any information on the subject.

" Mr. Parnell has affirmed that I have stated that ' under no circumstances would I give any promise, either now or hereafter, to any Irish party.' That assertion of Mr. Parnell's is not true.

" What really occurred is briefly as follows :—Mr. M'Carthy proposed to me that I, in concert with Mr. Gladstone and Mr. John Morley, should sign a letter binding ourselves to certain

DEC. 2.

terms propounded by Mr. Parnell, which letter was to be kept an inviolable secret. I confess I did not regard this as a practical transaction. I pointed out to Mr. M'Carthy that the condition of secrecy was wholly inadmissible ; that such a document could be of no value to Mr. Parnell or any one else unless its terms were made known ; and that, if it were otherwise, after what had occurred I did not attach any importance to Mr. Parnell's pledge of inviolable secrecy.

" So far from refusing to hold communication as to the settlement of Home Rule with any Irish party, what I stated was exactly the reverse. I told Mr. M'Carthy that the Irish party and the Irish nation possessed a far higher and more lasting security than any secret negotiation or individual pledges, in the unquestionable political fact that no party and no leaders could ever propose, or hope to carry, any scheme of Home Rule which had not the cordial concurrence and support of the Irish nation, as declared by their representatives in Parliament.

" I added some words of sympathy for the painful difficulties in which the Irish party now found themselves, and said that the present moment of confusion did not afford an occasion on which it was possible to enter with any advantage upon the discussion of the particulars of a future scheme of Home Rule.

" It will be seen, therefore, that both the spirit and the substance of my reply to Mr. Justin M'Carthy were exactly the opposite of what Mr. Parnell has stated. The other statements of Mr. Parnell in relation to my views and conduct are such as do not seem to me worthy of notice, except so far as to say that they are as opposed to the truth as that which I have just refuted.

" Your obedient servant,

" December 2."   " W. V. HARCOURT.

" December 2.

" Sir,—Mr. Parnell is reported to have yesterday informed his colleagues that a section of them had been in treaty with Mr. Labouchere and Professor Stuart to put him out of his position in the Irish Parliamentary party. This statement we desire emphatically to contradict. Mr. Parnell's attempt to turn off upon us the origin of a movement which arose entirely amongst his own colleagues has not the slightest foundation ; in fact, Mr. Sexton's version of the matter, in his reply to Mr. Parnell, is, so far as we are concerned, quite correct. We were seated together at about

8 o'clock on Tuesday evening, talking upon another subject, when Mr. Sexton approached us and asked us whether it was true that Mr. Gladstone had put on record his views with respect to Mr. Parnell's position in a letter addressed to Mr. J. Morley. We replied that it was so, and that we believed that the letter had already been sent to the Press for publication. On Mr. Sexton expressing a wish to have a copy of this letter, we procured him one from the Press agency to which it had been sent.

" We are your obedient servants,

" H. LABOUCHERE.

" J. STUART."

NATIONAL LEAGUE MEETING.

On the evening of the same day the usual fortnightly meeting of the National League was held at the League offices in Dublin. Current events gave it unusual importance, and the attendance was the largest which has been seen for some years. Every reference to Mr. Parnell elicited enthusiastic cheers, while the names of Messrs. Healy and Sexton were received with groans and expressions of scorn. Several Roman Catholic priests were present. Mr. Thomas Mayne, an ex-M.P., was elected to preside.

It was announced that the organizing committee of the National League had passed the following resolution the previous night :—" We, the members of the organizing committee of the Irish National League, express our full and complete confidence in Charles Stewart Parnell as leader of the Irish Parliamentary party in the British House of Commons, he having been duly elected leader for the present Session. We deprecate the attempt made to displace him from a position which he has so usefully and honourably filled." (Cheers.)

The CHAIRMAN, referring to the present crisis, said that the final decision in the matter should rest with the Irish people, no matter what might be done in Westminster. (Cheers.) The Irish people denied and repudiated the right of any Englishman, no matter how high his position, socially or politically, even though he was a friend of Ireland from his cradle—which Mr. Gladstone was not—(A voice.—" A Coercionist." Cheers. Another voice.—" The grand old conjuror." Laughter.) He was sorry to see that the letter of Mr. Gladstone was regarded by some worthy members of the Irish party—(Loud cries of "No, no, no," and a voice.—"Unworthy members." Cheers.)

MR. M'CARTHY, Drogheda.—"Place hunters," and a voice.—"Chief Justice Healy (hisses), who sold the interests of Father M'Fadden." (Loud cheers.)

The CHAIRMAN said these men had not looked upon the letter as they in Ireland did. The issues now before the people were well defined. These issues were two. The first was that the Irish party had become a portion of the Liberal party (cries of "No, no, no ") whether tail or head. That was the issue raised by Mr. Gladstone, from whom they would be bound in future to take their commands, and the first essential to the alliance between the two parties was that they should throw overboard the man who had made that alliance a possibility. (Cheers.) They would get nothing from either of the great English parties for love. (Hear, hear.) They would get the best terms from the party who came in first at the next election, and, as to the Liberal alliance, he felt that Mr. Thomas Sexton (hisses) did not believe what he said when he stated that the only hope for Home Rule was an alliance with the Liberal party. He (the chairman) believed he was the only gentleman present who had been a member of the Irish Parliamentary party, and after nine years of personal contact with Mr. Parnell he could tell them that, if Home Rule was to be won in their time, it could only be won by Charles Stewart Parnell. (Cheers.) He knew every member of the Irish Parliamentary party, and he could tell them that there was not one out of the 86, except Mr. Parnell, who could lead the party. (Cheers.) In the black history of Ireland he could tell them, as one who had mixed in private and public conversation with Mr. Parnell, there never was a man who had done so much for the Irish cause as their great leader. (Cheers.) No Washington, no Napoleon, ever did so much for his native land as that done by the Irish leader. No matter what came, whether they got Home Rule in seven weeks or seven years, Charles Stewart Parnell was the man that would lead them.

MR. J. SHANKS, T.C., said he was glad that his first act as a member of the central branch of the Irish National League was to propose a vote of confidence in Mr. Parnell. He moved the adoption of the following telegram :—

" To Parnell, M.P., House of Commons, London.—The Central

Branch of the Irish National League sends greeting to Charles Stewart Parnell, the elected leader of the Irish people, and assures him of their undivided allegiance to him and the Irish cause, and fully confirms the resolution passed by the organizing committee at their meeting last night.—THOMAS MAYNE, Chairman.'' (Cheers.)

The REV. FATHER BEHAN and MR. AMOS VARIAN.—No, no.

At this point there was considerable excitement and confusion, the cheers for Parnell being loud and repeated, while the shouts of '' No, no,'' were distinctly heard. Order was not restored until after repeated appeals from the chairman. Several panes of glass were broken in one of the doors, owing to the great crush and excitement. MR. SHANKS resuming, said that no doubt the offence charged against Mr. Parnell was a very unfortunate one. This announcement was received with cries of '' What about Sexton ?''

The REV. FATHER HURLEY, of Kildare, seconded the resolution, and said he had pleasure in raising his voice for God and country, and in defence of the deliverer of this country, Mr. Parnell. (Loud cheers.) He admired that maxim of O'Connell—Religion from Rome, politics from home (applause)—and referring to the Norman invasion, he said that the people, having listened to the voice of the hierarchy, had brought ruin to the country. (Loud cheers.)

MR. OLDHAM supported the motion. He said that if the Bishops had expressed an opinion on this question a week ago the people would have regarded their pronouncement on the moral aspect of the case ; but after the publication of Mr. Gladstone's letter, this had become a political question, and a political question it remained to-day, and any position that the Bishops might take now must be put into the scale as a political weapon. (Cheers.) He believed that the people could within the next month put sound material into the Irish party, and then they could present to the enemy a solid Irish square. Mr. Baker also supported the motion.

The CHAIRMAN then announced that it was desirable to telegraph the resolution to Mr. Parnell at once (Loud cheers.) He declared the resolution carried with acclamation. (REV. FATHER BEHAN, shouting.—No, it is not passed with acclamation.) At this announcement the cheering for Parnell recommenced, and

amid cheering for Mr. T. Harrington and Mr. J. J. Clancy, the
meeting adjourned.

MEETING OF THE IRISH PARTY—FIFTH DAY.

The meeting of the Irish Nationalist party, which was adjourned from the night of Tuesday, December 2, was resumed on
Wednesday, December 3, in Committee-room No. 15, the members
assembling at 2 o'clock. Mr. Parnell appeared to be in the best of
spirits, and expressed the utmost confidence as to the result of
the contest in which he is engaged. When he entered the Committee-room at 2 o'clock a considerable number of members had
assembled. During the afternoon there was a full attendance.
Mr. Parnell presided.

At 20 minutes past 2 MR. PARNELL said,—I think we have
enough members present to proceed with our business. Mr.
Campbell will go on reading telegrams. But first I ought to state
that I communicated with the Serjeant-at-Arms to know how long
we might remain here this evening after the rising of the House,
and he sent me a message to inform me that we might remain
until 7 o'clock, and not any later.

MR. HEALY.—I would like to see them sending the police to
turn us out. I think, Sir, it would be well for the Whips to inform the Serjeant-at-Arms ——

MR. PARNELL.—Mr. Campbell must go on with the reading ——

MR. HEALY.—Inform the Serjeant-at-Arms that this party will
decide for itself when we shall leave the House of Commons.

MR. PARNELL.—I shall not undertake to send any impertinent
message to the Serjeant-at-Arms or any other member of the House
of Commons, which has granted us the privilege of using this
committee room.

MR. HEALY.—It is no privilege ; it is a right.

MR. O'KELLY.—I understood we agreed that the proceedings of
this meeting should be conducted on Parliamentary lines. The
rule of the House of Commons is that all business should cease
at 6 o'clock on Wednesday, and it will cease here as well as in
other parts of the House.

MR. HEALY.—And there is another rule that the business of
the House should begin on Wednesday at 12 o'clock, and we did
not begin until 2 o'clock.

Mr. PARNELL.—You could have raised that last night, when the hour for commencement was discussed, and, as I understood, agreed to by the unanimous wish of the meeting.

Mr. SEXTON.—I trust that the business of the meeting will proceed, and if any member wishes· to prolong the period of sitting it can be raised at 7 o'clock, but at present the meeting should proceed.

Mr. PARNELL.—I merely thought it my duty to put you in possession of the information at my command.

Mr. HEALY.—I thought it my duty to put the meeting in possession of my views too.

Mr. CAMPBELL then proceeded to read the telegrams.

Mr. CLANCY, who resumed the debate, said that the last week had been to him a week of absolute torture, and though he had had some difficulty in making up his mind he had made it up at last. He disclaimed any intention to dictate to the party in his Leinster Hall speech. He supported Mr. Parnell on that occasion on several grounds, one of which was that he believed then, as he believed now, that Mr. Parnell had not ceased to possess all the qualifications for a leader. (Cheers.) Then came Mr. Gladstone's letter, which staggered him. He felt that a great deal of harm had been done, and that possibly the Home Rule cause might be injured by Mr. Parnell's retention of the leadership. He had been induced to give his vote by the belief that all they had gained in recent years, including the conversion of Mr. Gladstone and the Liberal alliance, had been gained by the manifestation of the absolute independence of the Irish party. Had they not shown in a hundred ways that they were independent? All the concessions of recent years would be still *in nubibus*, and Mr. Gladstone's conversion to Home Rule would still be in the womb of the future. (Hear, hear.) He was not prepared to characterize Mr. Gladstone's letter as an open and barefaced effort at dictation. (Hear, hear.) But no matter how mildly or considerately worded that letter, the effect of it was to tell them that, if they did not get rid of Mr. Parnell, they should get rid of Mr. Gladstone. (Hear, hear.) That seemed to him, whether Mr. Gladstone intended it or not, to be an absolute threat, to which the representatives of Ireland could not, without sacrificing the highest interests of the country, have submitted for one moment. (Cheers.) By deposing Mr.

Parnell they would destroy not only the independence but the
unity of the party (hear, hear), thus bringing back the internal
dissensions which for generations past had kept them helplessly
at the feet of the English. In his opinion, if Mr. Parnell was
deposed there would no longer be a united Irish party. (Hear,
hear.) He contended that they could not pluck Mr. Parnell from
his position as leader of the party without causing a terrible conflict. (Cheers.) It could not be done except after a storm which
would shake the whole Irish world. (Cheers.) His own desire
was to avoid a conflict which he was quite certain would postpone
even an attempted settlement of the Irish question for the present generation. (Cheers.) Another consideration with him was
one which had arisen out of the circumstances of Saturday
night's meeting at the Westminster Palace Hotel. He need not
narrate once again the facts on that subject. Mr. Parnell offered
to retire if Mr. Gladstone, Sir W. Harcourt, and Mr. John Morley
would give certain guarantees. Mr. Gladstone's reply might be
summed up by saying that he refused to answer. (Hear, hear.)
Mr. Gladstone said in the first place that he did not think it
right to interfere in the internal discussions of the Irish party.
He had, however, interfered with them already. (Hear, hear.)
He had also said that he could not treat with the leader of the
Irish party, and he himself could not understand why Mr. Gladstone had refused to treat with Mr. M'Carthy.

MR. M'CARTHY said that he told Mr. Gladstone that he did
not come from the Irish party, but from a hastily-summoned
meeting.

MR. CLANCY said he did not think he had said anything contrary to that. Mr. Gladstone had also said that he could not
give the guarantee because it could not be kept secret. Would he
give it to be made public? Why should it not be made public?
(Loud cheers.) It could not be kept private, and he himself intended to ask them to insist that it should be made public. Mr.
Gladstone had made the present situation in which they found
themselves.

MR. M. J. KENNY.—Not in any sense.

MR. CLANCY.—In the name of God, what did you mean by your
vote of Tuesday? What did you mean, after giving that vote, by
coming down and proposing to reverse it after Mr. Gladstone's
letter? Proceeding, Mr. Clancy contended that it was Mr.

Gladstone's letter which caused many members to alter their opinions. Mr. Gladstone made the situation and he could end it (Mr. PARNELL.—Hear, hear), and the millions of the Irish race throughout the world would convict him of insincerity if he stood in this tremendous crisis upon a point of punctilio or etiquette or technicalities. A nation's cause was at stake. (Hear, hear.)

MR. PARNELL.—Two nations. (Hear, hear.)

DR. TANNER.—One man.

MR. CLANCY said that Mr. Gladstone should come down from his high place when he knew he could settle the question. If Mr. Gladstone did not do it he himself could only come to the conclusion that he had not made up his mind to give them a satisfactory measure of Home Rule, and that they would lose nothing by retaining Mr. Parnell and losing the Liberal alliance. He himself would not sit in an Irish Parliament which had not the control of the constabulary. That question was at the very bottom of their demand. (Cheers.) They also wanted the settlement of the land question in their hands. Mr. Gladstone had no land policy ; he had not even the policy of voting for the present Bill ; he was going to vote against it. The Liberal party was going to vote against it.

MR. T. HEALY—So did we last night.

MR. CLANCY declared that the Liberal party at present had no land policy, and as the Irish party had a distinct policy they were entitled to ask Mr. Gladstone what his policy was. Those matters having been made public, it was imperative that the matter should be settled. They were bound to get this thing cleared up. If they failed they ceased to be not only an independent party but a Nationalist party. (Cheers.) He appealed to his friends to treat this matter seriously and considerately, and to bring to an end, if possible, this terrible crisis which had been wringing the heart out of them all the week. He begged their acceptance of the amendment he was about to move.

MR. SEXTON.—Before Mr. Clancy concludes, as he has made a most important proposal—namely, that certain suggestions should be made to Mr. Gladstone as to the declaration of his policy on vital questions in regard to Ireland—I presume Mr. Clancy is authorized by Mr. Parnell to make some further communication.

MR. CLANCY.—Certainly ; but let me understand you exactly.

MR. JOHN REDMOND.—Do I understand you to ask, Mr. Sexton, if Mr. Clancy is entitled to make a further communication that, if these assurances are of a satisfactory character, Mr. Parnell will resign the leadership of the party ?

MR. SEXTON.—My inquiry was directed to that point.

MR. REDMOND.—Well, that is so. (Cheers.)

MR. CLANCY.—I have authority for stating that, if assurances are given after the manner suggested in this amendment, Mr. Parnell will retire. (Cheers.) The amendment was as follows :—

" That, in view of the difference of opinion that has arisen between Mr. Gladstone and Mr. Parnell as to the accuracy of Mr. Parnell's recollection of the suggestions offered at Hawarden in reference to suggested changes in and departures from the Home Rule Bill of 1886 on the subject of the control of the constabulary and the settlement of the land question, the Whips of the party be instructed to obtain from Mr. Gladstone, Mr. John Morley, and Sir William Harcourt, for the information of the party, before any further consideration of this question, what their views are with regard to those two vital points." (Cheers.)

MR. T. M. HEALY.—I wish to put a question to the meeting as a matter of procedure. I am sorry Mr. Parnell is not here. I speak in presence of the Press, but I would suggest that, if necessary, the representatives of the Press here present should be asked to suspend their report upon any particular point, because I think it would be most inexpedient that our discussion on this matter, in case we accepted the amendment, should go before the world, and that the whole world should know practically the result of our Cabinet Council. (Cheers.)

MR. CLANCY.—I think the suggestion you are now making is so important that Mr. Parnell ought to be present. (Cheers.)

Mr. Parnell was then sent for.

After some discussion MR. SEXTON proposed that the discussion should be adjourned until noon on the following day, for the purpose of discussing Mr. Clancy's amendment. Mr. Parnell having returned and resumed the chair, MR. SEXTON, addressing him, referred to the terms of Mr. Clancy's amendment, urging that the amendment did not bear immediately or obviously on their proceedings at the conference during the week, but the statement of Mr. Clancy and Mr. Redmond, that if the communications were satisfactory Mr. Parnell would retire, had given him much gratification. It enabled him to hope that Mr. Parnell would voluntarily resign his position at the head of the party, under circumstances which would enable those who differed now to agree that he had made his retirement from public life the means of securing an advantage to his country. (Cheers.)

Mr. HEALY, who spoke with much emotion, said that, if Mr. Parnell felt able to meet the party on the points put forward, his voice would be the first, at the very earliest moment possible, consonant with the liberties of his country, to call him back to his proper place as leader of the Irish race. (Loud cheers.)

Mr. CHANCE submitted, in opposing the adjournment, that Mr. Clancy's proposal raised a false issue, and could by no possible chance lead to a settlement. (Cries of " No, no.")

Mr. M. J. KENNY said he fully adopted the opinions of Mr. Sexton.

Mr. PARNELL said Mr. Sexton had asked a practical question, as to whether his retirement from the leadership of the party and from public life would be governed by the decision of the party or his (Mr. Parnell's) own view as to the satisfactory nature of the replies of those statesmen to the questions on the two vital points of the control of the Irish constabulary and future powers of the Irish Parliament regarding the land question. That was a sudden question, and it would be fair to give him 24 hours to consider the subject between then and noon on Thursday. (Hear, hear.)

On the motion of Mr. SEXTON the meeting then stood adjourned until noon on the following day, Thursday, December 4.

DECLARATION OF THE IRISH ROMAN CATHOLIC HIERARCHY.

On this day, Wednesday, December 3, the following important document was issued by the Standing Committee of the Roman Catholic Archbishops and Bishops of Ireland, and approved by the undermentioned Prelates :—

" Address of the Standing Committee of the Archbishops and Bishops of Ireland to the clergy and laity of their flocks :—

" Very Rev. and Rev. Fathers and Fellow-countrymen,—The Bishops of Ireland can no longer keep silent in the presence of the all-engrossing question which agitates, not Ireland and England alone, but every spot where Irishmen have found a home. That question is—Who is to be in future the leader of the Irish people, or, rather, who is not to be their leader ? Without hesitation or doubt, and in the plainest possible terms, we give it as our unanimous judgment that, whoever else is fit to fill that highly responsible post, Mr. Parnell decidedly is not. As pastors of this Catholic nation we do not base this our judgment and solemn declaration on political grounds, but simply and solely on the facts and circumstances revealed in the London Divorce Court. After the verdict given in that Court we cannot regard Mr. Parnell in any other light than as a man convicted of one of the gravest offences known to religion and society, aggravated as it is in his case by almost every circumstance that could possibly attach to it so as to give to it a scandalous pre-eminence in guilt and shame. Surely Catholic Ireland, so eminently conspicuous for its virtue and the purity of its social life, will not accept as its leader a man who is dishonoured and wholly unworthy of Christian confidence. Furthermore, as Irishmen devoted to our country, eager for its elevation, and earnestly intent on securing for it the benefits of domestic legislation, we cannot but be influenced by the conviction that the continuance of Mr. Parnell as leader of even a section of the Irish party must have the effect of disorganizing our ranks, and ranging as in hostile camps the hitherto united forces of our country. Confronted with the prospect of contingencies so disastrous, we see nothing but inevitable defeat at the approaching general election, and, as a result, Home Rule indefinitely postponed, coercion perpetuated, the hands of the evictor strengthened, and the tenants already evicted left without the shadow of a hope of being ever restored to their homes.

"Your devoted servants in Christ,

"+MICHAEL LOGUE, Archbishop of Armagh and Primate of All Ireland.
"+WM. J. WALSH, Archbishop of Dublin and Primate of Ireland.
"+T. W. CROKE, Archbishop of Cashel.
"+JNO. MACEVILLY, Archbishop of Tuam.
"+JAS. DONNELLY, Bishop of Clogher.
"+JAMES LYNCH, Bishop of Kildare and Leighlin.

" +Francis J. MacCormack, Bishop of Galway and Kilmac-
duagh.

" +John MacCarthy, Bishop of Cloyne.

" +Wm. Fitzgerald, Bishop of Ross.

" +Bartholomew Woodlock, Bishop of Ardagh and Clon-
macnoise.

" +Thomas Alphonsus O'Callaghan, Bishop of Cork.

" +James Browne, Bishop of Ferns.

" +Abraham Brownrigg, Bishop of Ossory.

" +Patrick M'Alister, Bishop of Down and Connor.

" +Patrick O'Donnell, Bishop of Raphoe.

" +John Lyster, Bishop of Achonry.

" +Edward M'Gennis, Bishop of Kilmore.

" +Thomas M'Givern, Coadjutor Bishop of Dromore.

" +John K. O'Doherty, Bishop of Derry.

" +Michael Comerford, Coadjutor Bishop of Kildare and
Leighlin.

" +Thomas M'Redmond, Coadjutor Bishop of Killaloe.

" +Nicholas Donnell, Bishop of Canea.

" Dublin, Dec. 3, 1890."

MEETING OF THE IRISH PARTY—SIXTH DAY.

The meeting of the Irish party was resumed at half-past 12 on
Thursday, December 4. Mr. Parnell took the chair, and proposed to go on reading the telegrams.

Mr. Sexton suggested that they should avoid reading documents of a necessarily contentious description.

Mr. Parnell assented, and said,—I understood from you, Mr.
Sexton, that the condition that I should retire from public life was
not insisted upon.

Mr. Sexton.—I said nothing about public life, nothing whatever. (Hear, hear.) I never had in contemplation in the proceedings of this party that this party should dictate anything
more than its own chairmanship. (Cheers.)

Mr. Parnell.—I think that we had better have the resolution
read, and then I shall be in a position to make my statement.

Mr. T. Healy.—I would suggest, as the resolution has not been
put from the chair, and as we agreed practically to interrupt the

proceedings on a statement from Mr. Redmond, who also was allowed to interpolate his observations—

Mr. PARNELL.—Very well, it need not be necessary to read the resolution. The consideration which I have been able to give to this most important matter has been assisted by a consultation with my friends, and I may say in the first place that Mr. Sexton will be the first to admit that he asks us to some extent to enlarge the scope of the amendment as it was put before the meeting by Mr. Clancy. He asks me, in reference to those two most important requirements of his—requirements that I consider he is perfectly entitled to make, that I do not in the slightest degree object to his making, and that I am glad that he has made—he asks me to state that, in the event of the information to be obtained from Mr. Gladstone, Mr. Morley, and Sir William Harcourt being satisfactory to the party, I should consider then that the question of the chairmanship had been determined. I wish to show him in what way that request enlarges the resolution or the amendment. The amendment requires that we are to ascertain, before any further consideration of this question of the chairmanship, the views of Mr. Gladstone, Mr. Morley, and Sir William Harcourt for the information of the party with regard to these two vital points. Mr. Sexton asks me before we have obtained this information to bind myself practically to accept without any further consideration of the question the definite judgment of the party upon the matter. Now, I wish to say with regard to that proposal at once that, having placed myself in the hands of my friends in regard to this matter at the commencement, I could not agree to surrender my responsibility or any part of my responsibility. My responsibility is derived from you to some extent, to a large extent, but it is also derived from a long train of circumstances and events in which many of you, and I speak to you with great respect, have had no share. My position has been granted to me, not because I am the mere leader of a Parliamentary party, but because I am the leader of the Irish nation. (Hear, hear.) It has been granted to me on account of the services which I have rendered in building up this party, in assimilating prejudices, in smoothing differences of opinion, and in keeping together the discordant elements of our race within the bounds of moderation all over the world. And you, gentlemen, know, and I know, that there is no man living, if I am gone, who could succeed in reconciling the feelings of the Irish people to the provisions of the Hawarden proposals. (Hear, hear.) I have explained to you why I cannot surrender my responsibility in this matter, but I will go on to say, further, that, since you ask me to declare beforehand my views upon these important questions, since you ask me to surrender to you beforehand my judgment upon these matters, I claim that this party in the face of their constituencies should by solemn resolution announce what their judgment is. (Cheers.) While not apprehending, as I said yesterday, any difference of opinion (hear, hear), while believing as I do that I shall be found certainly not in advance of the sentiment of the party upon these matters, I claim that you, since you wish to take from me the responsibility which to-day is mine and which can only be surrendered by my act (cheers), that you should state, for the information of your constituents and for my information, what your definite judgment is with regard to the two important questions of the control of the constabulary and the land question. (Cheers.) In order to facilitate your coming to a conclusion, I have drafted a resolution, which, if you wish and think proper, I will move :—

" That, in the opinion of the Irish Parliamentary party, no Home Rule Bill will be satisfactory or acceptable to the Irish people which will not confer the immediate control of the Irish police on the executive responsible to the Irish Parliament ; and, secondly, which does not confer upon the Irish Parliament full power to deal with the land question."

I put this resolution before you for your consideration, for your judgment. It is, of course, capable, if you desire it, of amendment and of modification, but let me lay some further considerations before you. My word has been grievously challenged with regard to the accuracy of my statement as to the Hawarden communications, but no attempt has been made to contradict me (hear, hear), no attempt has been made to say in what single respect inaccuracy exists, no attempt has been made to show, if there is inaccuracy, what the correction for the inaccuracy ought to be. In other words, although I have been contradicted by a wholesale system of slander, we have not been informed, we have not been told, that the constabulary will be given. Now, gentlemen, it is for you to act in this matter. You are dealing with a man who is an unrivalled sophist ——

Mr. BARRY.—Which one ?

Mr. PARNELL.—The grand old man.

Mr. BARRY.—I don't believe it.

Mr. PARNELL.—You are dealing with a man with whom and to whom it is as impossible to give a direct answer to a plain and simple question, as it is for me impossible to give an indirect answer to a plain and simple question. (" Oh, oh," and " Hear, hear.") You are dealing with a man who is capable of appealing to the constituencies for a majority which will make him independent of both the Irish party and the Tory party at the next general election. And if I surrender to him, if I give up my position to him, if you throw me to him (" No, no," " Order," and cheers), I say, gentlemen, that it is your bounden duty to see that you secure value for the sacrifice. (Cheers.) How can you secure this value ? You can secure this value by making up your minds as to what these provisions in the Bill should be, and by going to him as the representatives of the Irish people and by telling him that this is your mind. Mr. Healy reminded me the other day that I had agreed to the provisions of the Home Rule Bill of 1886, under which the control of the constabulary was not immediately granted to the Irish Parliament. Well, gentlemen, Mr. Healy will also remember that just before the introduction of that Bill I called together a meeting of my leading colleagues, of whom he was one, and submitted the provisions of that Bill to them as soon as I knew what they were going to be. Mr. O'Kelly and Mr. Sexton, I think, were also present, so was Mr. Michael Davitt. I took counsel with all the men of authority, so far as I could reach them at the moment, in the Irish party. I said :—

" Here is the Bill. It is a Parliament hit, it is nothing more. I have been told to-day by Mr. Gladstone that it is for us to take or reject that Bill, and if we undertake the responsibility of leaving it, he will make a statement in the House of Commons to-night declaring that he can do no more, and that the responsibility and the want of solution for the Irish question must rest upon us."

I said :—" Here is the Bill with all its defects, absence of suffi-

cient control of the police ; will you take it or will you leave
it ?" And my colleagues said to me that they would accept it
pro tanto, reserving for Committee the right of enforcing and, if
necessary, reconsidering their position with regard to these
important questions. It is not fair to throw upon my shoulders
the whole burden and responsibility of these matters. (Hear,
hear.) It is not fair, gentlemen, it is atrociously unfair, to use
against me passages of acquiescence, general acquiescence, very
general acquiescence, with regard to the details of this measure
in the bygone days. I can say this—that nothing I have ever
done or said upon this or any other Irish question has been
spoken or done otherwise than out of an earnest regard for the
interests of the people. (Hear, hear.) I can say that I have
not been governed by any personal consideration whatever, and
that if anything or any principle has been sacrificed, I have
always been willing to offer myself up as the first victim. My
responsibility ceases when your responsibility commences. Consider well before you assume it. I gladly divest myself of it.
It will no longer be possible for you to say to the constituencies, "Parnell betrayed us by entering into a treaty
with this Grand Old Man behind our backs, and kept it
secret from us until the last moment, and then divulged it for
his own purposes." You will not be able to put upon my back
the responsibility for my shortcomings, and Heaven knows they
are many and great. You will not be able to point to this omis-
sion or to that deficiency in the future Irish measures as attri-
butable to my neglect or to my weakness, whichever you like to
call it, because whatever will have been done you will have done
it yourselves. I was willing—and this is the extent of my guilt,
and I admit it freely—I was willing to have done my best to recon-
cile the prejudices of the Irish people in reference to the control
of the Irish police. I was willing to have risked my position in
that direction ; to have done perhaps what I ought not to have
done—to have gone beyond my duty ; and Mr. Gladstone knows
well that in striking me down he strikes down the only man who
could make that measure acceptable to Ireland. (Cheers.) And
was I under these circumstances to keep my lips sealed and
closed ? Was the Hawarden seal to be kept on my mouth after
Mr. Gladstone himself had put it out of my power to remain any
longer silent (hear, hear) with any sort of regard to the interests

of Ireland and my public duty ? Now, I know this old gentleman well.   It is not sufficient here to call him a grand old man ; that is not sufficient adulation to offer at the shrine of the Gladstonian greatness.   I know not what further incense to offer, but I do say this—having been in communication with him since 1882 upon many important subjects and topics connected with Ireland—I can tell you, gentlemen, I have never yet succeeded in getting a straight answer to a single straight question from him, and they have been many and numerous that had to be laid before him.   I am quite willing, under those circumstances, to resign to you the task of negotiation, but not until I see you have recognized, and that you fully understand, your own responsibility.   That is my view.   (Mr. Parnell again read his resolution.)

Mr. T. M. HEALY.—That is an amendment to Mr. Barry's resolution.

Mr. PARNELL.—It occurs to me at first sight that the better course to adopt to conduct the discussion on this subject is, as a substantive motion, as having been called for by the amendment of Mr. John Clancy, that motion being kept alive as well as the question connected with it.   I beg leave to say, in conclusion, that if the Irish party adopt my resolution on this subject, and take the necessary steps to ascertain from Mr. Gladstone, Mr. John Morley, and Sir William Harcourt what their views are with regard to these two vital points, and if the party, after consideration and consultation, should decide that those views are in accordance with the views of the party on these points as above expressed, then I shall place myself in the hands of my friends and retire from the position of chairman of the party.   I would propose, after the first resolution is adopted, or anything resembling it is adopted, to move a further, with regard to a matter of detail, in these terms ;—

" That a sub-committee be appointed by the party, consisting of the Whips, of five members from those who were in a majority, and of five members from those who were in a minority on Colonel Nolan's amendment, and that to those people be intrusted the duty of selecting from amongst themselves three delegates from each side to seek an interview with Mr. Gladstone, Sir William Harcourt, and Mr. Morley for the purpose of ascertaining whether their views are in accordance with the views of the party on those points as above expressed, and whether they will agree to embody those views in their Home Rule Bill, and make them vital to the measure."

Mr. T. M. HEALY said he had heard with considerable amazement the extraordinary speech just delivered. They were placed in a remarkable position. They had adjourned the meeting until that day in order to ascertain whether the proposal put forward by Mr. Clancy was really a *bonâ-fide* one. They were prepared to accept the principle of Mr. Clancy's amendment. They were prepared to stand or fall ——

MR. PARNELL.—Excuse me, Mr. Healy, there must be something before the chair.

MR. T. M. HEALY.—There is your speech, and I will answer it.　-

MR. PARNELL.—I think Mr. Clancy's amendment should be seconded first.

MR. CAMPBELL.—There is nothing before the meeting.

MR. T. M. HEALY (warmly).—I am before the meeting.

MR. CAMPBELL.—I repeat there is nothing before the chair. (Hear, hear.)

MR. T. M. HEALY.—I am before the chair. ("Hear, hear," and cries of "Order.")

MR. CAMPBELL.—To put the matter in order, I beg leave to second the amendment of Mr. Clancy.

MR. T. M. HEALY, continuing, said he would invite their friends on the opposite side, even Mr. Campbell, to show some little sense of discretion. His side were prepared to accept the principle of Mr. Clancy's amendment—namely, to obtain from the Liberal party satisfactory assurances on the two points alleged by Mr. Parnell to be in contest. What would follow? When their Whips came back from the Liberal leaders, who was to decide whether the interview was satisfactory or not? They put the plain question to Mr. Parnell, and he asked—and it was a very natural request—that he should be allowed 24 hours to determine it.

MR. PARNELL.—I only took 12 hours.

MR. T. M. HEALY.—I am sure we would be very glad to have granted you 24 days. Mr. Parnell has refused ——

MR. PARNELL.—I have not. That is an entire misrepresentation of my position.

MR. T. M. HEALY.—I am putting the view as your speech

struck me, and I am endeavouring to do so against a flood of obstruction.

MR. PARNELL.—If Mr. Healy is going to complain of the tone of my speech ——

MR. T. M. HEALY.—I am not going to make any complaint. I am about to address myself to the political ingredients of the speech and not its tone. Mr. Parnell has refused to submit this matter to the judgment of his party. (Cries of " No, no.").

MR. PARNELL.—Not at all. Nothing of the sort.

MR. T. M. HEALY.—And he has proposed new conditions. (" Hear, hear," and " No, no.") They had adjourned last night in the hope of peace, on a distinct proposal made by him to know whether Mr. Parnell in this matter was going to rely not only on the judgment of his party by 44 votes to 29, but on the judgment of men, including Mr. Richard Power, Dr. Kenny, Mr. Leamy, Mr. Conway, and of leading friends on the other side.

MR. PARNELL.—Certainly, they are all entitled to judge it just as well as I am.

MR. HEALY, continuing, asked what was the value of discussing Mr. Clancy's amendment if Mr. Parnell would not accept the judgment of his party ? Were they fools to spend their time in elaborating the amendment, which on being accepted was to have no value ?

MR. PARNELL.—Not at all.

MR. HEALY said there were present some 73 members out of 86, and, according to Mr. Parnell's view, if there were 72 to one, and that one was Henry Campbell, he would refuse to submit himself to the judgment of his party.

MR. MAHONY.—You are mistaken.

MR. HEALY.—Why, if I am mistaken, does Mr. Parnell want Mr. Clancy's amendment withdrawn ? (Cheers and " No.")

MR. PARNELL.—I do not.

MR. HEALY.—Why does he want other proposals substituted ?

MR. PARNELL.—Because you made an additional proposal yourself in Mr. Sexton's speech, not included in Mr. Clancy's amendment.

MR. HEALY.—Precisely ; because we wanted to know what we were discussing Mr. Clancy's amendment for. Mr. Healy, continuing, said he would ask Mr. Parnell, supposing they agreed to send to the Liberal leaders, and, as Mr. Clancy requested, ask the Liberal leaders for an answer on the two questions, would he submit to the decision of the majority of the party as to whether the answers were satisfactory or not, and if they pronounced them satisfactory would he retire ?

Mr. PARNELL.—If the party assume the responsibility by adopting my resolutions, undoubtedly, yes. (Cheers.) If the party take my responsibility off my shoulders by adopting these two resolutions, and declare their opinion upon these two important questions before their constituencies, undoubtedly, yes—I retire and accept your judgment. (Cheers.)

Mr. HEALY said the question they were discussing was Mr. Clancy's resolution, and he would ask Mr. Parnell, with regard to that resolution, for an answer.

Mr. PARNELL said he had told them his views on the resolution. He had said that it did not free him from his responsibility, and that he declined to do anything unless the party assumed the responsibility, which he was willing to yield.

Mr. HEALY.—I invite the attention of the meeting to this fact. Mr. Clancy's resolution is practically Mr. Parnell's resolution. (Cheers.)

Mr. PARNELL.—I beg your pardon, nothing of the kind.

Mr. HEALY.—Is Mr. Clancy here ?

Mr. CLANCY.—I am.

Mr. HEALY.—I say your resolution is Mr. Parnell's resolution.

Mr. CLANCY.—My resolution is my own. (Cheers.)

Mr. HEALY said his foundation for the statement was that when he had asked Mr. Clancy to let him see his resolution he (Mr. Clancy) refused, unless with Mr. Parnell's sanction.

Mr. CLANCY said he was acting as a friend to Mr. Parnell, and he thought it right to consult him.

Mr. PARNELL said he had read the resolution twice before he was summoned into the room, and he had not grasped its full meaning until that morning.

Mr. HEALY said that Mr. Parnell had had the resolution before him for two days.

Mr. CLANCY.—He had not. I had the resolution in my pocket.

Mr. HEALY.—When did Mr. Clancy first show Mr. Parnell the resolution ?

Mr. CLANCY.—I do not think I ought to be catechized in this way.

MR. HEALY said they asked Mr. Clancy and Mr. Redmond, if this resolution were accepted, and if, thereupon, deputies were sent in conference to the Liberal leaders, and there was a satisfactory reply, would Mr. Parnell retire, and Mr. Redmond said, " Yes," honest man that he was.

MR. LEAMY.—What is the use of going on in this way ?

DR. FITZGERALD.—This is a nice way to make the " golden bridge." I ask Mr. Healy to withdraw that imputation.

MR. HEALY.—I say Mr. Redmond is an honest man.

DR. FITZGERALD.—That means we are all thieves. (" Hear, hear," and " No, no.")

MR. HEALY.—If Mr. Redmond feels that my statement about him is in the least degree offensive ——

MR. REDMOND.—What statement ?

MR. HEALY.—I said you were an honest man, Mr. Redmond. (Laughter, and " Hear, hear.")

DR. FITZGERALD.—I must ask Mr. Healy to keep himself within the bounds of some sort of decency.

MR. HEALY, continuing, said that was the position last night. They then said, " Who is to be the judge of the satisfactoriness of the decision ? "

MR. PARNELL.— That was a question left unprovided for in the resolution, and that is a question which has been defined by my speech—that when the party assume the responsibility and take the responsibility off my shoulders on to their own, they shall be the judge.

MR. HEALY.—As far as I can gather, the majority of the party is willing at once to assume that responsibility (cheers), and, if you will only allow Mr. Barry's resolution to be withdrawn, and allow our resolution, which you refused to allow to be put on Monday last, to be put now, the party will at once proceed to its executive responsibility. (Cheers.) Mr. Healy went on to say that his colleagues met the amendment on the previous day in the fullest spirit of reconciliation.

DR. FITZGERALD.—You cried over it.

MR. HEALY said they were in hopes at any rate that it would be accepted. But now what Mr. Parnell wanted was that Mr. Clancy's amendment should be withdrawn, and necessarily also Mr. Barry's resolution, in order to enable Mr. Parnell's resolution to be put forward. There would be no question of leadership before the party. (Hear, hear.) Mr. Clancy's amendment and Mr. Barry's resolution would be withdrawn, and then on the question of the chairmanship being withdrawn the party would be engaged in discussing, not the present leadership, but the prospects of a Home Rule Bill. (Hear, hear.) Did Mr. Parnell think they were children? (Cheers.) Mr. Parnell complained of Mr. Gladstone not giving a straight answer. Had they had straight conduct and straight answers since last night? (Hear, hear.) No. A question had been asked on Mr. Clancy's amendment, and to that question they had not received the straight answer which Mr. Parnell boasted he was always enabled to give. (Cheers.) They were to be trapped into the withdrawal of Mr. Clancy's amendment and necessarily of Mr. Barry's proposal, because when he asked Mr. Parnell whether his proposal was to go as an amendment or a resolution he said a resolution.

Mr. PARNELL.—It is indifferent to me whether you have it as an amendment or a resolution. It simply contains my views on the question Mr. Sexton put to me. I regret you do not consider it a straight answer, but it is my answer, and upon that answer I will stand or fall before the country.

Mr. HEALY.—Then you will fall. (Cheers.) And now that both sides have made up their minds, what is the use of further debate? (Cheers and interruption.)

Mr. LEAMY.—Away with him! Away with him!

Mr. JOHN O'CONNOR.—Crucify him! (Cries of "Oh, oh.")

Mr. CONDON.—I think that is an expression that should not be made use of. (Hear, hear.)

Mr. SEXTON.—Mr. Parnell, I think you will agree with me that the interests of good order cannot be advanced by observations which, under the circumstances, are nothing but blasphemous. (Cheers.)

Mr. J. O'CONNOR rose to explain.

Mr. HEALY.—Allow me to proceed. Mr. Healy went on to say that they would vote Mr. Parnell's deposition, be it that day, to-morrow, Saturday, or Sunday.

COLONEL NOLAN.—Not Sunday. I will not sit on Sunday. (Laughter.)

Mr. HEALY—Colonel Nolan will probably bring out his cavalry and artillery to the hills (laughter and cheers) now that a speech has been delivered appealing to what a certain gentleman in the

Special Commission called the hillside men. (Cheers.) Our position is plain and unmistakable.

MR. PARNELL.—Hear, hear.

MR. HEALY.—Your position is plain.

MR. PARNELL.—Hear, hear.

MR. HEALY.—Let us come then to the issue. (Cheers.) You declare that the country is for you. Go to it. (Cheers.)

MR. PARNELL.—So we will. (Cheers.)

MR. HEALY asserted that they were all bound by a solemn pledge that the minority would be bound by the majority.

MR. CAMPBELL.—I have taken no such pledge.

MR. HEALY said they had given their pledges in writing " to sit, act, and vote with the majority of the party " (cheers), and now the hillside men were to be appealed to. They had ascertained that their debates were a mere consumption of time, because when they were terminated no respect would be paid to their decision. Mr. Parnell declared in advance that he would defy it. (Cheers.) He would tell Mr. Parnell that he was no greater than the majority of that party. (Loud cheers.) Judged by every constitutional principle that party was the register of the authority of the Irish nation. (Cheers.) He repeated that every one of them had taken a solemn pledge—" that I will sit, act, and vote with the Irish party, and that if it should be declared by the majority of two-thirds of the party that I have failed to do so, I will resign my seat." (Hear, hear.) The pledge to respect the decisions of the party and be bound by the majority was absolute. (Hear, hear.) Yet they were to be told in the end by Mr. Parnell, " I have no regard for your decision. I have been talking here simply against time. I deride your authority and I appeal against it." (Cheers.) No man with an intellect superior to that of a sparrow would be misled by the sophistries of that deliverance. (Cheers.) " I tell you and those who move bogus resolutions," added Mr. Healy, " that we are the brains of the country and not its brogues." (Cheers.) These resolutions have been organized by Dr. Kenny. (" Hear, hear," and " No, no.")

DR. KENNY.—Mr. Healy pays me a high compliment, but I assure him that he is wrong.

MR. HEALY.—We know the machinery. We see the ropes and the pulleys.

DR. KENNY rose to order. He said it had been freely bandied about, that he went back to Dublin to organize the National League. He declared on his honour there was not one single iota of foundation for that statement, and he would make his denial as particular as any man liked.

MR. HEALY.—It is sufficient. There is not a man in the party will dispute your word.

DR. KENNY said there were men who had made such statements. He had wired saying he had heard of no meetings, and did not think any ought to be held ; but if the people chose to express their views, they could not help it.

MR. HEALY gladly withdrew the suggestion with regard to Dr. Kenny, whose mere assurance would give validity to any declaration he would make in the mind of any member of the party. (Hear, hear.) But let him (Mr. Healy) say, with regard to the resolutions, that they knew the machinery. They heard the creaking of the cranks. Every winch and pulley that could be employed had been gathered together to set them in motion, and he would only say, so far as concerned their effect on himself, that he would rather retire and emigrate, beggared and outcast, to an African swamp, than allow his judgment as an independent representative of the people to be influenced by any consideration which his conscience did not recommend. (Cheers.) Mr. Parnell had said that an atrociously unfair use had been made of the fact that he (Mr. Parnell) accepted the Home Rule Bill of 1886.

MR. PARNELL.—With reservations on certain points.

MR. HEALY said " Quite so." No such complaint had been made. They were delighted that Mr. Parnell accepted the Home Rule Bill of 1886. They were delighted that he got the Home Rule Bill of 1886. His name had been praised all over the country for having obtained it, and the only observation they made was neither in the nature of a complaint that he had accepted it, nor to give rise to a supposition of grievance against him ; but they simply pointed out that, having accepted that Bill, they did not see how he could, in the manifesto, complain that Mr. Gladstone had refused to give him satisfactory assurances in a sense further than what he (Mr. Parnell) had accepted in the Bill of 1886.

MR. PARNELL.—No, I beg your pardon.

MR. T. HEALY.—I am only explaining that we make no complaint against you.

MR. PARNELL.—You make a distinct statement of fact. The discussion at Hawarden was taken upon departures from the Home Rule Bill of 1886, as admitted by Mr. Gladstone, and it was in reference to those departures that I felt myself placed in this embarrassing position.

MR. HEALY said he was only explaining that Mr. Parnell was not entitled to say that atrociously unfair taunts had been levelled at him for accepting the Bill of 1886. The taunts were not for accepting the Bill, but for saying that Mr. Gladstone was in a plot with a section of the Irish representatives whom the Liberals had undermined.

MR. PARNELL.—I did not say that Mr. Gladstone was in the plot.

MR. HEALY.—Well, that there was some intrigue by which the Liberal representatives had sapped the Irish representatives to induce them to destroy you and fling you to the ravenous English wolves, because you were unwilling to accept an Irish Parliament in which the police would not be immediately controlled, and in which we should not have the right to settle the land question. Proceeding, Mr. Healy said they founded their complaints not on Mr. Parnell's attitude in 1886, but on his attitude in 1890. Mr. Parnell had referred to his calling his colleagues together in 1886 to consult them before the Home Rule Bill.

MR. PARNELL.—I called together Mr. Dillon, Mr. O'Brien, yourself, Mr. Sexton, Mr. M'Carthy, Mr. O'Kelly, Mr. Dwyer Gray, and Mr. Davitt.

MR. HEALY said " Quite so " ; but he (Mr. Healy) took entire issue with the position now assumed by Mr. Parnell, who was evidently now shaping his course towards " the hillside men," when he said that he submitted the proposals to them in 1886, and told them certain things which they accepted. They did accept the Bill, and they now rejoiced and gloried in it. But the attitude of Mr. Parnell in conference that night was not the attitude stated by him to-day. At that time they were discussing, not the police, not the land question ; in those days of 1886 it seemed a mighty great thing to get the control of an Irish Parliament (hear, hear), and the limitation of a few years put upon the

K

control of the Irish constabulary did not trouble them very much. (Hear, hear.)

Mr. Parnell.—Put your limitation into the Bill as it was put into that Bill.

Dr. Kenny.—There was no limitation. (Cries of "There was.")

Mr. Healy said the way Mr. Parnell showed statesmanship was this; they were cavilling over the details, or, rather, he should say, over the absence of certain provisions in the Bill. Some men demanded a Custom-house; some question like that was raised and Mr. Parnell rose from the table and said—and it clenched and ended the discussion—" Gentlemen, two great statesmen have left the Cabinet. You have now an opportunity of wrecking another Cabinet," whereupon they all said, " Good evening." That was the way in which the discussion was concluded.

Mr. Parnell.—I communicated to you the message which was given to me that, if we did not accept that Bill as it stood, the Cabinet would resign in a body, and my reason for communicating that message to you then was that you might share the responsibility of those proceedings with me. You did share it, and I shared it with you, and I say to-day before you put yourselves into a similar position, the next time, on the next introduction of the Home Rule Bill, be sure that a similar message will not be hurled at your head, and be sure that the majority of the Liberal party will not be against you on that occasion, and that you will not have lost the controlling voice which has been given you.

Mr. Healy said if a similar message was hurled at their heads, what could they do more than last time ? (Hear, hear.)

Mr. Parnell.—You can secure the ground now if you like, and if you have the courage. (Cheers.)

Mr. Healy rejoined that when the message was hurled at their heads their chairman, statesman as he was, accepted the Bill, and they accepted it. They met in the same room—but under what happier circumstances !—and Mr. Parnell introduced Mr. Michael Davitt. Mr. Parnell then said, in effect, We have had differences with the Liberal party ; there may have been some soreness and ill-feeling, but it would be a fatal error if we did not close with this offer and, further, to put it on record at once that this Bill is in principle accepted by the Irish party. Now what was the position ? The party was asked to secure the ground in advance. He would secure the ground if they gave him some millions of men and some artillery, but without them they would be in the future as they were in the past. Some leaders would put to the party the question :—" Will you accept this Bill or will you smash the Cabinet ?" That was Mr. Parnell's alternative in 1886, and he, himself, ventured to think that there was sufficient statesmanship yet left in the benighted majority who opposed Mr. Parnell now to take a course as states-manlike as that of their leader in 1886. Six months after the Hawarden interview, when, on the occasion of his birthday, Mr. Parnell was entertained at the Westminster Palace Hotel by his colleagues, he undertook to hold aloof from all English parties " until an English party arose which would concede to Ireland the just rights of the Irish people."

Mr. PARNELL.—Hear, hear.

Mr. T. M. HEALY.—Will he cheer what follows ?

Mr. PARNELL.—Every word of it. Read it.

Mr. T. M. HEALY.—I will read every precious word. (Read-ing) :—" That time has since come." Where is the cheer for that ?

Mr. PARNELL.—Hear, hear.

Mr. T. M. HEALY.—I have extracted it at last. Rather feeble, I suggest. (Reading) :—" That time has since come about when an English party—a great English party under the distinguished leadership of Mr. Gladstone—has conceded to Ireland those rights, and has enabled us to enter into an honourable alliance, honourable and hopeful for our country "—with a garrulous old man—

Mr. PARNELL.—That is your interpolation.·

Mr. HEALY (reading) :—" Honourable for the great English party, an alliance which I venture to believe will last." What broke it off ? (Loud cheers.)

Mr. PARNELL, COLONEL NOLAN, and DR. FITZGERALD each replied " Gladstone's letter."

Mr. T. M. HEALY.—It perished in the stench of the Divorce Court. (Loud cheers.) On the 30th of June last—the date of this speech—Mr. Parnell was satisfied with the Liberal alliance.

Mr. PARNELL.—I believe now that if that letter had not been

written that alliance would have been fully maintained. (Hear, hear.)

Mr. T. M. HEALY replied that that letter was merely a statement on the part of Mr. Gladstone that he would not be able to work with Mr. Parnell. It contained no statement departing from political principles. Mr. Gladstone was called a sophist and a garrulous old man, who never gave a straight answer, and yet they were to go hat in hand to him. Mr. Parnell had trampled on his gray hairs and bespattered them with mud, and then proposed that he should be asked for terms. Mr. Gladstone might say, " I am insulted by the chairman of your party, and if he cannot refrain even amongst yourselves from terms of abuse and anger towards me, how can I give an answer which I may be told is to lead to his political destruction ?" That was the matter which they were anxious to debate that afternoon. Mr. Parnell recommended the Gladstonian principle to the Irish nation, and declared in advance that their prejudices might be safely allayed, and that they might safely accept the aid of Mr. Gladstone's genius. He himself retained his opinion of the entire transaction. Nothing had occurred since the 30th of June to change his opinion of Mr. Gladstone, or to turn him back to the career of hatred towards the English people, out of which Mr. Parnell led him. (Hear, hear.) He should maintain his position, and invite his countrymen to do the same. They would go into this fight armed, as they believed, with every feeling of patriotism. They would go into the fight putting forward the claim that they were on the side of prudence, of justice, and of right (loud cheers), and, whatever taunts might be addressed to him in the course of this feud, he would endure them as they had endured ten years of slavery in the House, and, whatever were the issues, he should not shirk stating them of only to the people, and with the people be the verdict. (Loud cheers and counter cheers.) If Mr. Parnell should go down, he was only one man gone. Heads of greater leaders had been stricken on the block before now for Ireland, and the Irish cause remained. (Cheers.)

Mr. J. REDMOND said Mr. Healy's speech was a string of insults from beginning to end, and nothing but the weighty responsibility resting upon every man in the room upon this question restrained him from resenting Mr. Healy's imputations as

he believed they deserved to be resented. (Hear, hear.) He
denied absolutely the accuracy of the representation of the situation by Mr. Healy. Deliberately or otherwise, Mr. Healy had
absolutely misrepresented the position taken up by the chairman
yesterday. Mr. Clancy moved a resolution, and there had been
no suggestion that the two subsequent resolutions were in the
least inconsistent with Mr. Clancy's. He himself believed that
even yet there might be an amicable settlement if only they were
animated by a desire to deal reasonably in this matter. After
Mr. Clancy's resolution, Mr. Sexton asked if he was correct in
assuming that, if these communications were held with Mr.
Gladstone, and if satisfactory assurances on two vital points
were obtained, Mr. Parnell would resign the leadership. They
all agreed to this, yet one would think, to listen to Mr. Healy,
that there had been some receding from the position. Mr. Sexton
having received his assurances, he asked whether the majority of
the party or Mr. Parnell was to be the judge whether the assurances from Mr. Gladstone were satisfactory. Everybody who
heard the inquiry realized the fact that that was the crux upon
which would turn the attempt to settle the matter. He believed
that Mr. Parnell's statement had been misunderstood by Mr.
Healy and misrepresented. He did not want to impute bad faith
to Mr. Healy, though he had bandied accusations against them
pretty freely.

Mr. HEALY.—What accusations did I make ?

Mr. REDMOND.—You accused us of proposing bogus resolutions,
of taking up a position that was not *bonâ fide*, of wasting time
for the purpose of causing delay, and of an attempt to rig the
country.

Mr. HEALY.—I adhere to all those statements.

Mr. REDMOND.—Then what is the point of the interruption ?

Mr. HEALY.—I thought it was something terrible.

Mr. REDMOND.—I don't know anything more terrible than
accusations of bad faith and falsehood to your colleagues and
country. (Cheers.) Mr. Redmond went on to ask whether it
was unreasonable for Mr. Parnell to ask for security that the
Irish Parliament should have the control of the police and power
to settle the land question, and before surrendering his position
to ask from the majority an expression of opinion on those points.
When Mr. Parnell had made it absolutely certain that the Home

Rule Bill would be a reality and not a sham, then he would place his future in the hands of a majority which he knew was hostile to him at that moment. (Cheers.) How could that be a change of attitude ? The change of attitude was on the part of Mr. Healy. (Hear, hear.) He characterized Mr. Healy's speech as the worst-tempered and most hysterical speech that was ever delivered by a man in the position of a leading politician. He appealed to Mr. Sexton to say what difference there was between Mr. Parnell's attitude yesterday and to-day. When Mr. Clancy's amendment was moved Mr. Parnell was asked a question, and in reply he had given an answer that would be received in Ireland as it was received by his colleagues, as another proof of his soundness of purpose and his devotion to the cause which had led to the very threshold of victory. (Hear, hear.) His opponents were men who were willing to accept the vague assurances of Mr. Gladstone as to the future of Home Rule. They were men who were willing to sacrifice Mr. Parnell without thought or heed of what that sacrifice would entail. They were going to sacrifice the one man who was capable of serving the nation. (Cheers.) They had in Mr Parnell the greatest Irishman since the days of Hugh O'Neill, and if he were driven out they would be obliged to take inferior men. But they had got him, and why should they drive him out ? He believed that in the moment when by an adverse vote of the party Mr. Parnell was driven from the chair and public life the Irish race throughout the world would be rent in twain. The one hope of safety for Ireland and the Home Rule cause was that Mr. Parnell should remain at his post, or else abdicate it having obtained for Ireland security for the settlement of that question. If he, Mr. Parnell, obtained that security for Ireland and then retired, he believed the Irish race would consent to his temporary withdrawal from the position he now occupied. (Cheers.)

Mr. SEXTON said he had listened to Mr. Parnell's speech with profound attention, and was sorry to say he had no option but to add that he had heard it with deepest disappointment and most piercing regret. (Hear, hear.) His sorrow was more permanent than any anger could be, and he should endeavour in the solemn words he would now address to the party to secure that his language should bear no trace of anger. (Hear, hear.) He wished from his heart that the speech of Mr. Redmond had answered to his avowed desire, but it was a peculiar quality of his intellect that whilst in one sentence, in its form and its substance, he seemed to appeal to the spirit of conciliation, in the next breath he proceeded to imputation, innuendoes, and even to open charges which appeared to him (Mr. Sexton) to render conciliation impossible. Mr. Redmond had accused Mr. Healy of making use of threats. Let it be remembered that Mr. Healy himself and others had been exposed in the course of that lamentable contention to the most offensive charges and the most abominable insinuations. (Hear, hear.) Mr. Healy's speech, however it may have touched them in point of form, was impregnated and possessed by the spirit of a great constitutional argument. (Hear, hear.) Mr. Healy said that he was prepared to follow his convictions to the point of action. Could any man opposite say less ? Mr. Sexton said that never to his knowledge in the course of political history had there been cast upon any body of public representatives an imputation so injurious and so undeserved—that they were acting in an unpatriotic spirit because against the position of any man whatever they preferred the cause of their nation. (Cheers.) They stood by Mr. Parnell so long as they thought it within the range of human possibility that the continued leadership of their party by Mr. Parnell was compatible with any remaining national hope of the freedom of their country (cheers), but at a certain stage it ceased to be a question of clamour and became a question of political force. (Hear, hear.) They were elected by the people of Ireland to conduct the Parliamentary cause. Their first duty, therefore, was to guard the Parliamentary position (hear, hear), and as soon as it became apparent to them that the result of Mr. Parnell's retention of his leadership would be infallibly to draw away from the Liberal camp a sufficient proportion of the electors of the country to render victory impossible, as soon as the supreme interest of Ireland became visibly and undeniably concerned, their duty was, when the cause presented itself as between a nation and a man, to call upon the man to retire, and to stand indomitably by the nation. (Loud cheers.) But of all that had happened to pain and humiliate him, nothing had excited in him those feelings more potently than the argument that the cause of Ireland without Mr. Parnell became a hopeless cause. (Hear, hear.)

Mr. REDMOND.—Who said that ? (Cries of " Order.")

Mr. SEXTON said that the standing argument upon the other side was that the retention of Mr. Parnell was necessary for the salvation of Ireland. (Cheers.) He contended that no man was necessary. Whether the chairmanship were or were not left vacant, the party was composed of honest men, and independent men, and never more than at the present time had they given such painful proof of their independence. That party was, and would be, dominated by the spirit of the Irish people themselves, and no matter who might lead, the pitiable calumny against the Irish nation would not come true, that that party would ever be the tail of any party. (Cheers.) It was clearly suggested that Mr. Parnell's leadership was indispensable. It was perfectly possible for that party to elect a man with great knowledge, with remarkable culture, and with an intellectual ability which would enable him to cope in any emergency with even the most sophistical statesman. He, for his part, had no other ambition but to serve his country in the ranks. (Cheers.) He declared there was no personal ambition in the party which need stand in the way of an ample and efficient leadership. Never in political history was there a party constituted so full of mutual regard and respect, and so possessed and interpenetrated by the spirit of confidence and of friendship. (Cheers.) Let any man say what he would, that party was bound together by links of steel which no man, and no question of leadership, could injuriously affect ; and if they were to change their leader it would be possible for them to surround him with a Cabinet ; and in this connexion he had told Mr. Parnell that in his retirement he could nominate the committee—conclusive proof that he (Mr. Sexton), at any rate, in the future government of the party thought there should be no taint of hostility to him (Mr. Parnell) or anything which could operate detrimentally to Ireland. (Cheers.) He felt obliged to refer to the language employed towards Mr. Gladstone. They had long been a nation in the valley of the shadow of death. Generations of their countrymen had yearned in vain and had died without finding their prayer granted. What had Mr. Gladstone done for Ireland ? At a time of his life when he had a natural claim for repose he had prolonged his labours for the sake, and for the single sake, of securing the freedom of Ireland. (Cheers.) Who would say that for the last four years any man of the Irish party had laboured with more ardour than Mr. Gladstone ? (Hear, hear.) He had to encounter the heat of the whole nation and the prejudices of race and creed. He set himself to the task with a strong resolution, and in his (Mr. Sexton's) judgment he had performed it so far with unrivalled intellectual power, with the ardour and energy of youth, and with the most extraordinary success. (Cheers.) The *Freeman's Journal* had spoken of him (Mr. Sexton) as Mr. Gladstone's man. (Laughter.) He appealed to his friends opposite—and he thought they would always be his friends in private life (cheers)—did anybody in that assembly think he was Mr. Gladstone's man ? (Cheers.) He had never spoken to Mr. Gladstone but once, when the right hon. gentleman spoke to him in the House. Any attempt to misrepresent the position of Mr. Gladstone was discreditable to the generosity of the Irish race. He was not Mr. Gladstone's man. (Cheers.) In all humility he said he was Ireland's man. (Cheers.) And he was not prepared to allow any man to become Ireland's master. (Cheers.) They called Mr. Gladstone a dictator. What option had Mr. Gladstone ? He did not speak with haste. The letter was published, he (Mr. Sexton) admitted, with regrettable haste. (Cheers.) But he (Mr. Sexton) had heard—he was not in a position to declare it—that before that letter was published those who authorized the publication of it were under the fixed impression that the communication which had passed between the Liberal leaders and the Irish members, and the substance if not the terms of the letter itself, had come to the knowledge of the Irish party. Lord Salisbury won the contested elections of 1886 by only one vote in 40, and did any one say that the storm of feeling which had recently been excited over England would not probably detach from the Liberal strength a greater number than one in 40 ? Did any one say that Mr. Gladstone was wrong in concluding that if the situation remained unchanged his position as leader would be futile ? Yesterday he (Mr. Sexton) asked Mr. Parnell, upon view of Mr. Clancy s resolution, what authority would determine, in the event of a reply from the Liberal leaders upon the proposed negotiations—what authority would determine whether the reply was satisfactory or not. (Hear, hear.) Mr. Parnell's reply was in these words :—" I have every belief and I feel every confidence in such an issue as that placed before the Irish party—the question as to securing any future important provisions, and as to the power of the Irish Parliament—that there will be no difference of opinion between me and the party as to whether these future declarations are satisfactory or not." Why, then, was the position changed?

MR. PARNELL.—It is not changed. There is not an atom of change so far as you are concerned.

MR. SEXTON said he exerted himself assiduously last evening by conference with some of his friends to secure an honourable and amicable settlement, and he might say their hopes were such as did not now appear to him to correspond with the result. (Hear, hear.) He (Mr. Sexton) complained that Mr. Clancy on the previous evening declined to show him the amendment. Why was it denied to them until the moment before they rose to discuss it? Mr. Clancy's amendment was in effect a trap-door resolution. Mr. Redmond must have known that the party would only conclude that satisfactory assurances would be assurances satisfactory to the majority of the party. Now, however, closer questioning had discovered the fact that if they were to assent to Mr. Clancy's amendment they might meet there weeks hence or months, and find themselves in the position in which all their efforts would be of no avail.

MR. PARNELL.—No.

MR. SEXTON, continuing, said Mr. Parnell would be as absolutely dictator of the situation as he was at present.

MR. PARNELL.—I am not dictator of the situation at present.

MR. SEXTON.—It appears to me that Mr. Parnell will not deny that the majority of the party have the right to decide what is satisfactory as to the assurances.

MR. PARNELL.—I am not denying it. (Cheers.) I think this is a storm in a teacup.

MR. SEXTON said a situation had been created which none of them might be able to end. The American mission had been ruined, and their race in America were in danger of being torn by dissension. It was, therefore, of the utmost importance that they should secure some speedy solution of the crisis. How did Mr. Parnell propose to secure that? Mr Parnell asked them to turn aside from Mr. Clancy's amendment, which was his own, and to consider other and different proposals.

MR. PARNELL said he was quite willing, if it was so wished, that they should carry out the matter of Mr. Clancy's amendment.

Mr. Sexton.—If I understand Mr. Parnell correctly he said that upon the adoption of Mr. Clancy's amendment it was unequivocally understood that the majority of the party would have the right to determine, without these resolutions, whether the replies, if any, of the Liberal leaders are satisfactory. If that is so it alters the situation.

Mr. Parnell.—I never heard a word of objection to these resolutions until Mr. Healy's speech. I simply put forward these resolutions as a means of carrying out the scope of Mr. Clancy's amendment.

Mr. Sexton.—Mr. Parnell refuses to let us go into conference with the Liberal leaders unless we first bind ourselves as to the terms of the reference.

Mr. Parnell.—No.

Mr. Sexton said they might then proceed on the assumption that the resolutions were not to be moved. Here was the first submitted to Mr. Parnell :—" That, in the opinion of the Irish Parliamentary party, no Home Rule Bill will be satisfactory or acceptable to the Irish people which will not confer the immediate control of the Irish police on an Irish Executive responsible to an Irish Parliament ; and, secondly, which does not confer on the Irish Parliament full power to deal with the Irish land question.

Mr. Parnell, referring to his first resolution, said,—I believe that is the view of the party, and all I have to say is that if you take these proposals to the Liberal leaders, and if you say that the answer of the Liberal leaders upon those two points is satisfactory to you, and if you decide that it is so satisfactory by resolution, it will be satisfactory to me. (Loud and general cheering.)

Mr. Sexton.—In that case will these resolutions be withdrawn ?

Mr. Parnell.—I have not moved them. But I shall propose that the party should express its opinion upon the answer by resolution. I want simply to have an expression from the party, either first or last, so that the responsibility should be thrown off my shoulders.

Mr. Sexton suggested that if Mr. Clancy's amendment were carried the delegation should wait upon Mr. Gladstone himself.

Mr. Parnell.—I should insist strongly upon the three leaders,

Mr. Gladstone, Sir W. Harcourt, and Mr. Morley, being present, for reasons which I can give if necessary.

Mr. SEXTON asked Mr. Parnell if he would resign if, by vote, the majority of the party decided the answer of the Liberal leaders was satisfactory ?

Mr. PARNELL.—Certainly ; you might have had that at the beginning of the meeting, if you had not had Mr. Healy's speech.

Mr. HEALY.—No, Sir ; if we had not your speech.

Mr. SEXTON asked whether there would be any objection to appoint with the Whips one or two representatives of each section of the party as members of the delegation.

Mr. PARNELL.—So four or five of them could be formed into a committee and retire to consider the subject.

Dr. KENNY thereupon moved that the chairman, Mr. John Barry, Mr. Leamy, Mr. Sexton, Mr. T. M. Healy, Mr. Justin M'Carthy, and the two Whips be formed into a committee.

Mr. BARRY said he did not distinctly understand the position, and suggested that Mr. Parnell should make a distinct statement as to what his position would be in the event of the answer of the Liberal leaders being satisfactory. (Cries of " Oh, oh.")

Mr. PARNELL (vehemently).—Mr. Barry, I tell you this. I have stated with distinctness over and over again what my course will be, and I will give no further answer. (Loud cheers.)

Mr. BARRY.—I say this for myself, that I am not satisfied. (Cries of " Oh, oh.")

Mr. SHEEHY.—Mr. Parnell's statement is perfectly sufficient.

Mr. SEXTON said they all agreed that if Mr. Clancy's amendment was adopted the delegation would proceed to the English Liberal leaders, and if the answer was satisfactory Mr. Parnell had declared that he would voluntarily and of his own accord relinquish the leadership. If those negotiations, which appeared to him to stand upon a satisfactory basis, were carried to a successful issue, he believed that what otherwise might have been the decline of Mr. Parnell's career, and what might be treated as his fall, would be memorable as having been accompanied by one of the most distinguished achievements of his life. (Cheers.)

Mr. W. REDMOND, who spoke with emotion, claimed his right to put one question. (Cries of " Order.") In face of what had taken place within the last five minutes, who was the man who would say that Charles Stewart Parnell (renewed cries of

" Order ") was animated by any personal motive, or that he was not acting for the love of Ireland, and the love of Ireland alone ? (Loud cheers.)

Mr. Barry.—I do not believe he is. (Cries of " Oh !")

Mr. Sexton, continuing, asked that Mr. Clancy's amendment should be put from the Chair, and then if any man had anything to say against it let him say it. For himself, he would tell his friends to accept the amendment.

Mr. Healy suggested that before the amendment was put they should have an opportunity of considering its exact terms, and proposed that it should be suspended for a time.

Mr. Parnell.—That comes back to my suggestion.

Mr. O'Kelly appealed to them as representatives of Ireland, and in the name of the Irish race, to pass the amendment as it stood. (Hear, hear.) He believed that the declarations of their chief would be carried out to the letter, and he appealed to them not to interfere with the settlement, and perhaps to-morrow they would once more be a united party.

In the course of a discussion on the question of appointing a committee to consider the terms of the reference to be made to the leaders of the Liberal party,

Mr. Healy said he would like to substitute for his name on the committee the name of Mr. Arthur O'Connor.

Mr. Sexton.—I have a similar feeling, as I have taken a highly contentious part. (" No, no.")

Mr. Parnell read the resolution.—" That, in view of the difference of opinion that has arisen between Mr. Gladstone and Mr. Parnell as to the accuracy of Mr. Parnell's recollection of the suggestions offered at Hawarden in reference to suggested changes in and departures from the Home Rule Bill of 1886, on the subject of the control of the constabulary and the settlement of the land question, Mr. Justin M'Carthy, Mr. Parnell, Mr. Sexton, Mr. Healy, Mr. Redmond, and Mr. Leamy, together with the two Whips of the party, be instructed to take steps to obtain from Mr. Gladstone, Mr. John Morley, and Sir William Harcourt, for the information of the party, before any further consideration of this question, what their views are with regard to these two vital points."

The resolution was put, and Mr. Parnell declared that the Ayes had it. Mr. Barry challenged this, and called for a division. Mr. Parnell took a show of hands. Mr. Barry and Mr. Chance again held up their hands against the resolution, which was declared carried amid cheers.

The meeting adjourned to 12 o'clock on Friday, December 5.

Mr. Flynn asked whether it would not be well, in view of the naturally heated proceedings, that the same rule as formerly should be observed with regard to publication.

Mr. Parnell.—The report has gone already.

Mr. A. O'Connor asked whether the eight gentlemen who had been named were to go and request an interview with Sir William Harcourt, Mr. Morley, and Mr. Gladstone.

Mr. Parnell said the details must be left to the committee. The resolution was that they were to take steps to obtain from those gentlemen, for the information of the party, their views with regard to these vital points.

Mr. T. Healy said he had a strong objection to go on any such delegation.

Mr. Parnell.—That is a matter which the committee can settle when they meet.

The proceedings then terminated, and the members of the delegation remained in private consultation as to the means to be adopted to carry out the wishes of the meeting.

MEETING OF THE IRISH PARTY—SEVENTH DAY— NEGOTIATIONS WITH MR. GLADSTONE.

In pursuance of Mr. Clancy's resolution adopted by the Irish party on December 4, the members therein named, namely Mr. Justin M'Carthy, Mr. Parnell, Mr. Sexton, Mr. T. Healy, Mr. Redmond, and Mr. Leamy, together with the Whips, Mr. R. Power and Mr. J. Deasy, met and selected from their number Messrs. Sexton, T. Healy, John Redmond, and Leamy as a deputation to seek interviews with Mr. Gladstone, Sir William Harcourt, and Mr. John Morley.

The following account of the delegates' proceedings is taken from the official report presented by them to the Irish party on Saturday, December 6.

The Whips addressed to Mr. Gladstone, Sir William Harcourt, and Mr. John Morley severally, the following letter :—

" House of Commons, Dec. 4, 1890. Sir,—We are directed to inform you that at a meeting of the Irish Parliamentary party the following gentlemen have been appointed to seek an interview with you—viz., Messrs. Leamy, John Redmond, Sexton, and T. M. Healy—to inquire, for the information of the party, as to the manner in which the Liberal leaders would be prepared to treat certain subjects in the event of their being in a position in a future Parliament to deal legislatively with them. The subjects in question are the settlement of the agrarian difficulty in Ireland and the control of the Irish police. A similar request has been addressed to Sir William Harcourt and Mr. John Morley. We have the honour to remain your obedient servants,

" RICHARD POWER,   } Whips."
" JOHN DEASY,   }

The following were the replies received :—

" House of Commons, Dec. 4, 1890. Gentlemen,—I have the honour to acknowledge the receipt of your letter of this day. Whilst expressing my sense of the honour you have done me in desiring to learn from me ' the manner in which the Liberal leaders would be prepared to treat certain subjects in the event of their being in a position in a future Parliament to deal legislatively with them,' you must permit me to point out that I have no authority to determine such matters, and that Mr. Gladstone alone, as leader of the Liberal party, can speak in its name. You will understand, therefore, that it is from no want of courtesy that I find myself precluded from accepting an invitation to an interview such as you have been good enough to propose to me. I have the honour to remain your obedient servant,

" W. V. HARCOURT."

" House of Commons, Dec. 4, 1890. Gentlemen,—I am extremely sensible of the honour of your invitation, but it is strictly the duty of Mr. Gladstone, as the leader of the Liberal party, to determine the time and manner of stating the plan of dealing with the subjects mentioned in your letter which he would be prepared to recommend to his party and to Parliament. I must therefore very respectfully beg you to excuse me from intervening under the present circumstances in the way that you propose. Yours faithfully,   " JOHN MORLEY."

"1, Carlton-gardens, Dec. 4, 1890. Gentlemen,—So far as I comprehend the tenour of the letter I have just had the honour to receive, I understand that it is proposed by you to constitute a body with the assistance of Sir William Harcourt, Mr. Morley, and myself, which body is to deliver to you assurances as to the course which the Liberal party, if in power, would take in a future Parliament with regard to two of the many important particulars connected with any plan of Home Rule. I would on no account attempt to fetter in any way your liberty of communication in any quarter to which you may think proper to address yourselves, but I regret to be unable to enter upon the joint consideration of any matter submitted to me in combination with a selection of my friends and former colleagues which has been made neither by me nor by the Liberal party of this country. I leave it to you to consider how far this leaves it open to you to prosecute further your request, and I think it best at the present moment to abstain from touching upon any point except the one I have just raised. I remain, dear Sirs, yours faithfully,

"W. E. GLADSTONE."

The official report proceeds :—

" In consequence of the views expressed in these letters, the following communication to Mr. Gladstone was prepared by the committee and addressed to him by the Whips :—

" ' House of Commons, December 4, 1890. Sir,—We have the honour to acknowledge the receipt of your courteous reply to our inquiry. The names of Sir William Harcourt and Mr. John Morley were suggested with a view to greater convenience and facility of consultation. We are now instructed to say that we shall regard an interview with yourself, either alone or with any of your political friends whom you may be pleased to select, as for the purpose of enabling us substantially to discharge the commission with which we have been intrusted. We have the honour to remain your obedient servants,

" ' RICHARD POWER,
" ' JOHN DEASY.

" ' The Right Hon. W. E. Gladstone.' "

On receipt of this reply, Mr. Gladstone consented to see the delegates. The interview took place at 1, Carlton-gardens, at half-past 12, on Friday, December 5. The official report says :—

" In accordance with a memorandum previously agreed upon

between the delegates, the views of the party were submitted to Mr. Gladstone by Mr. Sexton. The following are the terms of the memorandum :—

" ' Clause 21 of the Home Rule Bill of 1886.—(1) To ask that subsection (a) of the clause be applied to the Royal Irish Constabulary as well as to the Dublin Metropolitan Police, and that subsection (b) of the clause be omitted.

" ' (2) To ask that Mr. Gladstone shall state whether the Liberal leaders intend to deal with the land question themselves in the Imperial Parliament, either by purchase or on the lines of the measure introduced by the Irish party and supported by the Liberal party, or by remitting the question to the Irish Legislature.

" ' (3) To ask that any proposals of the Liberal party in pursuance of the two foregoing articles shall be treated by them as vital.'

" Mr. Gladstone, in his reply, spoke from a written document, and the delegates agreed upon the following memorandum as containing their joint recollection of what he said to the effect that while he was willing at all times to confer with Irish members on questions affecting their country, such a conference was barred when it was sought for the declared purpose of determining a question of recollection as to the Hawarden conversation. Mr. Sexton asked if he felt it within his province to say whether the barrier could be removed, and in what way. Mr. Gladstone said that it was not within his province to make a suggestion which might be regarded as an interference with the independence of the Irish party. Mr. Redmond asked, if this barrier were removed, might it be hoped that these conferences would proceed. Mr. Gladstone replied that in that case he would regard the matter as if the barrier had not existed. As the deputation was leaving he remarked that, as regarded the police, he would have little difficulty in speaking.

" The statement made by Mr. Gladstone to the deputation was made from a written document, a copy of which was forwarded to the delegates. It is as follows :—

" ' I have never been indisposed to converse freely with Irish members on Irish policy, and there is nothing which I have heard from Mr. Sexton in the statement he has just made which in any degree tends to produce such indisposition. I have no opinion

L

or intention of any kind to conceal, but since writing my letter of last evening I have read in the papers of to-day the report of the proceedings of the Irish party at their last meeting. I find there is no appointment of a deputation, but, as far as I understand, you have been delegated by a committee which (*a*) is composed of certain persons ; (*b*) appointed to dispose of a question of a difference of recollection as to the purport of an interview at Hawarden.

" 'I fear that there is here a preliminary bar to any communications on the matters you desire to open. I acknowledge no such difference of recollection. I can say or do nothing which should imply that the general purport of that interview is matter of doubt. Besides my own recollection and written notes, and the recollections of my former colleagues founded thereon, I rely on the recollections of the other party to the interview conveyed in communications with one or more individuals and in public speeches both immediately after the visit and again when several months had elapsed. Viewing as a whole the language used by me in my letter to Mr. Morley, and in my published letter of last Saturday, I cannot, apart from any other difficulty, enter into a discussion having for its object to dispose of a difference of recollection which I do not acknowledge to exist. Further, I may say that the question raised by my letter to Mr. Morley was a question of leadership, representing what I found to be the views of the Liberal party of Great Britain, and having no connexion with Home Rule or its conditions. But what is now requested of me makes the question a question of Home Rule, and I am asked to open a new discussion on a separate ground. The British Liberal party is enthusiastic for Home Rule, but the trust which it has committed to me does not authorize me to open such a discussion in connexion with the question of leadership, on which they entertain a separate and decided opinion.' "

In order to remove the barrier referred to by Mr. Gladstone, the delegates then unanimously decided, in consultation with Mr. Parnell, Mr. Justin M'Carthy, and the Whips of the party, to recommend the party to rescind Mr. Clancy's amendment and to adopt the following resolution :—

" That the following members of the party—viz., Mr. Leamy, Mr. John Redmond, Mr. T. Healy, and Mr. Sexton—are hereby authorized to request a conference with Mr. Gladstone for the

Dec. 5.

purpose of representing the views of this party, and of requesting an intimation of the intentions of himself and his colleagues with respect to certain details connected with the following subjects : —First, the settlement of the Irish land question ; second, the control of the Irish constabulary force in the event of the establishment of an Irish Legislature.''

With this object the delegates met their colleagues in No. 15 Committee Room at 4 o'clock.

MR. REDMOND moved and MR. SEXTON seconded the rescission of Mr. Clancy's resolution, which was carried unanimously.

MR. REDMOND moved and MR. SEXTON seconded the substituted resolution stated above, which was carried, MR. BARRY and MR. CHANCE dissenting.

The official report records that, in pursuance of the foregoing resolution, the Whips addressed the following letter to Mr. Gladstone :—

" Sir,—We have the honour to inform you that at a meeting of the Irish party, held at 4 o'clock this day, the accompanying resolutions were unanimously passed. We are directed by the gentlemen named in the second resolution to request the favour of an interview.''

The following reply was received from Mr. Gladstone late the same night :—

"1, Carlton-gardens, Dec. 5, 1890.

" Gentlemen,—I have the honour to acknowledge the receipt of your letter transmitting to me two resolutions of the Irish Parliamentary party. By the first of these resolutions, the subject of our correspondence is entirely detached from connexion with the conversation at Hawarden. In the second I am requested to receive a deputation which, besides stating the views of the party, is to request an intimation of my intentions, and those of my colleagues, as to certain details connected with the subject of the settlement of the Irish land question and with the control of the Irish constabulary force in the event of the establishment of an Irish Legislature.

" As your letter reached me during the early hours of the sitting of the House, I have had the opportunity of learning the views of my colleagues with regard to such a declaration of intention on two out of the many points which may be regarded as vital to the construction of a Government measure of Home Rule. I may be permitted to remind you, as I mentioned to the deputation this morning, that the question raised by the publication of my letter to Mr. Morley was a question of leadership, and that it is separate from, and had no proper connexion with, the subject of Home Rule. I have arrived at the conclusion that I cannot undertake to make any statement of our intentions on those or any other provisions of a Home Rule Bill in connexion with the question of the leadership of the Irish party. When the Irish party shall have disposed of this question, which belongs entirely to their own competence, in such a manner as will enable me to renew the former relations, it will be my desire to enter, without prejudice, into confidential communication, such as has heretofore taken place, as occasion may serve, upon all amendment of particulars and suggestion of improvements in any plan for a measure of Home Rule.

" I may venture to assure you that no change has taken place in my desire to press forward on the first favourable opportunity a just and effective measure of Home Rule. I recognize and earnestly seek to uphold the independence of the Irish Parliamentary party no less than that of the Liberal party. I acknowledge with satisfaction the harmony which, since 1886, has prevailed between them, and, when the present difficulty is removed, I am aware of no reason to anticipate its interruption. From what has taken place on both sides of the Channel in the last four years I look forward with confidence, as do my colleagues, to the formation and prosecution of a measure which, in meeting all the just claims of Ireland, will likewise obtain the approval of the people of Great Britain.

" I shall at all suitable times prize the privilege of free communication with the Irish Nationalist party, and I will finally remind you of my declaration this morning that, apart from personal confidence, there is but one guarantee which can be of real value to Ireland. It is that recently pointed out by Sir William Harcourt in his letter of December 2, when he called attention to " the unquestionable political fact that no party and no leaders could ever propose or hope to carry any scheme of Home Rule which had not the cordial concurrence and support of the Irish

nation as declared by their representatives in Parliament."
With this statement of my views and those of my colleagues I
anticipate that you will agree with me in the opinion that there
would be no advantage in a further personal interview.

" I have the honour to be, gentlemen, yours faithfully,

" W. E. GLADSTONE."

CHAPTER V

RUPTURE OF THE IRISH PARTY—MR. PARNELL'S DEPARTURE FOR IRELAND.

Saturday, December 6, was the eighth and last day of the meetings of the Irish party. The members assembled at 1 o'clock in No. 15 Committee Room.

Mr. PARNELL took the chair, and said :—

Gentlemen,—This meeting is assembled for the purpose of receiving the report of the delegation appointed at the last meeting of the party to request a conference with Mr. Gladstone for the purpose of representing the view of this party in respect to certain details connected with the following subjects. First, the settlement of the land question, and, secondly, the control of the Irish constabulary force, in the event of the establishment of an Irish Legislature. I wish to know whether the delegates are present and are prepared to present their report.

Dr. KENNY (who was received with cries of "The delegates, the delegates") said,—I beg to move that the delegates be requested to retire to prepare a report for the information of this meeting, and that the sitting be suspended pending their return. ("Hear, hear," and "No, no.")

The proposal was seconded by Mr. MAHONY and opposed by Mr. T. HEALY, and, after a short but heated debate, was put to the vote. On a show of hands being taken, 25 were for the resolution and 34 against.

The resolution was therefore declared lost.

Mr. T. M. HEALY.—I have a motion to make which will put the meeting in order :—"That communications between this party and the Liberal leaders be read, as well as the report of the delegates' interview with Mr. Gladstone, already agreed to and signed by them."

Mr. E. Harrington.—I would appeal to my friend to take a different view. We all know what the object of our meeting yesterday was, and we all expected to have a report for this meeting. I may say nothing whatever about what has occurred since, and I am surprised that Mr. Sexton, who would be one of those to bring forward this report, did not support Dr. Kenny's motion. (Cries of " Order.") I do not want to be personal.

Mr. Sexton.—I will answer you.

Mr. Harrington.—I know nothing of the report, and I want now to know all about it. (Hear, hear.)

Mr. John Barry.—It is quite ready.

Mr. E. Harrington.—How do I know it is ready, or why should you know it before it is presented ? (Hear, hear.) I am as much of a partisan as you are, and I may tell you I am prepared to meet you on any ground. (Cheers.)

Mr. Barry.—The four delegates say it is ready.

Mr. Kilbride did not think there was any necessity for a resolution, and added,—"In God's name let the delegates now retire to report."

Mr. Parnell.—Well, then, will the delegates retire ?

Mr. Sexton said he should have been willing to retire, but he agreed with Mr. Healy that there was no necessity to put them under a formal direction, and he thought the delegates could add nothing to the material before the chair. If they were pressed to report, all they could do was to make a catalogue of the documents.

Mr. Parnell.—Hear, hear. Put the documents in the order in which they must be presented.

Mr. Redmond claimed that every step taken by the delegates since the appointment of the delegation should be recorded and put before them in proper sequence. If he had considered Dr. Kenny's resolution an insult to the delegates, he should have resented it as readily as Mr. Sexton; but the matter was important, and not one or two letters, but all of them, should be placed before the public. He appealed to the three other delegates to go with him into the next room for ten minutes, and come back with a report.

Mr. Barry.—Well, fire away. (Cries of " Go.")

After some further discussion, in which Colonel Nolan and Mr. Sexton took part,

Mr. John O'Connor made an earnest appeal in favour of the delegates retiring to prepare the report.

Mr. W. Redmond said he certainly thought that the delegates should retire at once. (Hear, hear.)

Mr. W. A. Macdonald failed to understand Mr. Healy's tactics. Mr. Healy had begun by saying—" Withdraw the resolution and we will retire, and the thing will be done in five minutes." It was not withdrawn, but was put in the ordinary way; but how did that alter the case ? He hoped they would not stand upon technicalities, but that the delegates would at once give them the report.

Mr. Justin M'Carthy deprecated any waste of time in debating this question, and suggested that they should leave it to the delegates to make the report in the form they thought best.

Mr. Parnell, at Mr. Healy's request, read that gentleman's resolution.

Mr. Parnell then said,—I will shortly explain why I object to the adoption of the resolution of Mr. Healy. My objection may be contained in a single sentence,—that I do not.think any piecemeal account of this matter should go before the country. (Cheers.) This business is, owing to circumstances which are not in the control of the meeting, becoming very conflicting. It consists of a number of communications made by our delegates to the Whips of the Liberal party, to Mr. Gladstone, to Mr. Morley, and to Sir William Harcourt. Some of these communications I have. I have been endeavouring--much assisted by the courtesy of the delegates—to keep myself informed of the subjects occupying the attention of the delegates during the interviews. I have here some documents which I have endeavoured to collect as the matter went on, but I have not got them all. I believe these documents are forthcoming ; but it is absolutely necessary, to enable you to understand what has been done ——

Mr. T. M. Healy.—What documents do you require ?

Mr. Parnell.—I cannot tell.

Mr. Healy.—You have got all we have got. (Hear, hear.)

Mr. Parnell.—I don't accuse Mr. Healy or any one else of suppressing any of the documents.

Mr. Healy.—You have got everything that is there.

Mr. Parnell.—Of course I have got everything that is here. (Laughter.)

Mr. Healy.—Everything that exists. (Hear, hear.)

Mr. Parnell.—The documents I have not got are in existence and capable of production for this meeting, and I submit they ought to be produced. How is it possible for you to understand this position unless the full information is put before you? (Hear, hear.) The only persons who can put the full position before you are the delegates. There is no blame attaching to the delegates for not having prepared their report. Up to late last night the delegates, after a series of complicated communications, were in waiting for Mr. Gladstone's formal and definite reply. That reply was not received till 10 o'clock. The delegates were good enough to assemble in my room at the Westminster Palace Hotel to consider the entirely new situation which has been created by that reply. I suggested to the delegates, while the matter was fresh in their memory, to put down on paper their recollections, as far as the recollections coincided, and the conversation which took place with Mr. Gladstone at the interview yesterday. This they were kind enough to do, and this recollection of the conversation is what Mr. Healy terms in this resolution the report of the delegates' interview with Mr. Gladstone, already agreed to and signed by them. It is true it was agreed to as containing the joint recollections of the delegates of this most important interview. I did not ask them to go any further. I said to them, "Put down so much on paper, but I don't wish to ask you to consider the question individually or go any further on the present occasion than putting in writing your joint recollections." That is all that has been done by the delegates in regard to framing a report—absolutely all. That memorandum is here amongst the papers I have in my possession, and will undoubtedly form a portion of what the delegates have to report to you. But it cannot possibly be the sole report. What I want is that these important events shall be placed before you in a collected form so that you may understand how the matter rests. I do not understand why we have got into this tangle. You seem to think that I am in some way so deep that you cannot trust me to take a single step without supposing that I am endeavouring to drag you into some quagmire or morass. I assure you that there is nothing further from my intention. All that I wish is that you be put into possession of all information possible from the delegates, which information is to be put into an orderly and regular fashion and will form portion of our proceedings. I will ask Mr. Healy how far he is acting in accordance with his deliberate judgment of what is just and right in this matter when he asks us to go into the consideration of this grave and momentous position in a fragmentary fashion. (Hear, hear.)

MR. T. M. HEALY reciprocated the courtesy and friendliness with which Mr. Parnell met them the previous evening. The first matter that arose was the communication from Mr. Gladstone to them. Then followed Mr. Gladstone's reply, and their reply to Mr. Gladstone. All these matters were in writing. Then followed their interview with Mr. Gladstone. On Friday night, on the suggestion and by the direction of Mr. Parnell, the four delegates agreed to draw up a memorandum of their joint recollections with regard to that interview. That, therefore, existed in writing. Then followed the rescinding of Mr. Clancy's resolution and the passing of Mr. John Redmond's resolution. Those things were in writing. Then followed a fresh communication with Mr. Gladstone and a fresh interview. Then followed Mr. Gladstone's reply, and that also was in writing. There was no matter in relation to this case from start to finish that was not in writing. He could not see, therefore, why his resolution did not, to use a theatrical phrase, " exactly fill the bill." The only report he would consent to make was this—to stick six pins into these different documents and join them together, and make that their report to the meeting. (Hear, hear.) If the intention were that they were to go outside—and having spent two or three hours the previous night in Mr. Parnell's room in hammering their brains and cudgelling their intellects— to draw up an exact memorandum of what had occurred, if they were to go further into the matter and take up time in trying to come to some further arrangement on the point, he declined. Every word that Mr. Gladstone uttered to the delegates in the first instance was read from a written communication, and in order that there might be no conflict as to its contents, he himself on the previous night advised that Mr. Richard Power should address a communication to Mr. Arnold Morley, who was present during the interview, with reference to the statement.

MR. PARNELL said Mr. Power had obtained that.

MR. HEALY said that everything that was done was under Mr.

Parnell's own eyes, and so careful was he on the previous night that he took two copies of the documents from Mr. Sexton. What were the documents that were not before him ?

MR. PARNELL.—I have not all the documents before me.

MR. HEALY said that must be the fault of Mr. Parnell's own Whip and supporter, Mr. Power.

MR. ARTHUR O'CONNOR thought that the drawing up of a formal report might protract the proceedings. He hoped they would have some regard for their dignity in connexion with the proceedings.

DR. KENNY contended that the meeting had a right to require a narrative of the events in consecutive order. (MR. PARNELL.—Hear, hear.) It was quite possible that the report might be a separate report by every one of the delegates ; but what they wanted was a simple narrative of the facts as they occurred reduced to writing. The delegates must give a narrative of the whole proceedings, and he said they were simply wasting time. (Loud ironical cheers from Mr. Parnell's opponents.)

MR. LEAMY.—We have no desire to waste time.

DR. KENNY.—It is ridiculous and insulting to insinuate that we are wasting time. (Cries of " Divide, divide.")

MR. E. HARRINGTON.—Rowdyism will not carry this.

MR. POWER, in the course of further discussion, said Mr. Redmond had prepared a short report.

MR. PARNELL remarked that there was nothing to prevent Mr. Redmond from giving his narrative of his share in the proceedings, but the question they were discussing was whether all the delegates should retire to make a joint report.

MR. HEALY —I am afraid if this thing goes on there will be more retiring than the retiring of the delegates.

MR. PARNELL said that upon Mr. Healy's amendment there was nothing to prevent Mr. Redmond, or any other delegate, from giving his account of what took place. At the same time it would be an immensely more convenient course if they would, without directing, allow the four delegates to retire and arrange the narrative for consideration.

MR. BARRY.—Well, put Mr. Healy's motion.

MR. REDMOND.—Will I be allowed to say one word ? (Cries of " No" and " Spoke.")

MR. SEXTON.—Hear Mr. Redmond.

MR. REDMOND repeated that the matter was so important that the country would claim to have a precise and chronologically arranged narrative of the different documents.

MR. HEALY said that could be done under his resolution, and that, if Mr. Parnell liked, he would add to his resolution the words "in chronological order."

MR. J. NOLAN said the deputation would only have been showing some courtesy in laying before the meeting a formal report, and he complained bitterly of the unnecessary waste of time that had taken place.

MR. BARRY called attention to Mr. Healy's proposal.

MR. PARNELL.—That does not carry out Mr. Redmond's proposal.

MR. HEALY.—That is what he said.

MR. REDMOND.—This is one of the things. I want not only the documents, but every event which led to them. (Cheers.)

MR. BLANE considered that the delegates were bound to give a report to the meeting that delegated them to conduct certain negotiations.

MR. O'KELLY said he thought they had a right to obtain the delegates' formal report on the matter. They had been engaged in proceedings of enormous importance, possibly the pivot on which the decision of the party should turn, and they had a right to demand that the history of the negotiations, which must have enormous influence, should be laid before them authoritatively. (Hear, hear.)

MR. MAHONY said that when he was speaking some time before Mr. Healy wished to retire with the other delegates. Why had he changed? What objection could there be to the delegates making that report when every one of them, even that ambitious gentleman Mr. Healy—(interruption, and cries of "Withdraw")—surely Mr. Healy did not hold a special licence to furnish taunts. (Hear, hear.) Mr. Healy took every opportunity of insulting them. ("No, no.") Well, he attacked as many of them as he could possibly find the opportunity. Mr. Healy would find that possibly they might be able to hit back. (Cheers.) Mr. Redmond was ready to make a report. Were they going to shut his mouth? ("No, no.") Well, if they carried Mr. Healy's motion they did shut his mouth.

MR. SEXTON.—No, no.

Mr. Clancy asked what objection they had to a formal report. If it were an easy matter, such as Mr. Healy and Mr. Sexton said it was, and could be done in ten minutes ——

Mr. Healy.—I was about to leave the room when stopped by Mr. Harrington's threats. (Hear, hear.)

Mr. E. Harrington.—Pardon me, now. I saw you leaving the room in an aggressive manner, as if inviting a following, and I told you to sit down—that neither now nor ever would you have a party. (Cheers.)

Mr. Healy rose to speak.

Mr. Harrington (in a loud voice).—You are doing everything to ruin the country. (Cheers, and cries of "Order.")

Mr. Healy (vehemently).—I repel the suggestion, and I retort it. (Counter cheers.)

Mr. Harrington.—I will say nothing now, but that we will find out. (Hear, hear.)

Mr. Clancy, resuming, said that it was agreed that the report could be done in five minutes.

Mr. Harrington.—Then let it be done now, in God's name. (Hear, hear.)

Mr. Clancy said that if the document were prepared no one could go outside its four corners hereafter, and that was an important consideration. (Hear, hear.) If there were any difference of opinion between the delegates there was no possible chance of that difference of opinion appearing there as a basis of discussion, for it would not be in the report.

Mr. John Redmond.—There is no difference of opinion.

Mr. Campbell appealed to Mr. Sexton, in the interests of peace and of the Irish race all the world over, to agree to let them have the documents, from which they could gather the facts, so as to be able to form their independent individual judgment on what had taken place.

Mr. Justin M'Carthy suggested that they should adjourn for luncheon.

Mr. R. Power seconded the motion.

Mr. Healy objected strongly to any adjournment. He thought that in a matter of that kind they should do without their luncheon. (Loud cheers.)

Dr. Fitzgerald urged that the delegates should be allowed to retire and consider their report, so that they might place before the country and the meeting a precise account of everything that had taken place. (Cheers.) Apparently, from the symptoms to be seen on the other side of the room, every man there knew the result of the negotiations which had taken place. He appealed to Mr. Sexton to retire with the other three delegates and place a plain issue before the party.

Mr. Sexton said the country was in an agony of suspense, and they found themselves led away day by day entirely from the main issue, which they would ultimately have to decide. Now, he did not think it would be proper for him at this stage to withhold the observation that the majority of the party had made up their minds (cheers and cries of "Oh, oh")——

Mr. Redmond.—They said that on Monday, too. (Hear, hear.)

Mr. Sexton (continuing) said they had made up their minds that these intolerably prolonged proceedings must be brought to a close to-day. If they could not be brought to a close by a motion from the chair, they must be determined in some other way. If his side were in a minority they would gladly retire ; but the fact that they were in a majority placed a deep obligation upon them. He was unwilling that the delegates should be called upon to consider a formal report. Certain communications had been made by them, and copies of the letters which they had written were in the hands of the officials ; and, in regard to the only matter which was not before them or in writing, the four delegates had already agreed to a narrative, committed it to writing, and verified it by their signatures. The majority of the party could not longer undertake the prolongation of the suspense to the country nor the strain on themselves. (" Oh, oh.") He could not endure it one day longer, and therefore, before the proceedings came to a close that day, they must ask Mr. Parnell to put a motion from the chair to determine the final question, or they would have to take such other measures as might be open to them. (Cheers.) In the course of his remarks. Mr. Sexton suggested an adjournment for half an hour, in accordance with Mr. M'Carthy's proposal.

Mr. Parnell.—It is proposed that we adjourn until a quarter past 3, and that in the interval we hope that the delegates will meet and come to some arrangement.

The motion for adjournment was then agreed to. On resuming after luncheon,

MR. PARNELL said,—Do you wish, Mr. Healy, to have your resolution modified ? I understand the delegates have come to some agreement as to the report they will present to us.

MR. HEALY said he moved his resolution believing that the object of the ·opposite side in desiring a report was that, the moment the report or any resolution about it was placed before the meeting, it was Mr. Parnell's intention to call upon some of his friends to move a further obstructive resolution upon that report.

MR. PARNELL said Mr. Healy must not impute motives or make assertions which he was not prepared to substantiate. He should confine himself to his resolution.

MR. HEALY said that, the delegates having agreed upon the report, thereby proving there was no conflict between them, he preferred leaving his motion with the meeting to be dealt with. Mr. Healy subsequently altered his resolution so that it read as follows :—" That the communications between this party and the Liberal leaders, as embodied in the report of the delegates, be read."

MR. PARNELL agreed to this.

MR. JOHN REDMOND then proceeded to read the report recording the negotiations with Mr. Gladstone described in Chapter IV. The substance of this document has .been given nearly *verbatim* above. It concludes as follows :—

" At all these conferences between the delegates, both before and after the written and oral communications above mentioned, the Whips and Mr. Parnell were present."

The report is signed—" Ed. Leamy, J. E. Redmond, Thos. Sexton, and T. M. Healy," and is dated December 6, 1890.

At the conclusion of the reading of the report a scene of great confusion arose, Mr. Abraham and Mr. John O'Connor rising together, and Mr. Parnell ruling that Mr. O'Connor had possession of the chair. Amid the confusion Mr. Abraham said he wished to move a resolution, and tried to read it, but he could not be heard. He thereupon handed it to Mr. M'Carthy, who rose, and was apparently about to read it, when Mr. Parnell, who throughout the scene remained standing, grasped the copy of the resolution from Mr. M'Carthy, saying, " I will not receive it." Mr. Parnell and Mr. M'Carthy then stood addressing each other amid cries of " Chair " and " Order."

Mr. PARNELL.—Until the party deposes me from the chair I am your chairman. (Loud cheers and counter-cheers.)

Mr. BARRY.—You are not our chairman. (Cheers, and cries of " Order.")

Mr. JUSTIN M'CARTHY addressed an observation to the chairman which could not be heard owing to the din.

Mr. PARNELL.—You attempted to move a resolution surreptitiously. (Cheers, and cries of " No.")

Mr. HEALY.—Give us back our document. (Cheers, counter-cheers, and interruption.)

Mr. PARNELL, in the midst of further disorder, still ruled that Mr. O'Connor had the chair, and Mr. BARRY exclaimed excitedly, " You're a dirty trickster." (Cries of " Order," " Chair," and interruption.)

Mr. PARNELL.—" Order, order." (Uproar.)

Mr. SHEEHY.—We will respect the Chair if it respects the party, but if the Chair does not respect the party we cannot respect the Chair. (Interruption.)

Mr. ARTHUR O'CONNOR.—I would appeal to my friends to manifest to the chairman, our late leader, every possible respect. He has called upon Mr. O'Connor. Let Mr. O'Connor speak. (Cheers and counter-cheers.)

Mr. T. HEALY was understood to state that Mr. O'Connor had not risen when Mr. Abraham was on his feet.

Mr. CORBET (warmly).—Healy, you will have to answer for this. (Cheers and counter-cheers.)

Mr. HEALY.—So will you, too.

Mr. PARNELL again called upon Mr. O'Connor, and repeated that he was their chairman until they deposed him.

Mr. HEALY.—Allow me to depose you. (Cheers and counter-cheers.)

Mr. PARNELL again called upon Mr. John O'Connor, but Mr. O'Connor was not allowed to proceed.

Mr. Sexton rose, and Mr. PARNELL exclaimed, " Silence, Sir. Mr. O'Connor."

Mr. SEXTON remarked that Mr. O'Connor was seated when Mr. Abraham rose, and Mr. ABRAHAM said that was true, but Mr. O'CONNOR denied it. Mr. SEXTON at last suggested that they should submit to the ruling of the Chair, and asked Mr. Parnell to call upon Mr. Abraham when Mr. O'Connor sat down.

MR. PARNELL.—Certainly. Of course it will be necessary for Mr. John O'Connor's resolution to be seconded.   ("Hear, hear," and ironical laughter.) I may state, for the information of the meeting, that I did not either see or hear Mr. Abraham until after I had called upon Mr. John O'Connor. (Hear, hear.)

MR. JUSTIN M'CARTHY said he had risen to a point of strictly Parliamentary order. As he was about to express that point some one handed him a letter of some kind, and the chairman struck it out of his hand. (Cheers.)

MR. PARNELL.—I took it out of your hand. (Cheers.)

COLONEL NOLAN.—No, no, he did not ·strike it out of your hand.

MR. M'CARTHY said he did not know what the letter contained or whom it came from. On that ground Mr. Parnell said he was going to act as chairman and suggest something that some one gave me, and that gave rise to the fearful storm that had been raging. (Hear, hear.) As to his point of order, when a difference of opinion arose between the Speaker and anybody in the House as to who had first caught the Speaker's eye, it was in the power of any man, and in his right, to move that that member be first heard, and not the other member.

MR. EDWARD HARRINGTON.—It was never done.

MR. T. M. HEALY.—Well done, Harrington.

MR. HARRINGTON.—Ill done, Healy. You will always get your answer from me, Healy. (Cries of "Order.")

MR. M'CARTHY.—I say it was moved by Mr. Cowan, of Newcastle, and carried against the Speaker. (Cheers.)

MR. PARNELL.—There was no such thing.

MR. M'CARTHY.—That point of order I was going to raise when our chairman struck the letter out of my hand and refused to hear me. (Cries of "No, no.")

MR. PARNELL.—Your friends refused to hear you by their clamour. (Hear, hear.)

MR. M'CARTHY.—You struck the letter out of my hand. ("Hear, hear" and cheers.)

MR. PARNELL.—You were about to put some resolution, thereby usurping my functions.

MR. M'CARTHY.—I was not.

MR. PARNELL.—That was my interpretation of your action.

MR. M'CARTHY.—You might have asked me what I was going

M

to do. I might have expected that courtesy from your hands.
(Cheers.)

Mr. PARNELL again called on Mr. John O'Connor.

Mr. T. M. HEALY.—I move that Mr. Abraham be heard.
(Cheers.)

Mr. PARNELL.—That motion is entirely out of order. (Hear,
hear.)

Mr. HEALY.—Put the motion.

Mr. PARNELL.—I refuse to put it. (Loud cheers.)

Mr. HEALY.—Then I will put it myself. (Cheers.)

Dr. FITZGERALD.—Who are you ? You are not the leader of the
Irish people. (Cheers.)

Mr. PARNELL.—Go on, Mr. John O'Connor.

Mr. JOHN O'CONNOR.—Mr. Healy has betrayed himself by his
haste into premature action. He is not leader yet. (Cheers.)
Permit me to say that I had endeavoured to catch your eye to
move this resolution, and had risen from my seat. (Cries of
" You had not.") The resolution I have to move is as follows :—

" That, having received from the delegates from this meeting a
report of the proceedings between Mr. Gladstone and the delegates of the party appointed to confer with him, and having read
Mr. Gladstone's letter of yesterday, we regret to learn, and we
call the attention of our countrymen to the fact, that although the
terms of the original resolution appointing the delegation were
specially altered to suit his views and to remove the barrier which
he stated stood in the way of the proposed conference, Mr.
Gladstone still refuses to enter into negotiations with the Irish
party, or to state his views on the two vital points submitted for
his consideration, except upon the condition that this party shall
first remove Mr. Parnell from the chairmanship."

He submitted that that resolution was not made with a view to
obstruction. He had heard the report of the delegates with very
great regret. As far as he possibly could, he would refrain from
saying anything offensive to Mr. Gladstone. But if there was
anything which would justify the charges made against Mr.
Gladstone—anything which would justify Mr. Parnell in his
statement that it was difficult to get anything out of Mr. Gladstone but what was indirect and uncertain—it was his conduct in
reference to these negotiations. (Cheers.) He rejoiced when the
delegates came to them to make an alteration in the terms of the

reference, and had thought it was only necessary to make the alteration in order to place Mr. Gladstone in a position to bring about a settlement of the question at issue and a determination of the crisis. He was borne out in that by the statements in the newspapers speaking for the Liberal party. To his intense regret, the hopes they entertained were broken. Why had Mr. Gladstone altered his mind? He had done so in obedience to English feeling—to manufactured English feeling. (Hear, hear.) But what had become of the noble idea that Ireland was to be ruled according to Irish ideas? He had thought that Mr. Gladstone would keep that idea in his mind, but he asserted that in his conduct towards this party he had parted from that position. (Cheers.) There could be no doubt that the feeling in Ireland and of the Irish people abroad was with Mr. Parnell and for his maintenance of the leadership. (Cheers.) He contended that any attempt of Mr. Gladstone and the Liberal party at dictation would be resented by the Irish people. Mr. Parnell's opponents were placing themselves unreservedly in the leadership of Mr. Gladstone. They said "No," but let them read Sir William Harcourt's letter, and he said " Treat with Mr. Gladstone."

MR. A. O'CONNOR.—He is not a member of the party.

MR. J. REDMOND.—The master of the party. (Cheers and counter cheers.)

MR. T. HEALY.—Who is to be the mistress of the party? (Cries of " Shame " and noise, several members calling out remarks which could not be distinguished in the uproar.)

MR. W. REDMOND.—They must be very badly off when they go to arguments like that.

A voice.—It is time.

MR. A. O'CONNOR.—I appeal to my friend the chairman. (Noise.)

MR. PARNELL.—Better appeal to your own friends ; better appeal to that cowardly little scoundrel there (noise), that in an assembly of Irishmen dares to insult a woman. (Loud cheers and counter-cheers.)

MR. A. O'CONNOR said he was going to appeal to his friend Mr. Parnell by saying that whatever painful duty they had to discharge, they should discharge it like gentlemen. (Cheers.)

MR. JOHN O'CONNOR said he pitied the Irish gentlemen, the representatives of a nation of gentlemen, who were obliged to accept the leadership of a coward who dared to insult a woman. (Cheers.)

Mr. CONDON protested against Mr. O'Connor's language, and said he, for one, was not under the leadership of any one.

Mr. JOHN O'CONNOR said that Mr. Parnell, as chairman of that party for the last eight or nine years, would be insisted upon by the Irish people to demand securities for those liberties which he had been commissioned to obtain for them before he disbanded his army. (Hear, hear.) The Irish people knew the history of their country, and knew from the quarrel between Grattan and Flood that the man who demanded securities for the preservation of their liberties was in the right. (Cheers.)

Mr. W. REDMOND.—And one of the men who defended Ireland's liberty was Parnell's ancestor.

Mr. J. O'CONNOR said that all their liberties had been taken from them, and a Parliament as was proposed, which would be allowed to make laws but not to enforce them, would be a sham, a mockery, and a delusion to the Irish people. With regard to the Hawarden conference, he defended Mr. Parnell's action in divulging its nature after having kept it secret so long before he was deprived of an opportunity of safeguarding the principles that he himself considered necessary. (Hear, hear.)

Mr. O'KELLY, in seconding the motion, thought that the answer which they had received from Mr. Gladstone was a warning to gentlemen on the opposite side. It was a new evidence of the danger of departing from absolute independence in dealing with the English parties in this country. While in one part of the response they were told that there was no desire to interfere with the action or the independence of the Irish party (hear), in another and most vital part of the communication it was clearly laid down that unless the party did a certain thing no communication would be held with the party. (Loud cheers.) The order had gone forth that before the new party could be recognized it must depose its chief. (Loud cheers and counter-cheers.) They who had been members up to this day of a united party would be no party to a transaction of that kind, and he was sure that in taking their stand by their leader they were acting for the benefit of their country and in the interests of their constituents, whose wishes, he believed, they were carrying out. There would be a grave responsibility upon the gentlemen who had announced their intention of becoming a separate party.

MR. ABRAHAM felt that any attempt to carry a Liberal majority at the next general election must prove unsuccessful if Mr. Gladstone should be induced by anything they did there to retire from the leadership of the party. (Cheers, and cries of " No.") He had, therefore, felt that Mr. Parnell should retire. (Cheers.) As he had not done so, however, he himself thought they would be wanting in respect to themselves if they did not bring matters to an issue. They ought to decide who should be their chairman. (Cheers.) The resolution in which they attempted to bring the discussion to an issue having been ignominiously treated by the chairman and torn to pieces in his hands —— (Cheers.)

MR. PARNELL.—That is distinctly untrue that I tore the resolution—quite untrue. (Hear, hear.)

MR. ABRAHAM would not enter into an altercation on the subject, but he repeated that the party would be wanting in respect to themselves and in duty to their constituents if they allowed the minority to continue the tactics by which the party had been made the laughing-stock of the world. (Cheers.) Mr. Parnell and his friends desired to appeal to Cæsar; unto Cæsar let them go. His own side would be willing to stand or fall by the same decision—the decision of the people. (Cheers and countercheers.) He would ask permission to move his resolution as an amendment to Mr. O'Connor's resolution—

" That we, the members of the Irish Parliamentary party, declare that Mr. Parnell's tenure of the chairmanship of this party is hereby terminated."

COLONEL NOLAN.—I rise to order. No one could construe that as an amendment.

MR. M. HEALY (to Mr. Parnell).—You declared Mr. Clancy's amendment, which had no possible connexion with the resolution, to be an amendment to the resolution.

MR. T. HEALY.—But circumstances alter cases.

MR. JOHN REDMOND said that Mr. Clancy's amendment was quite consistent with Mr. Barry's proposal, which was not that Mr. Parnell should be deposed from the chair, but that there should be an adjournment till Friday to enable Mr. Parnell to consider his decision.

MR. PARNELL.—I have now had the opportunity of examining

the original resolution proposed by Mr. John O'Connor, and the resolution suggested by Mr. Abraham as an amendment to it, and I rule that the resolution suggested by Mr. Abraham as an amendment to the original resolution is no amendment whatever to the original resolution. (Cheers, and cries of " Oh, oh.")

MR. HEALY.—Bravo, bravo !

MR. PARNELL.—Mr. Healy, I will not stand very much more from you. (Cheers.) I say it is no amendment whatever to the original resolution, and it can only be put as a substantive motion. (Hear, hear.)

MR. A. O'CONNOR said that those who, like himself, acquiesced mistrustfully, but yet acquiesced in the suggested conference with the Liberal leaders, did so in the hope that it might prove a golden bridge for the voluntary retirement of Mr. Parnell, with a sincere desire to bring the existing position to an amicable end, and to preserve the unity and amity of that party for the great work that yet remained to be done. (Hear, hear.) Their hopes had been dashed, and they now found themselves in the position in which they stood before Mr. Clancy's amendment was proposed. (Hear, hear.) Apparently now they were invited to resume the wearisome and, as it seemed to him, unseemly round of further amendments from only particular quarters, of successive adjournments, and of altercations of a not very dignified character. (Cheers.) They had already spent a whole week at that work, and the prospect of a formal decision had become more and more dim. (Hear, hear.) It was obvious that a determined minority, favoured by the chairman, who was personally interested (cheers), could, if they chose, indefinitely postpone the record of the decision of the majority.

MR. PARNELL.—Nothing of the sort.

MR. O'CONNOR said that, whatever might be the proceedings of the minority and whatever the decision of the chair, there was inherent in the majority right, power, and authority, some way or other, to define and record its position. (Cheers.)

MR. PARNELL.—I am bound to point out to the meeting a fact of which you must be very sensible, Mr. O'Connor, with your long experience, that up to the present moment you have not addressed yourself to a single portion of the resolution. (Cheers.) You are favouring us with a lecture about obstruction, on which you are undoubtedly well qualified to speak (laughter), but it is not the subject before the chair. (Hear, hear.)

MR. O'CONNOR.—My experience also tells me that when there is a motion before the chair it is right to move an amendment, and in my speech to lead up to that amendment. (Cheers.) I am endeavouring to come to it. We have been very moderate in this matter, and there is danger of our moderation being misconstrued. (Hear, hear.) We are in danger of appearing to the country as if shirking our duty. We are in danger of becoming the laughing-stock of the world. (Unanimous cheers.) I think this thing has gone on' long enough. (Cheers.) I think further words only a waste of time, and a loss of dignity, and therefore I invite my colleagues to make an end of the business. (Cheers.) The time has now come not to talk but to act. (Loud cheering.) We owe it to ourselves, to our party, to our country, to make an end of what is rapidly becoming a disgraceful farce. I ask the over-whelming majority of this party to decide now and at once to record their decision, if not here, then elsewhere. (Cheers.)

MR. PARNELL.—Mr. Arthur O'Connor knows perfectly well that that is not an amendment.

MR. A. O'CONNOR.—Very well, if it cannot be put here——

MR. T. M. HEALY.—Wait awhile, Arthur.

MR. LEAMY said they had heard a good deal of the old cries of obstruction. He was proceeding, when

MR. T. M. HEALY asked if Mr. Leamy was in order.

MR. PARNELL.—He is perfectly in order.

MR. T. M. HEALY.—I thought you ruled Mr. Arthur O'Connor out of order.

MR. PARNELL.—He chose to make a speech, and it will have to be answered. (Hear, hear.)

MR. LEAMY went on to say that if they were at all within their right to bring the charge of obstruction against Mr. Parnell and his followers, they might have done it in a manner which would show that they had some tenderness for the man who by the use of this very same weapon of obstruction, when he had very little support, brought their country to its present glorious position. (Hear, hear.)

SECESSION OF THE MAJORITY.

MR. JUSTIN M'CARTHY thought the time had come when they

ought to bring this debate to a close. (Hear, hear.) He did not want to say one word to increase the bitterness of a crisis like the present, but he had hoped up to last night that their chairman would still help them out of this terrible, this national, this organic difficulty. He was disappointed that Mr. Parnell had not lent them more assistance out of the dilemma, and he felt that they would be wasting time in further controversy, when it had been made clear that the door was to be barred against any definite settlement of the controversy in that room. (" Hear, hear " and " No, no.") He saw no further use is carrying on a discussion which must be barren of all but reproach, ill-temper, and indignity, and he would, therefore, suggest that all who thought with him at this grave crisis should withdraw with him from the room. (Loud cheers.)

MR. J. H. M'CARTHY (speaking amid interruption caused by members leaving the room).—I am a member of a constitutional party. (Cries of " Order," and noise.) I said it was my intention to vote with Mr. Parnell. I did vote with Mr. Parnell. I would have voted with him again if the decision had taken place to-night, as to my mind it has taken place. The question is over ; the majority has decided. I am sorry for the decision, but it is decided, and I go with the party. (Loud cheers and dissent.)

The majority of the party then left the room, leaving Mr. Parnell in the chair and the following members :—

Blane, A., South Armagh
Byrne, G. M., West Wicklow
Campbell, H., South Fermanagh
Clancy, J. J., North Dublin Co.
Conway, M., North Leitrim
Corbet, W. J., East Wicklow
Dalton, J., West Donegal
Fitzgerald, Dr. J. G., South Longford
Harrington, E., West Kerry
Harrison, H., Mid Tipperary
Hayden, L. P., South Leitrim
Kenny, Dr. J. E., South Cork
Leamy, Ed., South Sligo
Macdonald, W. A., Ossory Division, Queen's County
M'Kenna, Sir J. N., South Monaghan
Maguire, T. R., North Donegal
Mahony, P., North Meath
Nolan, Colonel J. P., North Galway
Nolan, J., North Louth
O'Connor, J., South Tipperary
O'Kelly, J. J., North Roscommon
Power, R., Waterford City
Quinn, T., Kilkenny City
Redmond, J., North Wexford
Redmond, W., North Fermanagh
Sheil, E., South Meath

When the meeting had again settled down,

COLONEL NOLAN said that now that Mr. Huntly M'Carthy had made a change, they made every possible allowance for the contending feelings which had drawn him in two directions - in one direction by his judgment and the wishes of his constituents, and in the other by family ties. Therefore not a word would be said in reprobation of the course taken by Mr. Huntly M'Carthy. The gentlemen who had left the room, he went on, had exercised a right, but it was the right of departing from that party. He went on to contend that they had had only two days of real debate—Monday and Tuesday—and yet they were told that they had exhausted the question. He was afraid that what had happened was of a totally different nature. The country, being enlightened by the debates of Monday and Tuesday, for the first time understood the position in which Mr. Parnell stood, and commenced to pronounce in his favour. A number of gentlemen were very much afraid that that process would go on, and so they were most anxious to terminate the discussion which would enlighten the people of Ireland as to the true position. (Cheers.) He went on to say that perhaps some people would like to understand the balance of English parties. There were 306 Conservatives, 68 Unionists, 86 of the Irish party, and 209 Liberals. Mr. Gladstone calculated that at the next election he would get an increase of 12 per cent., so that the numbers would be—Conservatives 250, the Unionists 53, the Irish members 86, and the Liberals 280. It was obvious from that that without the Irish party the Liberals would be able to do nothing, even if they took the Unionists into their camp. But some said the Liberals would get a greater gain than 70 seats, but there was one condition even of them getting the 12 per cent.—viz., the Irish vote. He had been a Whip for seven years, and had talked the matter over with all the leaders, and they could never make out that the Irish vote in England was worth less than 40 seats. Whether they would vote with the Liberals or Conservatives he could not tell, but he believed if Mr. Parnell were to go through those constituencies they would rally to give the Liberals a majority sufficient to give Home Rule. In concluding, Colonel Nolan said that whatever Mr. Parnell's position might be for the next two or three years, he would have ranked his name with that of O'Connell as the greatest Irishman for the last three centuries. (Cheers.)

DR. FITZGERALD repudiated with indignation the charges levelled by Mr. Healy against what he called "Irish hillside men and Irish brogues." He was a hillside man, but he remembered well the danger those hillside men had faced, rightly or wrongly, for the sake of Ireland. (Hear, hear.)

MR. W. REDMOND, in giving the reasons why he intended to follow Mr. Parnell's leadership, said that he had come solemnly to the conclusion that the only reason why the continuance of Mr. Parnell as leader was opposed was because it would not please Mr. Gladstone. (Cheers.) Mr. Parnell had offered to retire if they could ascertain from Mr. Gladstone what the Home Rule was that was to be proposed. Mr. Parnell could not have acted fairer than that. He himself would not remain in the House of Commons a single day if his leader were to be chosen by Mr. Gladstone, or any other English statesman. He for one would not, in the absence of assurances from Mr. Gladstone, consent to throw away the man who, above all others, had shown himself able to cope with the cunning of Mr. Gladstone and other English statesmen who deceived Irishmen in days gone by, and whose deceit would be practised again if they sent their leader from their midst. For those reasons he intended to persevere in that House, as far as he could, to maintain Mr. Parnell's leadership in that House. (Loud cheers.)

MR. BLANE said they were not unmindful of the fact that the Tenant Right party formed in 1852 was split up by men who had previously gone about the country making patriotic speeches. Those men were afterwards found on the bench sentencing unfortunate men in the dock for following the advice they gave them. Let them be careful that the days of Keogh were not coming again. He would say what he intended to tell his constituents, that a certain compact was entered into with Peter the Packer.

MR. LEAMY.—Enough. This is very injudicious. (Hear, hear.)

MR. PARNELL.—Mr. Blane, I wish to tell you that the Serjeant-at-Arms says we shall have to leave at 5 o'clock.

MR. BLANE.—Then I move the adjournment until Monday.

MR. PARNELL.—I will put the resolution. (Cheers.) I wish to say, in putting this resolution, that the men who have deserted from our party this evening have deserted on the eve of the day when we were about to return to our country, and that those men, while clamouring for a decision, clamoured for that decision because they dreaded the lightning of public opinion in Ireland. (Cheers.) I recognize the right of postponing a decision as long as the postponement of that decision gives time to the country to understand the issue. (Hear, hear.) I recognize the right of a minority not to obstruct, but to claim full and fair freedom of debate (hear, hear), where that freedom of debate gives the opportunity to the Irish nation to rally round us as it has done to-day. (Cheers.) It was this Irish nation that has consolidated round us from Ireland, America, England, Scotland, and every other direction that those men feared ; it was this Irish opinion they wished to stifle that they have recoiled from ; and it was this Irish opinion they fled from when they fled from this room this evening. (Loud cheers.) Gentlemen, we have won to-day. (Loud cheers.) Although our ranks are reduced in number, I hold this chair still. (Renewed cheering.) Although many of those who were our comrades have left us, Ireland has power to fill their ranks again. (Cheers.) Ireland has power to send us good men and true for every one of those who have left us, and I little know our gallant country if I am mistaken in the opinion that when she gets the opportunity she will freely exercise that power. (Renewed cheers.) They left this room because their position here was no longer tenable. (Hear, hear.) They saw they had arrayed against them that great force to which we must all bow— that great force without which none of them would ever have come here. (Hear, hear.) And, recognizing that position, they stand to-day in the most contemptible of all positions—the position of men who, having taken pledges to be true to their party, to be true to their leader, to be true to their country, have been false to all those pledges. (Loud cheers.)

The resolution of Mr. John O'Connor was then put to the meeting and carried unanimously, amid acclamation.

The proceedings then terminated.

MEETING OF THE MAJORITY—DEPOSITION OF MR. PARNELL.

The majority of the party, after leaving Committee Room No. 15, adjourned to the Conference Room, when it was found that 45 members were present. Mr. John Deasy, the Whip, was moved to the chair. It was in the first place moved by MR. ARTHUR O'CONNOR and seconded by MR. J. F. X. O'BRIEN :—

" That, acting under an imperative sense of duty to our country, we, the undersigned, being an absolute majority of the whole number of the Irish Parliamentary party, declare that

DEC. 6.

Mr. Parnell's term of chairmanship of this party is hereby terminated."

This having been carried, MR. T. M. HEALY moved, and MR. SEXTON seconded, the election of Mr. Justin M'Carthy as " Sessional chairman " of the party. It was also resolved, on the proposition of MR. CHANCE, seconded by MR. MOLLOY :—

" That a committee is hereby constituted to exercise jointly with the chairman the powers and discharge the functions hitherto attached to the chairmanship of the party ; and that this committee do consist of eight members of the party, to be chosen by ballot on Monday next at 2 p.m."

On the proposition of MR. ABRAHAM, seconded by MR. D. SHEEHY, the following declaration was agreed to :—

" We hereby solemnly renew our adhesion to the principle in devotion to which we have never wavered—viz., that the Irish Parliamentary party is, and always must remain, independent of all other parties ; and we further declare that we will never entertain any proposal for the settlement of the Home Rule question except such as satisfies the aspirations of the Irish people.

M'Carthy, Justin, Derry City (Chairman)
Abraham, W., West Limerick
Barry, J., South Wexford
Chance, P. A., South Kilkenny
Commins, A., South Roscommon
Condon, T. J., East Tipperary
Cox, J. R., East Clare
Crilly, D., North Mayo
Deasy, J., West Mayo
Dickson, T. A., St. Stephen's Green, Dublin
Esmonde, Sir T. H. G., South Dublin Co.
Finucane, J., East Limerick
Flynn, J. C., North Cork
Foley, P. J., Connemara Division, Co. Galway
Fox, J. F., Tullamore Division, King's County
Healy, M., Cork City
Healy, T. M., North Longford
Jordan, J., West Clare
Kenny, M. J., Mid Tyrone
Kilbride, D., South Kerry
Knox, E. F., West Cavan
Lane, W. J., East Cork

M'Cartan, M., South Down
M'Carthy, J. H., Newry
M'Donald, P., North Sligo
MacNeill, J. G. S., South Donegal
Molloy, B. C., Birr Division, King's County
Morrogh, J., South-East Cork
Murphy, W. M., St. Patrick's Division, Dublin
O'Brien, J. F. X., South Mayo
O'Brien, P. J., North Tipperary
O'Connor, A., East Donegal
O'Keeffe, F. A., Limerick City
Pinkerton, J., Galway City
Power, P. J., East Waterford
Reynolds, W. J., East Tyrone
Roche, J., East Galway
Sexton, T., West Belfast
Sheehan, J. D., East Kerry
Sheehy, D., South Galway
Stack, J., North Kerry
Sullivan, D., South Westmeath
Tanner, Dr. C. R., Mid Cork
Tuite, J., North Westmeath
Webb, A., West Waterford

At a late hour the same night an informal conference of the anti-Parnellites was held for the purpose of deciding what steps should be taken for strengthening the position of the party in view of the anticipated campaign against them in Ireland.   Mr. Justin M'Carthy presided, and the whole of the 45 members opposed to Mr. Parnell's retention of the leadership were present.   It was resolved—" That Messrs. Justin M'Carthy, Dickson, Murphy, Barry, Morrogh, T. Healy, and Sexton be constituted a committee, with power to draw up a prospectus for the formation of a limited company to establish and conduct a daily National journal in Ireland."   Mr. John Barry and Mr. Alfred Webb were added to the list of treasurers, and a subscription list having been opened to meet urgent needs, contributions to the amount of £1,020 were announced, every gentleman present subscribing.

PROCEEDINGS OF DECEMBER 8 AND 9.

Mr. Parnell spent the greater portion of the afternoon and evening of Monday, December 8, at St. Stephen's, but he was seen very little in the House of Commons.   He remained some time in the library, discussing with Mr. John Redmond and others his programme for the next few weeks.   Subsequently he proceeded to the smoking-room, where a considerable number of his supporters had gathered, and further conferences took place.

The following telegrams passed between Mr. O'Brien and Mr. Parnell :—

" To Parnell, House of Commons, London.—I shrink with horror from taking sides with you in a struggle which opens such appalling prospect of ruin and disgrace to our cause. Throughout this unhappy business I have refrained from saying one word personally offensive to you, and have read with deepest pain and disgust some of personal attacks made on you. And now before Ireland is irretrievably committed to a ruinous conflict I appeal to you, as a leader I have for ten years been proud to follow, and as a friend for whom I still feel warm affection, can you not see some way by which, while safeguarding your own reputation, the country may be saved from the utter destruction that threatens it ?   WILLIAM O'BRIEN, Hoffman-house."

To this Mr. Parnell cabled the following reply :—

" Had you wired prior to Saturday some suggestions from me might have succeeded. Now too late for me to rescue seceders from false position. Shall, however, be glad to see and consult with you on arrival in Europe."

———

ANTI-PARNELLITE MEETING.

In accordance with the decision arrived at on the previous Saturday night, the anti-Parnellites held a meeting at 2 o'clock on Monday, December 8, for the purpose of completing their arrangements in view of the impending contest in Ireland. The circulars convening the meeting had been sent to all the members of the Irish party, but, as was anticipated, only those opposed to Mr. Parnell's retention of the leadership put in an appearance. Mr. Justin M'Carthy presided, and upwards of 40 members attended. On the motion of Mr. SEXTON, it was agreed, "That this meeting of the Irish Parliamentary party, to which every member was invited, do hereby solemnly ratify the resolutions passed at the meeting held on Saturday last in the Conference Room of the House of Commons."

Sir Thomas Esmonde was appointed as an additional Whip to the party. It was then resolved, " That our chairman, Mr. Justin M'Carthy, be authorized, if he deem it expedient, to prepare an address to the Irish people at home and abroad on the present aspect of the Irish question with regard to the future policy of the party."

Mr. Deasy was empowered by the meeting to move for a writ for North Kilkenny, and the meeting then proceeded to elect a standing committee " to assist the chairman by their counsel and advice." Voting was by ballot, the method adopted being that in force at meetings of the National League. The Whips and secretaries of the party having first appointed scrutineers, each member present wrote on a slip of paper the names of eight gentlemen for whom he intended to vote. Then, the lists having been collected and analyzed, the first eight names were announced by the chairman as those of the committee, no other information being vouchsafed. These names were—W. Abraham,

J. Dillon, T. M. Healy, W. O'Brien, A. O'Connor, T. P. O'Connor, D. Sheehy, and T. Sexton.

A number of telegrams and letters having been read in support of the action taken by the majority on Saturday, the meeting adjourned until Tuesday, December 9, at 2 o'clock. The adhesion of Mr. Gilhooly and the O'Gorman Mahon has increased the voting strength of the anti-Parnellites to 52.

On Tuesday, December 9, Mr. Parnell received a telegram from Sir John Pope Hennessy, in which the latter declared that in view of the Bishops Manifesto, he could not as an Irish Catholic stand by Mr. Parnell.

At the adjourned anti-Parnellite meeting on the same day, Mr. Justin M'Carthy in the chair, Sir John Pope Hennessy's telegram to Mr. Parnell was read. It was agreed to telegraph at once to Sir John Pope Hennessy asking whether he would stand as an anti-Parnellite.

The following telegram addressed to Mr. M'Carthy was also read :—

" We are, of course, in cordial sympathy with your resolutions. As to the methods to be employed in the immediate future, owing to the impossibility of having adequate consultation by cable, we desire, as hitherto, to leave the responsibility to you, we cooperating by methods we believe best to secure Mr. Parnell's withdrawal and the reunion of the party.

" DILLON.
" O'BRIEN.
" O'CONNOR.
" SULLIVAN.
" GILL."

MR. PARNELL'S DEPARTURE FOR IRELAND.

Mr. Parnell left London for Dublin on the evening of Tuesday, December 9. He travelled by the night mail starting from Euston at 8 20. Mr. Richard Power, M.P., chief Whip of the party, was in waiting at the station, and was shortly afterwards joined by Mr. Barry, M.P. At 8 15 there was a rush of people who had gathered at the entrance to the station. Mr. Parnell had then arrived, and was escorted from his cab by about 20 of his Parliamentary supporters to the door of the carriage engaged for his conveyance, he having declined a special saloon which was offered him. Amongst those present were Messrs. E. Harrington, John O'Connor, Kenny, and Chance. While Mr. Parnell was thus accompanied to his seat in the train, Mr. T. Healy and his brother, Mr. Maurice Healy, entered the station and proceeded to a first-class compartment in the train, from which they witnessed the reception accorded to their late leader. In response to many inquiries Mr. Parnell said, " We will win—we will win," and he shook hands with many of those who crowded around him.

When Mr. Parnell entered his compartment the crowd gathered and called for a speech. Mr. Parnell, who seemed to be in excellent spirits, advanced to the window of the carriage, and, in addressing the gathering as " fellow-countrymen in England," said he was overwhelmed with the honour they had done him in appearing in such numbers to wish him " God speed " in the fight he had undertaken. It was just 16 years ago that they first assisted him in framing for his country a policy which he had never given up, and which, with their help, would be successful. He had never forgotten that help, and he asked them, exiles of Erin, to continue the support they had previously given. They would have no cause to regret that action or the fight upon which he entered that day, and his hope was that they would achieve the end which God had determined for them. These remarks were frequently interrupted by loud cheers and approving shouts. After the speech a rush was made by those present to grasp Mr. Parnell's hand, and the crowd followed the carriage in which Mr. Parnell stood as it moved out of the station, cheering as they ran along the platform.

———

The following leading article appeared in *The Times* on the morning after Mr. Parnell's departure for Ireland :—

" The brief but eventful Parliamentary Session that closed yesterday will be long remembered for its intense dramatic interest and its profound influence upon political relations. It has disappointed every reasonable forecast of its character and every ordinary calculation of results. The day before Parliament met there was nothing to indicate the approach of a storm which has brought to the ground the elaborate and laboriously constructed fabric of Opposition policy. There were, indeed, mutterings of discontent among the Nonconformists on account of the revelations made in the Divorce Court, but many Gladstonian writers and speakers had insisted that these revelations had nothing to do with political life ; the Nationalist party in Ireland and in the House of Commons had gone solid for Mr. Parnell, and Mr. Gladstone was as far as the Roman Catholic hierarchy from giving any sign of disapproval. In a few hours the whole situation was changed. Mr. Gladstone, apparently convinced that his noisy friends in the Press and on platforms had not rightly gauged the feelings of the constituencies, addressed to Mr. Parnell a request that he would temporarily efface himself, on the ground that otherwise Mr. Gladstone's retention of the leadership would become almost a nullity. What that oracular threat may have meant, we shall probably never know. Mr. Parnell did not trouble himself to inquire, but speedily put it beyond all doubt that he had not the remotest intention to retire, whether temporarily or otherwise, on any consideration whatever. Obstinacy on one side was met with obstinacy on the other. With trained docility, the ' items ' who had just been proving that the Irish people alone have the right to say who shall lead them, and that Mr. Parnell's private life has nothing to do with his fitness for political command, instantly turned round and demanded, in tones of outraged virtue, that their sacred movement should forthwith be purged from the stain of adultery. The priests and Bishops took courage to vindicate the moral law, upon which, notwithstanding the pressure brought to bear by the Vatican, they had permitted the Irish people to trample ; and the Nationalists were divided into two hostile camps by a difference of view concerning the best means of breaking up the Empire. From the purely Parliamentary point of view the immediate result was the total collapse of preparations, ostentatiously made and loudly trumpeted, for the obstruction of business. With unprecedented rapidity and ease the Government worked off their entire programme under cover of the furious battle raging in Committee Room No. 15. It still wants a fortnight to Christmas, yet members of Parliament are at liberty to go home and prepare to enjoy the festive season. There is evidence, however, that no undue haste was shown in taking advantage of the respite. The Government were bound by promise not to push things beyond the present stage, but had they been free to go on, it is doubtful whether much more progress could have been made.

Not a moment is lost by the two Home Rule factions in prosecuting their quarrel upon the larger battlefield where it now has to be fought. The Irish mail last night bore away from Euston a precious freightage of political and personal virtue. In one compartment were Mr. Parnell and his principal adherents, in another were packed Mr. T. M. Healy and other shining lights of the faction which, with a defective sense of humour, is now eager to be known as 'the patriots.' The honours of the start were undeniably with Mr. Parnell, who has evidently taken from the highest authority lessons in deportment in railway stations. His imitation of the accepted model of peripatetic propriety was remarkably accurate. He ensconced himself in a first-class compartment, after declining the too ostentatious luxury of a special saloon. Upon his modest retirement burst the sounds of popular enthusiasm, which were quickly ascertained to proceed from a great concourse of Irishmen bent upon doing him honour. There were cries for a speech, and then Mr. Parnell " advanced to the window of the carriage "—how well we know the phrase—and made his little oration after the approved model. There was the proper touch of humility, the proper thankfulness for this magnificent demonstration, the due declaration that he could never forget the support extended to him at a critical moment in a nation's history, and—last and subtlest stroke of all—the inevitable hint of special acquaintance and harmony with the decrees of the Almighty. The imitation was perfect, and was done with a perfect gravity which leaves it doubtful whether he intended an audacious parody, or whether a dangerous politician has acquired that *quasi*-belief in his mission which alone can make him more dangerous still. While this delectable scene was enacting at one part of the platform, the poor " patriots " were hiding their mortification in a compartment at another, It is a thousand pities that no sympathizing band could be found to give them what Mr. Parnell beautifully calls a " God-speed." If Mr. Healy could only have " advanced to the window " as well, and unburdened his swelling heart in a neat and appropriate speech after the best model, the comedy of the situation would have been complete.

There is dramatic fitness in the opening of the Irish struggle in Kilkenny, which enriches the language with a proverbial description of internecine conflict. Sir John Pope Hennessy has found it difficult to make up his mind, but has finally decided that as an Irish Catholic he cannot go against his Bishops. What a pity it is that Bishops who command such implicit obedience should have refused to put down outrage and fraud, and should have been so slow to pronounce even against adultery! It remains to be seen whether this obedient son of the Church will stand in the anti-Parnellite interest, but if he does there can be no doubt at all that the fight will be a lively one. Meantime Mr. Parnell will hasten to expound the situation as he views it to a meeting in Dublin, to which admission is to be by ticket. There may be some occult reason for an arrangement which on the face of it seems an indication of weakness. The expected manifesto from the other party is held back, possibly in order that it may include a reply to Mr. Parnell's Dublin speech. Evidently there is nothing useful to be done just now in America, for members of both parties are preparing to return to Ireland, Mr. Harrington in the interest of Mr. Parnell, and Mr. William O'Brien with intentions which at present seem a little obscure. His telegram to Mr. Parnell betrayed a degree of perturbation and indecision which might have won a less frigid reply ; and his second message, to correct some supposed misunderstanding of the first, has the air of considerable anxiety for the interview which Mr. Parnell coldly stated his willingness to grant. Judges of Irish sentiment think that Mr. O'Brien is the only man who has much chance of successfully rousing the country against Mr. Parnell, and in that case any weakness on his part would go far to spoil a very pretty fight. It is probable that we have not yet seen the last of the revelations with which Mr. Gladstone and his followers have been regaled. It may be expected that the general struggle in Ireland will be productive of much plain speaking all round. Enough, however, is already known of the characters of both factions to fill their English allies with unspeakable disgust, and to open their eyes to the fact they have so long ignored, that the representation of the elements in Ireland

DEC. 10. which alone can make a nation does not lie with any section of
the Parnellite party. Partisan prejudice dies hard, but the
application of the Rev. Newman Hall for membership of the
Nonconformist Unionist Association may perhaps be taken
as a sign of a salutary revulsion of feeling in Nonconformist
circles."

PRINTED BY GEORGE EDWARD WRIGHT, AT THE TIMES
OFFICE, LONDON

www.ingramcontent.com/pod-product-compliance
Lightning Source LLC
Chambersburg PA
CBHW030820270326
41928CB00007B/816